How to Do Everything™

iPad® 2

Joli Ballew

New York Chicago San Francisco Lisbon
London Madrid Mexico City Milan New Delhi
San Juan Seoul Singapore Sydney Toronto

The McGraw·Hill Companies

Cataloging-in-Publication Data is on file with the Library of Congress

McGraw-Hill books are available at special quantity discounts to use as premiums and sales promotions, or for use in corporate training programs. To contact a representative, please e-mail us at bulksales@ mcgraw-hill.com.

How to Do Everything™: iPad® 2

Product image used by permission from Apple, Inc.

Product photography used by permission from Dwight Eschliman Photography—eschlimanphoto.com. Model photo taken by and used with permission from Thayer Allyson Gowdy—www.thayerphoto.com. Image of Tiana Bahr in the iPad 2 used by permission from LemonLime Agency.

1234567890   QFR QFR   10987654321
ISBN   978-0-07-178091-9
MHID   0-07-178091-2

Sponsoring Editor Megg Morin	**Technical Editor** Janet Cloninger	**Production Supervisor** George Anderson
Editorial Supervisor Patty Mon	**Copy Editor** Margaret Berson	**Composition** Cenveo Publisher Services
Project Editor Vasundhara Sawhney, Cenveo Publisher Services	**Proofreader** Julie Searls	**Illustration** Cenveo Publisher Services
Acquisitions Coordinator Joya Anthony	**Indexer** Jack Lewis	**Art Director, Cover** Jeff Weeks
		Cover Designer Jeff Weeks

For Mom. I had no idea how much I'd miss you; you'd have loved the iPad.

Contents at a Glance

Contents

x **Contents**

PART VII   Appendixes

Acknowledgments

I've written five *How to Do Everything*™ books now, and have worked with just about everyone at McGraw-Hill. This book was one of my favorites, though. Everyone came together, at the same time, and with the same gusto. My Sponsoring Editor, Megg Morin, even purchased her own iPad, and we spent lots of time swapping stories and sharing our views on the latest and greatest apps. We both love iBooks; we both love Netflix. We both think watching TV on the iPad is awesome, and that Maps is the bomb. We've both spent way too much money on movies, books, and apps, even though we could have opted for free ones, but neither of us cares. I don't normally have such a close relationship with the people I work with, and I have a feeling Megg and I will remain friends for many years to come.

To get this book to market as soon as possible, we all worked long days and long nights. Everyone was crunching numbers, and everyone was pushed to their limits with regard to how much they could do within a given window of time. The people who worked directly with me on this book include Megg Morin, Janet Cloninger, Joya Anthony, Patty Mon, and Vasundhara Sawhney, and I'd like to thank them for all their hard work.

I'd like to call out Janet Cloninger for a moment, though. If I'm not mistaken, this was her first go-around as a technical editor. She went above and beyond the call of duty, editing chapters the day I sent them, and often within the hour (or hours, depending on the chapter's condition!). And because we were in a rush, I gave Janet permission to simply write over my words, if she felt so inclined, but she never did so. I'm sure I would have been happy with her work on that front too, though, because her comments were certainly informative.

Book writing takes a bit of family support too, and I'd like to thank mine for sticking by me through the months that I'm overworked, and the various times when I'm not. I put in some incredibly long 12-hour days toward the end of this journey, and my family left me alone and let me be. They let me slide on Monday and Thursday night dinners and didn't complain when I spent all day Saturday or Sunday at my computer.

I miss my mom, who passed away in 2009, and the sadness was especially heavy while writing this book. I know she would have loved the iPad, and I often wanted to call her on the phone and say something like "Hey Mom, you have to try iBooks!" or "Mom, check it out, I can see your house on Maps!" She was always a bit afraid of the computer, with all its pop-ups about updating antivirus software, installing operating system updates, and the thing freezing up from time to time, and toward the end she was just too sick to even care to try. iPhones and the like were too small for her, so she never got into that either. She would have loved the iPad, though, I know it. I wish she were here for this.

I'm proud of my dad, who at 90-years old still lives alone, drives, does his own shopping, and maintains his house all by himself. I'm only about 15 minutes away if he needs me, though, and he has a Jitterbug phone he's quite comfortable with. He's a happy guy, and it's nice to see him getting along on his own. He never complains and always agrees with me, and he trusts the decisions I make for him. Believe me, I know how blessed my life has been and continues to be, even with the tragedies that must occur because life is, well, life, and things will and do happen.

The rest of my family includes Jennifer, my daughter, a recent graduate of the University of Texas and a civil engineer (I never get tired of saying that); my son-in-law Andrew, a black belt in Karate and awesome physical education teacher; and Cosmo, my best friend and partner in life, who like Dad, always has a smile on her face and happiness in her heart. They all make my life very special indeed.

Finally, I'd like to thank my agent, Neil Salkind, who continues to surprise me with his talents, tact, personal support, and connections, and how he goes out of his way to keep me busy. He's a great friend, my biggest fan, and for some reason, thinks I can do no wrong. I'm sure I wouldn't be where I am today without him. I enjoy our emails, our phone calls, and our friendship, and am glad to have him on my side.

The publisher would like to add special thanks to Sue Carroll at Apple, Inc. for her help in securing the green light to use the iPad 2 product shot on this book's cover, and thanks go to Jenifer Guskay and Dwight Eschliman Photography, Maren Patton and Thayer Photographs, Inc., as well as Robin Harrington and Chaim Magnum at LemonLime Agency for their help in taking the photos and securing the needed permissions for the photographers and talent involved in that iPad 2 product shot.

Introduction

Congratulations on the purchase of your new iPad 2. You're going to be amazed at how versatile this device is, how many ways you can use it to stay in touch with others, and how many apps are available for you to play and work with. You'll love surfing the Internet on the go and on a screen you can actually see; you'll appreciate Maps when you need to get somewhere fast or find information about a business or restaurant; and in your downtime, you'll enjoy shopping at the iTunes Store for movies, podcasts, music, TV shows, and just about any other media imaginable, and watching and listening to that media on your iPad. I'm sure you're going to love FaceTime too, which lets you video chat with others, just like they used to do on that old cartoon, *The Jetsons.*

Here at McGraw-Hill, we're all amazed with the iPad. We're amazed at how great an HD movie looks in the Videos app, we're stunned at how fast we can surf the Internet, and we love all of the different ways we can share our photos. Picture Frame is awesome, as is Photo Booth, and we can create slideshows on the fly. iTunes offers iTunes U, where we can listen to lectures for free from colleges and universities all over the United States, including Stanford, Yale, and Berkeley, and we're all happy that for only about $15 a month, we can have Internet access with our iPad 3G, provided we're careful with the 3G plan and the amount of data we use.

The third-party apps are incredible too. iBooks offers a lot of free books, and we have full bookshelves. Netflix lets us watch movies, and the ABC Player lets us watch TV shows we missed the night before. Those of us that are Time Warner subscribers also enjoy the Time Warner app immensely. We can sit on the couch and answer our email on a keyboard that we can actually see, touch, and use effectively, and we can open all kinds of documents and pictures. With iWork apps, we can even work from anywhere.

We all sincerely hope that you are just as excited as we are. In this book we vow to teach you "all you need to know." In fact, I'm pretty sure we've introduced everything there is to the iPad here, with the exclusion of all of the third-party apps, of course. If we've left anything out or if you have any questions or comments, feel free to email me directly at joli_ballew@hotmail.com, or visit my Facebook group, How to Do Everything: iPad. It's open and everyone can join.

Without further ado then, let's get started. Here's what you'll learn in this book:

- **Chapter 1, Set Up and Discover Your iPad,** helps get you through the setup process, learn the parts of the iPad Home screen, sync your iPad, and learn touch techniques. You'll discover what's on the outside of your iPad, what model iPad you have, and what kind of data plan might be right for you (if you have the Wi-Fi + 3G model).

- **Chapter 2, iPad Basics,** shows you how to personalize your iPad, turn on Wi-Fi and connect to a free hotspot or your home network, connect via cellular connections using a Wi-Fi + 3G iPad, use the built-in search features to find data on your iPad, and how to type effectively, or at least well enough for now!

- **Chapter 3, Safari,** instructs you on using Safari to surf the Internet, use gestures to zoom and otherwise navigate a page, create shortcuts to web pages (called web clips) on your Home screens, bookmark sites you visit often, and organize those bookmarks. There's a lot more to Safari than you may have expected, and we'll cover it all here.

- **Chapter 4, Communicate with Mail,** walks you through setting up your email accounts in Mail, the iPad's email app. With accounts configured, you'll learn to send, receive, compose, organize, and work with mail. You'll also learn how to send pictures in an email, open an attachment, and add senders to your address book.

- **Chapter 5, Go Digital with iBooks,** shows you how to get iBooks, how to use iBooks, and how to browse and shop the iBookstore. You'll learn about Top Charts, where you can download free books, like *The War of the Worlds* by H. G. Wells and *Pride and Prejudice* by Jane Austen. You'll also explore all of the iBooks controls, including changing the font and font size for any book.

- **Chapter 6, Read News and Commentary, and Use Social Networks,** shows you how to locate your local newspaper online, read the *New York Times*, read blogs and listen to podcasts, and participate in social networking web sites like Facebook. You'll also learn to text with a popular third-party app and exchange instant messages with others using an app like AIM.

- **Chapter 7, Get and Use Apps from the App Store, and Incorporate Game Center** helps you learn how to locate, purchase, download, and install apps, and how to read reviews and ratings for apps or write your own. We'll introduce some of our favorite apps, and show you how to manage the apps you keep by backing them up, repositioning them on your Home screens, and deleting apps you don't want from both your iPad and your computer.

- **Chapter 8, Use Your iPod App,** shows you how to do virtually everything with your iPad's music player, from syncing to creating playlists to enabling and using Genius. You'll learn how to browse your music by category, and how to play, pause, and skip songs, and use onscreen controls, to name a few.

- **Chapter 9, Shop the iTunes Store,** shows you how to get what you want from the iTunes Store, including music, movies, TV shows, podcasts, audiobooks, and media from iTunes U. You'll learn how to rent movies too, and how to back up and sync your data to your computer. There's a lot more to iTunes than music!

- **Chapter 10, Take, View, Obtain, Manage, and Share Photos,** teaches you how to use the Photos app to...well...view, manage, and share your photos! You can create slideshows, pinch to zoom, skim all your photos quickly, set a photo as wallpaper, assign a photo to a contact, copy a photo so you can paste it in an email, and lots, lots more. With the optional Camera Connection Kit, you can also upload photos directly to your iPad, skipping the need to sync photos from your computer. Of course, we introduce the new Camera app, missing from the original iPad but available on the iPad 2. With it you can shoot digital pictures and video. It's a nice camera too!

- **Chapter 11, Take, View, Obtain, Manage, and Share Videos,** teaches you how to use the Videos app to watch movies you buy and rent from iTunes, watch music videos or podcasts you've acquired, and access media you've downloaded from iTunes U. You'll learn how to use the video controls and how to enable closed captioning too, should your media include closed captions. Of course, there's YouTube, and third-party apps such as Netflix and the ABC Player to explore too. You'll learn to use the video camera to take video, and how to share that video with others as well.

- **Chapter 12, Manage Contacts,** shows you how to input, sync, and manage contacts using the Contacts app. You can add contact information that's considered outside the box too, like birthdays and anniversaries. If you add an address, you can even tap the address on the Contact card to open Maps to view the location, or tap an email address to open a new message in Mail. It all works together!

- **Chapter 13, Manage Your Schedule,** teaches you how to use the Calendar app to sync calendars you already use, add events to a specific calendar, and even create new calendars on your computer and sync those to your iPad. You can create events that repeat, and you can create alerts too. You can even subscribe to others' calendars like those from your favorite sports team, your child's school cafeteria, and more.

- **Chapter 14, Use Maps,** guides you through the process of searching for locations, getting directions, and finding driving, walking, and even public transportation routes. You can view locations in various views too, including Classic, Satellite, Hybrid, and Terrain, and if a location has a picture for Street View, you can view it with a full 360-degree angle, so you'll know what you're looking for when you get there. You can also save bookmarks, share locations, and mark new locations on maps, as well as find a business's web site and phone number.

- **Chapter 15, Use Notes,** introduces the Notes app you'll use to create personal notes you can type quickly. There's no need to save a note, because they're all saved by default, and they are easy to delete or share, when applicable.

- **Chapter 16, Accessibility,** offers guidance on using the available Accessibility options on your iPad, including VoiceOver, Zoom, White-on-Black display, Mono Audio, and others. Other options are introduced, which, while they are not true accessibility options, will make the iPad easier to use if you have a visual, hearing, or mobility issues.

- **Chapter 17, Security,** shows you how to secure your iPad with a Passcode Lock, Restrictions, and parental controls. You'll also learn about securing Safari, avoiding phishing scams, and more. Finally, we'll show you how to configure Find My iPad, which lets you use location information to find your iPad if it's ever lost or stolen.

- **Appendix A, Settings,** lists all the things you can do in settings from enabling and disabling Wi-Fi to signing out of the App Store.
- **Appendix B, Troubleshooting,** describes some of the most common problems that iPad users encounter and their solutions.

PART I

Introduction to the iPad 2

1

Set Up and Discover Your iPad 2

HOW TO...

- Install iTunes on your computer
- Understand sync options
- Perform your first sync (or not)
- Configure default connection options
- Add headphones, microphones, and speakers
- Use the external ports and buttons
- Navigate the Home screen
- Explore accessories
- Understand the differences between iPad models (Wi-Fi only and Wi-Fi + 3G)
- Choose a data plan for the iPad 3G
- Understand the Status icons
- Create your first backup

Congratulations on your new iPad 2! If you've ever used an iPhone, a first-generation iPad, or an iPod Touch, you'll recognize that the iPad has similar features (except for its size). Once you've set it up, you'll see the familiar Home screen and applications like Mail and Safari, and you'll find you can touch the screen to interact with it, just as you can with many of Apple's devices. If you've never used an "iDevice," you're in for a real treat. Set it up, turn it on, and hold it in your hands; it's a nice fit! You'll marvel at how a simple touch can manipulate such a fantastic device, and you'll begin to uncover all of the things you can do with it.

In this chapter you'll set up and discover your iPad, including connecting it to your computer and downloading the proper software so you can register, sync, and back up your iPad. You'll learn how to use the external jacks and ports and what you can and cannot connect, how to navigate the Home screen, and how to connect Bluetooth devices, to name a few. You'll learn about some of the accessories you can purchase to make the iPad uniquely yours, and what data plans are available for the Wi-Fi + 3G model. Finally, you'll discover a little bit about some technical stuff too, like what an "accelerometer" is and what the iPad's "OS" consists of.

First Steps

There are a few things you have to do with (and to) your iPad before you can use it. You can't just open the box and turn it on. Although there is a "quick start card" in the box, we'll still carefully outline the required *first steps* here. They include:

- Connecting the iPad to your computer
- Installing iTunes
- Registering your iPad

Connect Your iPad to Your Computer

You have to connect your iPad to a computer to set it up. You can't use your iPad until you set it up, so this is a must-do thing. If you have more than one computer available to you, you should choose the one that contains your music, pictures, data, videos, and other items you want to put on your iPad once it's up and running. The computer you select should be the computer you use most often, and one that is always available to you.

The computer you use will also have to have iTunes on it, a software program you download and install from Apple. Don't worry, it's free, and it's easy to install. You'll use your computer along with iTunes to sync your data between your computer and your iPad, and to back up your iPad's settings and application data.

Additionally, you will have to have the following in place before you can get started:

- You must have Administrator rights on the computer so you can download and install iTunes to it.
- You must have the ability to obtain an iTunes store account, which includes having a PayPal account or a valid credit card. Additionally, you can redeem an iTunes card, if you have one.
- You must use a computer that
  - Has an available USB port
  - Is either a Mac and runs Mac OS X v. 10.5.8 or later, or is a Windows PC and runs Windows 7, Windows Vista, or Windows XP with SP3 or later
  - Is currently connected to the Internet

Note Your iPad should arrive fully charged, or at least charged enough to get started. If it isn't charged, refer to the section later in this chapter, "Charge Your iPad."

Now you're ready to connect your iPad to your computer. Because a majority of readers will have a Windows-based PC (Windows XP, Vista, or 7), we'll outline the steps for connecting to a PC here. However, connecting with a Mac is similar.

To connect your iPad to your Windows-based PC:

1. Connect the included white USB cable connector to the iPad and the computer. Plug the larger end into the iPad with the icon facing upward; plug the smaller end into an available USB port on your computer.
2. Press the Home button on the iPad. That's the round button toward the bottom of the iPad.
   a. If you see a USB symbol and the iTunes icon, iTunes is not installed on your computer. Install iTunes as outlined in the next section.
   b. If iTunes is installed on the computer, the iPad Home screen will appear. Skip the next section, "Install iTunes," and go directly to "Register Your iPad."

 The iPad should be associated with only one computer at a time. Attempting to plug the iPad into a different computer than the one used for setup could result in the loss of data.

Install iTunes

If iTunes is not yet installed on your computer, you'll have to install it. You'll also need an iTunes Store account. You'll use the iTunes program (which will soon be on your computer) to manage and sync data between your computer and your iPad. Some things you may opt to sync are your media (including music, videos, movies, pictures, music videos, TV shows, podcasts, and so on), and contacts, calendar appointments, and other data. You'll also need iTunes on your computer to back up and restore your iPad. If you already have and use a current version of iTunes and have an iTunes account that you use with another iDevice such as an iPod or iPhone, you can skip this section, although you may want to check iTunes for updates. The iPad 2 requires that you have iTunes version 10.2 (or later) installed.

Tip Chapter 9 shows you how to obtain media from the iTunes Store using the iTunes app installed on your iPad.

To download, install, and set up iTunes and obtain an iTunes Store account on a Windows-based PC (the steps for a Mac are similar but not exactly the same), follow these steps:

1. From your computer, visit www.apple.com/itunes/download.
2. Verify whether you want to leave the two options selected to receive email notifications from Apple (and if so, input your email address). If you do not want to receive email from Apple, deselect these items.
3. Click Download Now, shown in Figure 1-1.
4. Click Run, and when the download has completed, click Run again.
5. Click Next to get started.
6. Click I Accept the Terms in This License Agreement, and click Next.

Download iTunes Now

◉ 🔲 iTunes 10.2.1 for Windows
XP, Vista or Windows 7

◯ 🔲 iTunes 10.2.1 for Windows
(64-bit)

☑ Email me New On iTunes and special
iTunes offers.

☐ Keep me up to date with Apple news,
software updates, and the latest
information on products and services.

Apple Customer Privacy Policy

Email Address

[   ]

Download Now ○

FIGURE 1-1   Click Download Now to start the download process.

7. Configure installation options, including whether or not you want a shortcut to iTunes placed on your Desktop and to use iTunes as the default player for audio files. Do not change the location of the iTunes folder unless you know what you're doing!
8. Click Install. You may have to input administrator credentials or otherwise allow the installation on your PC.
9. Keep selected the option for Open iTunes After the Installer Exits. Click Finish.
10. When iTunes starts, you'll be prompted to agree to more terms of service. Click Agree.
11. When prompted to create an account, click Continue (and if you aren't prompted, click Store and Create Account).
12. Tick I Have Read and Agree to the iTunes Terms and Conditions (and you may actually want to read these); click Continue.
13. Click Next to begin the iTunes setup.
14. If you want iTunes to find and incorporate your music files, leave the default options selected, shown in Figure 1-2. Click Next.
15. If you want iTunes to keep your media folder organized, click Yes, Keep My iTunes Folder Organized. Otherwise, click No, I'll Change the File and Folder Names Myself. (We opted for Yes.)
16. Click Finish. Wait while iTunes adds your media files.
17. Click Done.

FIGURE 1-2   You have to set up iTunes after installation, and you should let iTunes find your existing music files.

Register Your iPad

After iTunes is installed on your computer, you can connect your iPad. When you touch the Home button (that's the round button on the iPad itself in the center of the bottom of the iPad), the Lock screen will appear. Use your finger to move the slide to the right to unlock the iPad. Once your iPad is unlocked, you'll have access to the Home screen.

Now, take a look at iTunes on your computer. You'll notice a prompt to register your iPad. To register your iPad and to create a new iTunes Store Account (Apple ID):

1. With your iPad connected to your computer, at the iTunes Welcome page, click Continue.
2. Tick I Have Read and Agree to the iPad Software License Agreement, and click Continue. (You can read this if you like.)
3. On the iTunes Account (Apple ID) page, either log in with an existing Apple ID or tick I Do Not Have an Apple ID. Click Continue.
4. If you do not have an Apple ID, work through the steps to create one. You'll also have to input a form of payment for future purchases. Click Continue when finished.
5. At the Register Your iPad page, fill in the required information. Click Submit when finished.
6. If prompted to try MobileMe, click Not Now. You'll learn about MobileMe later in this book.

FIGURE 1-3   Make sure your iPad is updated with the latest software.

7. On the Set Up iPad page, type a name for your iPad. On that same page, decide how you'd like to sync your music, photos, and applications. If you're unsure if you want to sync your iPad with every song and photo on your computer, deselect all three. You'll learn to set up syncing in the next section, and you can choose then exactly what you want to sync and what you do not.

8. Click Done.

9. The iPad's screen will come on, and it will show that syncing is in progress. If you have not selected anything to sync, it won't take long to complete.

10. To make sure you have the latest software on your iPad, go to iTunes on your computer, make sure your iPad is selected in the left pane, and from the Summary tab, click Check for Update (or Update). See Figure 1-3.

Note   If you already have an iTunes account that has not yet been authorized on the computer you're using, in iTunes, click Store, and click Authorize Computer.

Set Up Syncing and Perform Your First Sync

With your iPad connected and registered, and with iTunes open, you can now begin to configure how you'd like syncing to occur between your computer and iTunes. Syncing, at this particular moment anyway, is the process of copying data from your computer to your iPad, so that the data, pictures, music, movies, calendar appointments, contacts, and the like are on both your computer and your iPad. Once data has been copied to your iPad, any changes that occur later, either on your iPad or on your computer, will be synced back to your PC and the reverse, the next time you connect. You can configure syncing now or later, but we suggest you set up syncing now.

Tip   If you have duplicate songs in your Music folder, duplicate songs will be copied to your iPad. If you have duplicate contacts in your contact list, the same holds true. It's best to clean up your computer before syncing your iPad.

You can opt to sync certain types of data automatically, manually, or not at all. There are lots of options. Several of these options have their own tabs in iTunes, while a few are listed together under one tab. (For instance, the Info tab offers a place to sync, or not sync, contacts, calendars, mail accounts, and the like.) Table 1-1 summarizes the options.

TABLE 1-1   iTunes Tabs and Options

iTunes Tab	Data You Can Choose to Sync If Desired
Info	
Contacts from:	Outlook Google Contacts Windows Contacts Yahoo! Address Book
Calendars from:	Outlook Third-party calendars as applicable
Mail accounts from:	Outlook Windows Mail Apple Mail Third-party email programs as applicable
Bookmarks (Favorites) from:	Internet Explorer Safari Third-party web browsers as applicable
Notes from:	Outlook Third-party applications if applicable You can also replace information already on your iPad including contacts, calendars, mail accounts, bookmarks, and notes.
Apps	All apps or only apps you handpick
Music	Your entire music library Only the songs you select or only selected music from artists, playlists, and genres Music videos Voice memos Automatically fill free space with songs
Movies	All movies (your entire movie library) Only movies you select or the most recent movies on your computer
TV Shows	All TV shows Only TV shows you've yet to watch, most recent, or by other criteria
Podcasts	All podcasts Only podcasts you've yet to hear, most recent, or by other criteria
iTunes U	All iTunes U collections Only collections you've yet to hear, most recent, or by other criteria

TABLE 1-1 iTunes Tabs and Options *(continued)*

iTunes Tab	Data You Can Choose to Sync If Desired
Books	All books Selected books All audiobooks Selected audiobooks
Photos	All photos from a specific folder Only selected picture folders Include (or not) videos in those folders

 Note that many of these options in the Info tab are different on a Mac computer, and some vary on a PC depending on what software you have installed.

After you've decided what you'd like to sync and how, configure those options in iTunes:

1. Open iTunes on your computer.
2. Connect your iPad to your computer.
3. In the left pane, click to select your iPad, as shown in the illustration. Note that you can click the arrow to the left of your iPad's name to show the subcategories associated currently with your iPad and the data on it. (The arrow to the right is used to "eject," or disconnect, the iPad.)

4. Next, you'll click each tab to configure sync options. Most tabs work similarly, so we'll start with the Music tab:
   a. Click the Music tab.
   b. Tick Sync Music.
   c. Choose syncing options. If you opt to sync only selected playlists, artists, and genres, more options will appear, where you can handpick the music to sync.
5. Click the Photos tab.
   a. Click Sync Photos From.
   b. Note the default picture folder. In Windows 7, it's the My Pictures folder, and you can select a different folder using the arrows.
   c. To select only certain picture folders, tick Selected Folders. You'll see something similar to what's shown in Figure 1-4.
6. Repeat these steps to configure syncing options for the rest of the tabs.

Summary	Info	Apps	Music	Movies	TV Shows	Podcasts	iTunes U	Books	Photos

☑ **Sync Photos from** ⬚ My Pictures ⬚ ⬦   624 photos

○ All folders
◉ Selected folders
☐ Include videos

Folders

☐ 📁 2010-09-23 Pam
☐ 📁 70-680 Boot Camp JPEGS
☐ 📁 BlackBerry
☐ 📁 Camera Card Dec 2010
☑ 📁 Cats   116
☐ 📁 CES 2011
☐ 📁 Christmas 2010

FIGURE 1-4   You can select exactly the folders you want and no others.

7. When finished, click Apply.
8. If your iPad is still connected to your computer, the sync will begin immediately. If the iPad is not connected, syncing will occur the next time you connect it.

Tip   Once syncing is set up, syncing will occur automatically each time you connect your iPad to your computer.

Note   You can prevent syncing from automatically occurring between a computer and an iPad. The configuration change can be made in the Preferences dialog box from iTunes. On a Mac, in iTunes, click iTunes, and then Preferences; on a PC, in iTunes, click Edit, and then Preferences. In the Preferences dialog box, tick the following option: Prevent iPods, iPhones, and iPads from Syncing Automatically. If you ever decide to sync data, you can do so manually.

Charge Your iPad

Your iPad has a built-in battery that has to be charged to use it. To charge it, you connect the USB dock connector and a power adapter that shipped with it, and let it sit for a while to get a full charge. A charge should last a full day (10 hours or so) if you use your iPad constantly, or for a month if you rarely use it.

It's okay to keep the iPad connected to the charger when you aren't using it, but understand that a rechargeable battery's life is defined by how many times it is charged, and your iPad's battery won't last forever. We suggest you charge the iPad fully, use it until the battery is almost spent, and then, completely charge it again. Beyond that piece of advice, I'll add a few tips here to help you get the most from your battery.

To charge your iPad:

1. Locate the charging port on the outside of the iPad. It's a 30-pin connection and is located at the bottom of your iPad.
2. Locate the dock connector to USB cable that came with the iPad and connect it to the adapter.
3. Plug the adapter into a wall outlet.

To get the most from your battery while at the same time extending the battery's life:

- If you know you won't be using your iPad for a while, turn it completely off by holding down the Sleep/Wake button until a red Power Off slider appears. Move the slider to turn off the device.
- Lower the screen brightness by opening the Settings app and selecting the Brightness and Wallpaper menu option.

Note   For more information on the Settings app and available options, refer to Appendix A.

- When you aren't using Wi-Fi, 3G, Location services, and/or Bluetooth, turn those features off. You can access these settings in the Settings app.
- Use Airplane Mode in low- or no-coverage areas. This prevents your iPad from trying to obtain or maintain a connection with a Wi-Fi or 3G data network when one isn't available.
- Turn off Push notifications. Again, look to the Settings app under Mail, Contacts, Calendars.

Explore the Hardware

Your iPad is registered and ready to use, congratulations! So let's get going. First things first, though; spend a minute or two exploring the outside of your iPad before you start touching and tapping items on the Home screen, because you may want to connect something or adjust the volume while you explore.

There are several things on the outside of your iPad. There's a docking port that allows you to charge your iPad or connect it to your computer, a jack to connect headphones, a switch to mute or lock the screen orientation of the iPad quickly (this is user-configurable), Volume buttons to turn the volume up and down or mute the iPad quickly (hold down the volume down button), and a sleep button that also works to power the iPad on and off. You'll also find camera lenses, speakers, and a microphone, among other things.

Note   Although the iPad comes with a powerful speaker with rich, full sound, external speakers can improve on this. As you might guess, two or four (or more) speakers are better than one. However, you'll lose the portability when you opt for this type of setup.

Add Headphones or Speakers

Your iPad has the required port for connecting generic (nonproprietary) headphones and external speakers, neither of which are included with the iPad. You'll likely use headphones when listening to music, an audiobook, or when on an airplane; you might opt for a headset with an integrated microphone when using Skype or FaceTime; and you can use external speakers when watching a video (although the speaker built into the iPad is pretty good). Connecting is as simple as inserting the hardware into the proper port on the outside of your iPad.

Carefully turn your iPad in all directions and look for the following ports and features:

- **Home button**   The small round button on the front of the iPad near the bottom. Use it to access the Lock screen when the iPad is inactive, to access the Home screen when the iPad is in use, and to perform other tasks outlined in this book.
- **30-Pin Dock Connector**   The dock connector is located on the bottom of the iPad. This is where you connect accessories, such as the battery charger, docking stations, the Camera Connection Kit (optional), and other devices.
- **Built-in Speaker**   The speaker is behind the grid on the bottom right of the iPad, when holding the iPad in Portrait mode, under the Home button, on the right side.
- **3.5 mm Stereo Headphone Mini Jack**   A standard headphone jack that accepts generic headphones and headsets is located at the top of the iPad on the left.
- **Microphone**   The pinhole microphone is located on the top of the iPad, in the center, just above the front-facing camera lens.
- **Silent/Screen Rotation Lock**   This lock is located on the right side of the iPad near the top, just above the Volume buttons. Slide this switch to silence the iPad. You can change the function of this lock in the Settings app, from the General tab, to serve as a screen rotation lock instead.
- **Volume**   The Volume buttons are located on the right side of the iPad underneath the Screen Rotation Lock.
- **Sleep/Wake and On/Off**   The Sleep/Wake button is located on the top of the iPad on the right; just apply a short press. You can use this button to turn on or off the iPad as well; apply a long press and hold, and then opt to turn off the iPad when prompted.
- **Camera lenses**   The front- and rear-facing camera lenses are at the top of their respective sides of the iPad.
- **Micro-SIM card tray**   Located at the top, on the left side, and available only on AT&T Wi-Fi + 3G models. You'll need a SIM eject tool (or a paper clip) to gain access.

Locate and Use the Sleep and Volume Buttons

Look straight at the iPad Home screen and locate the physical Sleep/Wake button on the top-right corner of the device. It's at the top of the iPad, the part that is facing the ceiling as you hold it in portrait view. Now, locate the Volume buttons on the right side, also near the top.

Use the Sleep/Wake button to lock your iPad when you aren't using it, to prevent it from waking up when you touch it. While your iPad is sleeping, you can still listen to music and use the Volume buttons. To wake the iPad, press the Sleep/Wake button or the Home button to bring up the unlock screen. Press and hold the Sleep/Wake button to shut the iPad completely off and turn it on again.

Note If you haven't used the iPad for a few minutes, it'll lock itself automatically. You can lengthen or shorten the Auto-Lock duration by opening the Settings app, tapping General, and tapping the Auto-Lock option. For more information, refer to Appendix A.

As noted, the Sleep/Wake button can be used to put the iPad to sleep or to wake it up. When the iPad is asleep, it uses minimal battery power. In this state, the iPad can hold its charge for a long time (perhaps a month), so it's okay to use this mode as often as you like. You'll put the iPad to sleep when you want to blacken the screen and use the device again in the near future. In contrast, you'll completely power off the iPad when you know you won't be using it for a few days, or if you intend to pack it for travel.

The Volume buttons are used as you might guess; you press and hold the top button to increase the volume and the bottom button to decrease the volume. To quickly mute the iPad, you simply hold the bottom Volume bottom button until the device is silent or press the Silent switch just above it. You'll see an icon on the screen when you press either Volume button. See Figure 1-5.

FIGURE 1-5   When you adjust the volume, volume information is displayed briefly on the screen.

You can configure the maximum volume in Settings, under iPod.

Explore the Home Screen

The Home screen is what you see when you turn on and unlock your iPad, and it gives you one-tap access to everything that's available on it. In Chapter 2 you'll learn how to personalize this screen by moving the icons, and how to add or remove icons to make the iPad uniquely yours. For now, though, you'll want to explore what's on the Home screen already, and learn to navigate around in it. The Home screen icons are shown in Figure 1-6.

FIGURE 1-6   The Home screen comes with preconfigured icons for Apple's own apps.

These are the icons you'll see on the Home screen when you first turn it on:

- **Calendar** A fully functional calendar that allows you to create and manage events; configure reminders for events; view the calendar by day, month, and lists of events; and add new calendars by incorporating applications like Microsoft Office Outlook.
- **Contacts** An application you use to manage the contacts you create or add. You can easily add new or edit existing contacts, select a contact to communicate with, or share contact information with others.
- **Notes** An application that allows you to take notes easily. The Notes app looks like a yellow lined steno pad and allows you to create notes with a virtual keyboard, and then email them, delete them, or save them for future reference.
- **Maps** A full-fledged application for getting directions to local restaurants or points of interest, contacts' physical addresses, your current position (where you are), and for showing traffic, satellite views, typed directions, and more.
- **Videos** An option for managing the videos you own, and watching videos you get from iTunes.
- **YouTube** An application that allows you to quickly view YouTube video content, watch the most popular videos of the day, and search for videos you want to view. With YouTube, you can also mark your favorite videos so you can access them later or view similar videos easily. This is an app, though, and doesn't take you to the actual web site.
- **iTunes** An application that allows you to preview and purchase music and media on your iPad. (As with some of the other apps, you need to be online to access the iTunes Store.) Note that the iTunes app on the iPad is only a storefront and does not handle media management and playback as iTunes on a computer does.
- **App Store** The App Store is where you purchase and download apps, including those that enable you to engage in social networking, manage your finances, obtain additional information about products you plan to buy, play games, share data, and more. Think of anything you'd like to do with your iPad; there's likely an app for that!
- **Game Center** The Game Center makes it easy to find games, play games, and create an online gaming identity and keep track of the games you play and the scores you earn, among other things.
- **FaceTime** FaceTime lets you hold video conversations with anyone else using an iPad 2, iPhone 4, new iPod touch, or Mac over Wi-Fi. It works just as you'd expect a "video phone" to work, by assisting you in placing a call to a contact, initiating and holding a video conversation, and hanging up when your call is complete.
- **Camera** The Camera app offers access to the front- and rear-facing cameras, enabling you to take both photos and video, as well as hold video conversations with FaceTime.
- **Photo Booth** Photo Booth can be used to take pictures and apply effects to those pictures using either the front or rear camera lenses.
- **Settings** An application that enables you to turn on and off Wi-Fi; change sounds, brightness, and wallpaper; configure email, contacts, and calendar options; change Safari defaults; change iPod defaults; and more.

There are also four icons located across the bottom of the screen, on the Dock:

- **Safari**   A web browser for surfing the Internet. With it you can create bookmarks, set a home page, and perform common tasks associated with the Internet.
- **Mail**   A complete email solution. With Mail, you can send and receive email, save and manage email, and perform common tasks associated with emailing.
- **Photos**   An application for viewing and managing photos. With Photos, you can view slideshows, browse your photos, and even upload photos from a digital camera or media card (provided you purchase the Apple Camera Connection Kit).
- **iPod**   A complete music player that enables you to play and manage music. You can create playlists of your favorite songs or access playlists that have been synced from your home computer too, such as Most Played.

Tip   Tap any icon one time to open it. Tap the Home button to close it.

Navigate the Home Screen

Navigation isn't difficult; just touch any icon on the screen to open it. To return to the Home screen, press the Home button. That's it. It's what you do after you open an application that can change from app to app. Go ahead, touch any icon on the screen to open it, and tap the Home button to return to the Home screen.

If you're not sure what to tap, tap Notes. When you open the Notes app (included with your iPad), you touch once to bring up the keyboard, and use it to create your note, shown in Figure 1-7. Touch the keyboard icon on the virtual keyboard to make the keyboard disappear, and then use your finger to share the note, delete it, or otherwise manage it. Now, try a different app, perhaps Calendar. It won't take long for you to get the hang of it.

Click the Home button to return to the Home screen, if you haven't already, and this time click Photos. If you synced photos earlier in this chapter, they will appear here. Continue experimenting as desired, noting that some apps require you to connect to the Internet to use them (Maps, YouTube, iTunes, the App Store, Game Center, Safari, and Mail).

Learn Touch Techniques

There's more to navigating the icons and applications besides touching an area of the screen. You can "flick" up or down to scroll up and down in a screen, for instance. You can flick left and right to move between pages in an iBook. You can "pinch" (spread a finger and thumb outward or inward) to zoom in and zoom out on a photo, web page, email, or other item. You can "tap" to open a stack of photos in the Photos application, and you can "double-tap" to switch between full-screen and wide-screen mode in the Videos application or to zoom in on something. You can also *tap and hold* to select items, and *tap, hold, and drag* to move icons and data.

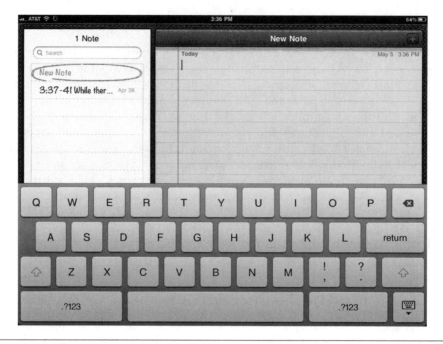

FIGURE 1-7   The Notes app is one of the easiest apps to use.

How to...   # Tap and Touch

The best way to get to know your iPad is to explore it. Perform these steps to learn how to use the touch techniques introduced in this section:

1. Touch the Photos icon to open Photos. If you have photos, you can
   a. Double-tap one to make it full screen.
   b. Double-tap again to zoom in.
   c. Use a pinching motion with your thumb and forefinger by pulling them together on the photo to make the photo small again.
2. Touch and hold an app icon on the Home screen for a few seconds. Once the icons begin to "jiggle," you can
   a. Drag to rearrange the icons on the screen, even the ones that run across the bottom of the screen.
   b. Press the Home button to stop the icons from "jiggling" and accept the new arrangement.
3. Touch and hold an app icon again to enable the "jiggle" mode, and then
   a. Drag to move an icon to the right until you have moved it "off" the screen. A new, blank screen will appear. Drop the icon.
   b. Click the Home button when finished.
   c. To visit additional Home screens, flick left or right.
4. Flick right to open the Spotlight Search screen.
5. Tap any icon to open the app associated with it; tap the Home screen to close the app.

You can open the Spotlight Search screen by tapping the Home button while on the first Home screen. (You can also flick left to right.)

Tip Tap and touch are used often in this book and are generally exchangeable terms.

Understand the iPhone OS

The iPad uses the iPhone OS. Although the iPad was initially touted as a tablet *computer*, it simply isn't. A tablet computer should, in the minds of most experts at least, run a full-fledged operating system, like the one used in an Apple Mac computer or a Windows-based PC. A full-fledged operating system allows the user to manipulate the computer at the disk level, restructure the files and folders stored on it (if desired), and install compatible hardware and their drivers, as well as any compatible software. You can't do much of that with the iPad; you can't manipulate the file structure, for instance, or install device drivers for hardware that may be connectable physically, but will not work.

Your iPad does have an operating system, though. While it does not run any version of the Mac OS X software that a Mac computer would run, it does run an OS. It runs a version of the iPhone's operating system. This operating system is locked down and heavily restricted; it can't be modified in many of the ways you'd modify a computer, and it can't fulfill many of the specialized tasks we ask of computers. So understand that when you want to do something with your iPad, like manage music, videos, or photos, you'll need to rely on what Apple provides, at first at least, and then you can move on to more fully featured apps as you gain experience with the iPad.

When you start to explore apps, a few notable apps can really improve what you can do with your iPad, such as iWork's Numbers, Keynote, and Pages, and can help you be more productive. iBooks, another app, enables you to turn your iPad into a digital book reader, complete with a built-in store for purchasing books. And Netflix enables you to watch movies on demand if you have a Netflix subscription.

Note Earlier in this chapter you learned a little about the applications located on the Home screen, including but not limited to Maps, Videos, and Contacts. There are additional features, though, like Spotlight for searching for data. As you work through this book, you'll learn about these things and others.

Explore and Purchase Accessories

Your iPad came in a box with a USB adapter, and a power adapter. As you may know already, though, there are other Apple accessories you can purchase, including a Camera Connection Kit, and a Standard Dock. You can also purchase various third-party keyboards and cases, among other things. In this last section, you'll learn about some of the additional accessories you can obtain, and what to look for when you do.

When you get a chance, visit www.apple.com and click the Store tab. There, you can take a look at all of the accessories available from Apple. Take a look at each of the following while at the store. You may find something you can't live without:

- Apple's wireless Bluetooth keyboard
- Apple TV
- The iPad Smart Cover
- Video adapters for an external monitor or projector
- Bluetooth-compatible speakers
- Camera Connection Kit
- Apple's in-ear headphones with compatible remote

Connect a USB Component

There's no USB port on the iPad. There is a USB Camera Connection Kit you can purchase, though, which allows you to connect a USB digital camera to your iPad. If you can connect a USB digital camera, physically at least, you may also think that you can also connect (and make work) a USB printer, USB scanner, USB mouse, or any other USB device. That's not the case at the moment, although you never know what the future holds.

Let's start with something we know will work, and connect a digital camera using the USB Camera Connection Kit.

To use the USB Camera Connection Kit to connect a USB digital camera:

1. Purchase the USB Camera Connection Kit from any Apple store, authorized reseller, or third party.
2. Connect the adapter to the 30-pin connection at the bottom of your iPad.
3. Using the camera's USB cable, connect the camera to the new hardware, or if you opt to use the Media Card Reader adapter instead, insert a media card. Turn on the camera, if applicable.
4. Click the Home button and move the slider to unlock the iPad, if necessary.

Did You Know? **iWork Is Available for Your iPad**

Apple's popular iWork suite of productivity applications is also available for your iPad. iWork apps include special editions of Pages, Keynote, and Numbers, software you can use to create and manage documents, presentations, and spreadsheets. The three apps are priced individually at $9.99 each, and can be downloaded directly through the iPad's App Store or through iTunes on your home computer.

FIGURE 1-8   It's easy to import images using the optional Camera Connection Kit.

5. Note that the pictures appear automatically on your screen.
6. To select images, tap them one time. Note that you can choose to import all of the pictures if desired. See Figure 1-8.
7. After selecting the images, click Import. You can then select Import All or Import Selected.
8. Wait while the import process completes.
9. When the import process is complete, you can opt to delete or keep the images on your card.

 Images imported directly to the iPad can be transferred back to your computer when you sync.

Connect a Bluetooth Device

A compatible Bluetooth device is a wireless device you can use with your iPad, such as a wireless headset, wireless speakers, or wireless keyboard. Because these devices are wireless, connecting them requires a little more effort than connecting devices that simply plug in (like headphones). Specifically, you have to "pair" the device with the iPad, and it is this process of pairing that allows the iPad to recognize and use the device. Pairing also allows the device and the iPad to agree on a Bluetooth frequency, so that they can communicate effectively without "crossing signals" with any other Bluetooth devices you may have installed. To connect a new Bluetooth device the first time (and you shouldn't have to repeat these steps):

1. Turn on your new Bluetooth device, insert batteries, or perform any other step to power the device.
2. Follow the directions for the device to make it discoverable.
3. Locate and tap the Settings icon on the Home screen.
4. Tap General.
5. Tap Bluetooth and move the slider to On.
6. Wait while the iPad searches for Bluetooth devices.
7. When it finds the device, type the device's passkey or PIN when prompted.
8. To turn off Bluetooth, again click Settings, then General, then Bluetooth. Move the virtual switch into the Off position.

If you're in the market for a Bluetooth device, make sure it's iPad compatible; not all devices will be.

Understand Wi-Fi and Wi-Fi + 3G iPad Models

iPads come in two models, each with varying amounts of internal memory. There's a Wi-Fi only model and a Wi-Fi + 3G model. The Wi-Fi only model enables you to get online via wireless routers, including those found in home and work networks and free Wi-Fi hotspots. Wi-Fi only models don't allow you to sign up for a data plan from AT&T or Verizon so that you can have additional Internet access using an integrated cellular connection. Thus, although you can access free Wi-Fi hotspots in coffee shops, hotel lobbies, libraries, pubs, gyms, and the like with your Wi-Fi only iPad, if you're away from these types of networks you won't be able to get online. This limits your ability to use the iPad on the go. When you're within range of a Wi-Fi network and you attempt to access the Internet, you'll be prompted to join the network, as shown in Figure 1-9.

The Wi-Fi + 3G model allows you to access the Internet over a conventional Wi-Fi connection, but also gives you the option of using AT&T or Verizon's prepaid Internet data service, which works over a 3G cellular network. This means that when you're travelling in a car, commuting on a bus, or away from a Wi-Fi network, you can get online using the 3G cellular network (provided you have 3G coverage in your area). Additionally, with Wi-Fi + 3G, you'll be able to use Assisted GPS (Global Positioning System) thanks to an integrated chipset not included on Wi-Fi only models. Of course, you'll have to pay for a monthly data plan to make this happen.

Note There are, of course, downsides to 3G service through AT&T and Verizon. You can't get access everywhere, and coverage can be spotty. When 3G is enabled, you'll use quite a bit of battery life, too. And don't forget that a 3G model costs quite a bit more than a Wi-Fi only model.

Select a Wi-Fi Network

JolisHomeNetwork

Cancel

FIGURE 1-9   You can join a Wi-Fi network in range.

Choose a Data Plan for Your Wi-Fi + 3G iPad

To get the most from your iPad, you really need always-on Internet access, especially if you travel or are away from your own home or business Wi-Fi network often. To have always-on access, you'll have to opt for a data plan. The data plan you choose depends on how much time you plan to spend on the Internet, and what you plan to do while there.

If you only want to check email, read online newspapers and blogs, and occasionally watch a video from YouTube, you might be able to get away with the least expensive option. As you can see in Figure 1-10, AT&T offers two plans, one that gives you 250MB of data and another that offers 2GB.

Many experts refer to the 250MB plan as "your mother's plan." Having 250MB of data will allow you to access the Internet, but with limited access. If you're unsure what 250MB is, consider this: One email with a large attachment can be somewhere around 2MB; a single song can be 3 to 4MB, and a video can be 8 to 10MB (or more). An hour of web browsing consumes about 40MB of data; watching a single high-definition video can consume upwards of 300MB. As you can see, this type of data usage can add up pretty quickly. Note that when you connect to the Internet on

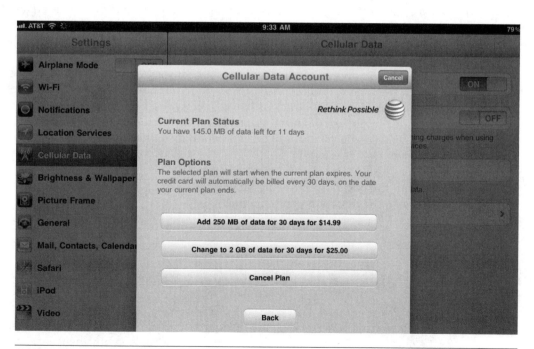

FIGURE 1-10   Opt for the least expensive plan, and later, if you need more, you can upgrade.

your iPad from a home Wi-Fi network or from a free AT&T Wi-Fi hotspot, you will not be charged for your data usage, though, so if you can work this into your surfing regimen, this plan may work. (Verizon offers similar plans and access.)

We suggest you start off with the 250MB plan, and then later, if you decide you need more data, you can upgrade your plan from Settings, in the Cellular Data section.

 AT&T will warn you when you're getting close to your monthly limit, and offer an available upgrade to unlimited service.

Understand the Built-in Sensors

Your iPad came with various sensors to help it perform tasks. The accelerometer, for instance, can sense when you turn the iPad from landscape to portrait view, and change the view of what's on the screen accordingly. The accelerometer, because it senses and understands the movement of the device, also enhances game play. You can move the iPad to simulate a movement, such as driving really fast around a sharp curve, and the game will respond accordingly.

There are other sensors you might not think too much about, but they are there. There's a sensor that identifies the current lighting, be it a sunny sky or a dark tunnel, and then adjusts the brightness of the screen to accommodate. And of course, Multi-Touch is a sensor. *Multi-Touch* technology is what enables you to tap or touch the iPad and have it respond.

GPS (Global Positioning System) is another sensor. With it, the iPad can access information from earth-orbiting satellites to find your current location or the location of another place (like a restaurant or library). Only the iPad 3G models have true GPS capability, due to the use of an integrated chip. Wi-Fi models of the iPad can also be used to provide a ballpark guess of your location by gathering information on nearby Wi-Fi hotspots.

Your iPad also has a built-in digital compass. With it you can discover your direction, but the best part of the digital compass is that it automatically repositions maps to match the direction you're facing.

Did You Know?   There's an iPad User Guide on Your iPad

To view the iPad User Guide, tap Safari, tap the Bookmarks icon, and then tap the iPad User Guide bookmark. While viewing the guide, you can also tap Add to Home Screen to make the guide easily accessible. You can even view the guide in other languages.

Understand the Status Icons

While you're using your iPad, various status icons will appear and disappear on the Home screen. The icons tell you how you are connected to the Internet, how much battery life you have left, and a few other things, all of which are summarized in Table 1-2.

TABLE 1-2   Status Icons and Their Meaning

Status Icon	Meaning
Airplane Mode	Shows that Airplane Mode is enabled. When this mode is enabled, you can't access the Internet or use Bluetooth devices.
3G	Shows that your carrier's 3G network is available and is currently being used to connect to the Internet. This option is available only on the Wi-Fi + 3G iPad models.
EDGE	Shows that your carrier's EDGE network is available and is currently being used to connect to the Internet. This is available on Wi-Fi + 3G iPad models.
GPRS	Shows that your carrier's GPRS network is available and is currently being used to connect to the Internet. This is available on Wi-Fi + 3G iPad models.
Wi-Fi	Shows that your iPad is connected to the Internet via Wi-Fi. The more bars, the stronger the connection.
Activity	Shows that there is activity. The activity can be network activity or app activity.
VPN	Shows that you are connected to a VPN (virtual private network). Generally, this is a network you use in an enterprise at work.
Lock	Shows that the iPad is locked.
Screen Rotation Lock	Shows that the screen's orientation is locked.
Play	Shows that something is playing, perhaps a song, audiobook, or podcast.
Bluetooth	Shows the status of a Bluetooth connection. If the icon is white, Bluetooth is enabled and a device is connected. If the icon is gray, Bluetooth is enabled but no device is connected. If the icon is not showing, Bluetooth is not enabled.
Battery	Shows the status of the battery and/or its charging status.

Connect and Create Your First Backup

If you've worked through this chapter from beginning to end, you now have some data on your iPad. If your iPad is still connected to your computer, disconnect it. Now, reconnect it. Your iPad will sync automatically (if that's what you've configured) and a backup will begin automatically as well, as shown in the following illustration.

iTunes

Syncing "Joli's iPad" (Step 1 of 4)
Backing up

2

iPad 2 Basics

HOW TO...

- Reposition icons on the Home screen
- Move icons off the Home screen
- Delete icons for third-party apps
- Change the wallpaper
- Turn on Wi-Fi
- Locate and connect to a free public Wi-Fi hotspot
- Connect to a private network
- Access the Internet using 3G
- Change your data plan
- Use Spotlight Search
- Type effectively
- Restore your iPad to its previous settings

You're eager to get started with your iPad by making it uniquely yours with new wallpaper, rearranging the icons to meet your needs, getting online, learning to type, and finding stuff! After you've worked through the exercises in this chapter, you'll be well on your way to understanding how to navigate all parts of your iPad. You can then use this knowledge to work through the rest of the book in any order you like.

 Chapters 1 and 2 should be read in sequential order. After you've finished Chapter 2, feel free to skip around.

Personalize the Home Screen

The Home screen on your iPad has several icons, all placed in a specific order out of the box, and a beautiful picture of what look to be air bubbles for wallpaper. You can change just about everything about this, though, by repositioning apps on the Home screen or moving apps to another screen (and out of your way), deleting icons for third-party apps you've decided you don't need or like, and by replacing the wallpaper with something else.

Manage Icons

Just because the icons are positioned a certain way when you unpacked your iPad doesn't mean they have to stay that way! If you aren't perfectly happy with the order of the icons on the Home screen, you can do a little tweaking. If you write a lot of notes, for instance, you can put the Notes app in the top-left corner of the Home screen for easy access; if you use Maps quite a bit, you can opt to put the Maps app at the bottom of the screen (in the *Dock*), and replace one of the four there currently or add it to them (you can have up to six); if you rarely access the Contacts app, you can move it off the main Home screen to a secondary screen with other apps you rarely use so that it's not in your way.

Tip   Yes, you can have multiple Home screens! You access any additional Home screens you create by flicking your finger to the left or right while on a Home screen.

If you read Chapter 1, you may have already tried the tap-hold-and-drag technique for repositioning icons, but we'll go over it here in more detail, just to make sure it's clear. Because there's a lot you can do with hiding, moving, and repositioning icons, there are five scenarios we'll cover:

- You want to reposition the icons on the Home screen.
- You want to change something about the four icons that appear across the bottom of the screen.
- You want to hide icons by moving them to a secondary Home screen.
- You want to delete an icon for an app you've downloaded and installed.
- You want to create a folder to hold apps that are alike.

To reposition an icon on the Home screen:

1. On the Home screen, touch and hold your finger on any icon.
2. Once the icons all start "wiggling," drag any icon to any area of the Home screen to move it there. See Figure 2-1.
3. Repeat Step 2 as often as desired, and then click the Home button to set the icons.

FIGURE 2-1   When repositioning icons, tap, drag, and once in position, drop.

To change icons on the Dock:

1. On the Home screen, touch and hold your finger on any icon.
2. Once the icons all start "wiggling," drag one icon from the lower area of the screen to the upper area. Repeat if desired.
3. From the upper area of the Home screen, drag an icon to the bottom area to add it there. Repeat as desired. You can have up to six icons on the Dock.
4. Click the Home button to set the icons.

To hide icons by moving them to a secondary Home screen:

1. On the Home screen, touch and hold your finger on any icon.
2. Once the icons all start "wiggling," flick any icon to the far right of the screen, as if you were trying to flick it off the iPad.
3. A new screen will appear, where you can "drop" the icon.
4. Flick left to return to the main Home screen, and repeat as desired. You can have multiple Home screens.

You can also delete icons for third-party apps you've acquired. When you delete the icon, the app is also removed from your iPad (and thus frees up space on your iPad for other things). Deleting icons and their apps from your iPad can help you keep it uncluttered and organized. It's important to note that the iTunes program on your computer will retain copies of apps you've acquired, including those downloaded directly on the iPad, which get automatically transferred to your iTunes collection when you sync it. If you ever want to reinstall an app you've deleted on your iPad, connect your iPad to your computer, and in iTunes under the App tab, select the app to sync.

You Can Reacquire an App Without Connecting the iPad to Your Computer

Once you've paid for an app, you can delete it from your iPad and download it again, for free, as often as you like. You can also download the app to other authorized iDevices, again, for free. You can authorize up to five computers and all of your compatible iDevices from a single iTunes account.

To remove an icon for a third-party app you've downloaded and installed:

1. On the screen that shows the third-party app, touch and hold your finger on any icon.
2. Once the icons all start "wiggling," look for any icon that offers a little X on it. These are the only icons you can delete.
3. Touch the X on the app to delete, and when prompted to delete it, touch Delete. See Figure 2-2.
4. Repeat Steps 2 and 3 as often as desired, and then click the Home button to set them.

We don't suggest you create any folders yet, because if you do, the instructions in this book won't match what you see on your screen. However, creating folders is a way to personalize the Home screen, and does bear an introduction here. To create a folder to hold apps that are alike (which you will hopefully do much later, after reading this book):

1. Choose two like apps you'd like to combine into a folder.
2. On any screen, touch and hold your finger on any icon.
3. Once the icons all start "wiggling," drag one icon to the top of the other.
4. To rename the folder, tap the X and type a new name. See Figure 2-3.

FIGURE 2-2 You can delete icons for third-party apps you've downloaded by clicking the X in the top corner of the icon.

FIGURE 2-3   You can create folders to organize similar apps.

5. Tap outside the new folder to close it.
6. Continue to drag icons into this folder as desired; to remove icons from it, drag them from the folder back to the Home screen.
7. Tap the Home button when finished.

Change the Wallpaper

As noted earlier, the picture on the Home screen is called the *wallpaper*. You can change the wallpaper to any picture you can get onto your iPad (like a picture you've taken with a digital camera), or any picture that Apple has provided for you (and there are several). If you don't have any of your own pictures yet, that's okay. You can always return here to set your favorite image as wallpaper when you do.

You can also assign a picture to the Lock screen. That's the image you see when the screen is locked, but the display is on. In other words, it's the picture you see on the page that shows the slider to unlock the iPad before using it. The Lock screen is shown in Figure 2-4. I've already changed the image here, and it shows the lake and mountain wallpaper.

To change the wallpaper for the Home screen, the Lock screen, or both on your iPad:

1. On the Home screen, touch Settings.

Tip   If you created an additional Home screen page, you may have to flick left or right to find the Settings icon.

2. In the Settings page, touch Brightness & Wallpaper. See Figure 2-5.
3. In the right pane, touch the arrow next to Wallpaper, also shown in Figure 2-5. (You can actually touch anywhere in the white box showing the two current screens.)

FIGURE 2-4 The Lock screen with a new image applied

FIGURE 2-5 You can access a lot of options from Settings, including Brightness & Wallpaper.

FIGURE 2-6   Select a picture and then choose where to apply it.

4. If you have pictures on your iPad, you'll see them in the resulting screen. If you do not have your own pictures yet, you'll only see the Wallpaper option. Click any folder to view the pictures in it. Any other folders shown below Wallpaper are your own personal photos you've synced or imported.

5. If you see a picture you like, tap it, and click one of the following options, shown in Figure 2-6:
   - **Set Lock Screen**   This is the screen you see when the iPad is locked.
   - **Set Home Screen**   This is the image you see on the Home screen, under the Home screen icons.
   - **Set Both**

6. To return to the Settings window, click Back, and then click Wallpaper. You can also simply click the Home button on the iPad.

 To set different pictures for both the Lock screen and the Home screen, perform these steps twice.

Access the Internet with Wi-Fi

If you read Chapter 1, you know the difference between Wi-Fi and Wi-Fi + 3G iPad models, and you understand the differences between connecting to the Internet using a Wi-Fi connection versus using a 3G connection. If you didn't read Chapter 1, the sidebar here provides an explanation. That said, in this section you'll learn about connecting to a Wi-Fi network to gain Internet access, something you can do with either the Wi-Fi only or the Wi-Fi + 3G iPad model. In the next section you'll learn about connecting to the Internet with 3G, something you can do only if you have the Wi-Fi + 3G iPad model and sign up and pay for a data package from AT & T or Verizon.

Turn on Wi-Fi

Your iPad has an option that enables you to turn on and off the Wi-Fi feature at will. When Wi-Fi is enabled, you're telling your iPad "Hey, I want you to look for Wi-Fi networks, and keep searching until you find one!" Because the iPad then constantly searches for networks, battery power is drained more quickly than if it isn't. So, when you don't need Wi-Fi access, it's best to turn this feature off. You'll be asked to disable Wi-Fi when you're on a plane too, so you need to know where this feature is and how to get to it quickly.

Wi-Fi vs. Wi-Fi + 3G

There are two models of the iPad. The first is Wi-Fi only and the second is Wi-Fi + 3G.

The Wi-Fi model connects to the Internet only one way, when you are within range of and have permission to use a Wi-Fi network. You may have a Wi-Fi network in your home or at work, and you can locate free Wi-Fi networks in coffee shops, hotels, libraries, and similar establishments. You must be within range of a Wi-Fi network to get Internet access. There is no other way to get online.

The Wi-Fi + 3G model connects to the Internet in two ways. One is through a Wi-Fi connection, described in the preceding paragraph. The other is through a 3G connection available via cellular networks, access to which is offered by a company like AT&T or Verizon, both cellular phone and Internet providers. If you have a Wi-Fi + 3G model, you can get online at free Wi-Fi hotspots, at your wireless network at work and home, and, when those aren't available, from a cellular network. Note that you have to pay for a 3G data plan to obtain cellular access.

Caution Wi-Fi must be enabled to see and connect to wireless networks like the one in your home or your local library.

If you have a home network and have already opened Safari or YouTube while exploring, you may have already connected to your own home network. That's because by default, Wi-Fi is on, and when you try to access the Internet, your iPad will let you know about available wireless networks. If you were prompted about your own network and input your security code or passphrase, you're ahead of the game and already connected!

To turn on and off Wi-Fi and to connect to an available network:

1. From the Home screen, click Settings. (To view the Home screen at any time, click the Home button.)
2. In the left pane, tap Wi-Fi.
3. Move the slider for Wi-Fi to Off or On, as desired. Remember, Wi-Fi must be turned on to connect to Wi-Fi networks. See Figure 2-7.
4. If you want to be notified when Wi-Fi networks are available, move the slider for Ask to Join Networks to On. This is also shown in Figure 2-7.
5. If networks are available, you'll see them under Choose a Network. If you see a network you'd like to join now, you can
   a. Tap the network in the list.
   b. Enter the password, if applicable, and click Join.
6. Click the Home button to return to the Home screen.

FIGURE 2-7   Wi-Fi must be enabled to choose and connect to a network.

Locate a Free Hotspot

With Wi-Fi enabled you can now seek out and join free, unsecured Wi-Fi networks in public places like your local coffee shop. These free and open networks are called Wi-Fi hotspots. Before you can connect you have to find a local hotspot, though, and that's detailed here.

To locate a free hotspot near you:

1. Visit www.google.com and search for Free Wi-Fi Hotspots, followed by your zip code. You'll probably see several results.
2. Browse through the results to locate a Wi-Fi hotspot near you.
3. If Step 2 does not result in a viable hotspot, try either of the following (and understand there are many other options to try):
   a. Navigate to www.free-hotspot.com and type your zip code to see the results.
   b. Navigate to www.openwifispots.com, and enter location information to see the results.

Connect to a Free Hotspot

With a free Wi-Fi hotspot in your sights, it's time to take a walk or a drive and learn how to connect to it. Keep in mind that some establishments will require you to purchase a cup of coffee, a beer, or a bite to eat for the privilege of using the hotspot (or maybe you have to get a library card), so once you get there, inquire about the rules. When you're ready to connect, verify that the following settings are enabled:

- In Settings, for Wi-Fi, Wi-Fi is set to On.
- In Settings, for Wi-Fi, Ask to Join Networks is set to On.

When you're sure you are within range, and you've verified that the settings are properly enabled, from the Home screen, tap Safari. You should see a notification that a network is available. Tap it to join the network. The next time you're within range, you should be connected automatically. If you don't see a prompt, tap Settings, tap Wi-Fi, and under Choose a Network, tap the network to join.

Note On the slim chance the network is not listed under Choose a Network, click Other. Then type the name and password for the network.

Connect to a Private Network

If you have a wireless network in your home, you can connect to it with your iPad. If there is a secured wireless network where you work, at your parent's house, or at a friend's, and the owner or administrator of that network will give you the information required to connect, you can access the Internet from that network too. So before you try to connect to any private network, obtain the required information for the personal Wi-Fi network you want to connect to (which is generally referred to as a passcode, password, or something similar). You'll need to input this information when prompted during the authentication process the first time you connect. You should not need to input it again unless the security information for the network changes.

With the security information at hand, you can connect to a secure, personal network:

1. From the Home screen, tap Settings.
2. Tap Wi-Fi.
3. Verify that Wi-Fi is enabled.
4. Under Choose a Network, tap the arrow beside the network you'd like to connect to. (If it's not listed, tap Other.)
5. Type a name, if required, and type the password.
6. Click Join.

Because the iPad is not a computer, you won't be able to access files and folders on resources connected to the network. You will be able to access the Internet, though, and for free! You will not be charged for nor will you accumulate data usage on any prepaid plan when you're connected to a local wireless network like this one.

Note You'll learn about Safari in Chapter 3.

Access the Internet with 3G

If you have a Wi-Fi + 3G iPad and pay for a data plan, you can access the Internet when you're away from private wireless networks and Wi-Fi hotspots (provided you are in an area with coverage). With this combination, you can access the Internet from anywhere, at any time. Connecting with 3G is automatic. If you try to access the Internet and your iPad can't find a Wi-Fi network, it'll connect with 3G. You don't have to do anything, except leave Cellular Data enabled.

Note If you have a Wi-Fi only iPad but now want 3G service, there's no way to upgrade.

Enable or Disable Cellular Data on the Wi-Fi + 3G Only

You know you can enable and disable the Wi-Fi feature on your iPad when you aren't using it. Generally you do this to save battery power. You can also enable and disable Cellular Data. You will want to disable Cellular Data when you've met your data usage limit for the month (and don't want to renew right away) or if you're out of the country and aren't sure what charges you'll incur if you leave it on.

You may also opt to disable cellular data when you don't need to access the Internet and don't want data to be sent to your iPad automatically. Some apps receive data from the Internet routinely, such as a social networking app that gets status updates from your friends behind the scenes. If you don't need to view these updates and are keeping an eye on your data usage, you can disable the Cellular Data feature when you aren't using the iPad.

To disable Cellular Data and enable it when you need it again:

1. Tap Settings.
2. Tap Cellular Data.
3. Use the slider for Cellular Data to switch from On to Off. See Figure 2-8.
4. Click the Home button to return to the Home screen.

FIGURE 2-8 You can easily turn off the Cellular Data feature.

Change Your Data Plan

You may have noticed on the Cellular Data page, which you saw in Figure 2-8, that you can also tap View Account. You'll see this if you have already signed up for a cellular data plan. You can change your plan from here too, so if you ever decide to cancel your plan or change the data usage, do it here.

 If you haven't yet signed up for a data plan and you want to, do it at the Cellular Data page in Settings.

Search for Anything

Spotlight Search is a built-in feature on the iPad. You can access Spotlight Search by tapping and holding the Home button for a second or two, and then letting go. You can also flick from left to right on the default Home screen. You can search for almost anything from the resulting Spotlight Search screen. Additionally, you'll find a small Search window in several iPad app windows like Calendar, Contacts, Maps, YouTube, App Store, iTunes, iPod, and Mail. You can use this window to search inside an app for something specific, like a song or an artist, or a specific contact or event. You use the search window the same way you'd use a search engine on the Internet; you simply type in keywords. As you type, results are filtered automatically in apps that contain personal data, and suggestions are offered for apps like iTunes that offer data you can download.

Try the Search option in the iPod.

1. Open the iPod app.
2. Tap once in the Search window.
3. Use the keyboard to type the last name of any artist in your library and view the results.
4. Click the X in the Search window to clear the results.
5. Type a word you know is in a specific song title. View the results. This time, all of the songs with that word in the title appear (and perhaps other data, if it matches an album title or band name). See Figure 2-9.

		Q Love ⊗
Shuffle ⤬		
A Deeper Love - (Tri...	Studio All-Stars	Music From Sister Act 1...	4:42
(Love Is Like A) Heat...	Studio All-Stars	Music From Sister Act 1...	2:55

FIGURE 2-9   Type any word that's in a song title to see all songs with that word.

As noted earlier, you can access the full Spotlight Search page by flicking right while on the Home screen. You can also click the Home button if you're on the Home screen to access this page. From here you can search the iPad for data. Results in this list will include matches from contacts, applications, music, podcasts, videos, audiobooks, notes, mail, and events.

To use the Spotlight Search page to search your iPad:

1. While on the Home screen, flick right. (Note you can also click once on the Home button.)
2. In the Search window at the top, type any keyword.

3. The results will appear automatically.
4. To perform another search, use the back key on the keyboard to erase what's in the Search window, and type another keyword or tap the X at the right end of the Search window to clear what's written.

> **Tip** Whenever you tap somewhere that requires you to type, the virtual keyboard will appear. For information on how to type effectively, see the next section, "Type Effectively."

Type Effectively

When you search for something on your iPad, you have to type what you're looking for in the Search window. Typing a word or two is pretty easy, and doesn't require much instruction. However, as you progress, you'll do more and more typing, and will need to know how to type effectively. Here are a few tips now to get you started, and we'll scatter other tips throughout the book as needed.

To type effectively, try these tips and tricks:

- When typing, if you press the wrong key on the virtual keyboard, simply slide your finger to the correct one and tap it. A letter is not input until you lift your finger from the screen.
- Tap and hold specific letters, like c, l, e, y, u, i, and others to see additional characters you can insert. For instance, tap and hold the key that has the comma and the exclamation point to access an apostrophe.

- Tap the up arrow (that's the SHIFT key) on the virtual keyboard before typing a letter to capitalize it.
- Tap the up arrow key and slide to a letter to capitalize it. To type a period and a space, quickly tap the space bar two times.
- If you've enabled Caps Lock in Settings, in General, in Keyboard, double-tap the SHIFT key (up arrow) to enable Caps Lock.
- Tap the number key (.?123) to access a secondary keyboard that includes numbers, and then type a number.
- Tap the symbol key to access a secondary keyboard that includes symbols and punctuation. To access this key, click the number key first.
- While you're typing, the Dictionary may suggest a word before you've finished typing the word. To accept the word, tap a space or hit the RETURN key, or hit any punctuation key. To reject the word, continue typing the word as you want it. (Tap the X next to the word to help your iPad learn the word.)

Restore Your iPad's Settings

Your iPad offers a way to revert to previous settings, so if you've made changes to the Home screen and want it to look as it did out of the box, you can reset the Home screen icons. You may have also input network settings you're unhappy with now, and you can reset those easily as well. You can also reset other things, like the Keyboard Dictionary, and even erase all content and all settings.

To reset any of the settings you've changed so far, and to reconfigure the settings to work like they did out of the box:

1. Tap Settings.
2. Tap General.
3. At the bottom of the screen, tap Reset.
4. Tap the settings to change, shown in Figure 2-10. Note that opting to erase all content and settings will remove all of the personal data you've added so far, and chances are you don't want to do that.
5. Click Reset to apply the changes.

So when would you want to erase all of your personal data and settings? When you sell your iPad of course! You can be sure that new models of iPads will be released, and you may want to trade up. That's why the iPad offers the option of erasing all content and settings. The next model of the iPad may have a media card slot. Future models may have a paper-thin slide-out keyboard or other new hardware features. Whatever happens, there will likely come a time when you want to sell your current model and purchase something better. Before you do, you'll need to restore your iPad to its factory settings.

When you restore the iPad to factory settings, you make it appear brand new again, at least on the inside! After it's restored, there will be no trace of your email accounts, messages, photos, videos, applications, iBooks, or anything else; it's returned to the

FIGURE 2-10   If you've made changes in this chapter and want to reset the Home screen layout, tap Reset Home Screen Layout here.

state it was in when you purchased it. You must do this before selling it to erase all of your personal data, and to make it easier for the next person to personalize.

To restore your iPad to factory settings:

1. Click Settings.
2. Click General.
3. At the bottom of the right pane, click Reset.
4. To reset your iPad to factory settings, tap Erase All Content and Settings.
5. Click Erase to verify.

PART II

Internet and Email

3

Safari

Safari is the web browser that comes preinstalled on your iPad and you can use it to surf the Internet. It's a full browser; with it you can locate anything on the web, view just about any web page, view lots of types of web media, save and manage bookmarks for web sites you visit often, and lots more. You can explore varying views, you can zoom in and out of a page, and you can have multiple web pages open at once.

If you've never used Safari and have always used a browser like Internet Explorer, Safari won't take much getting used to. The navigation bar is clean and contains easy-to-recognize icons, and there are some pretty smart features that just might take you by surprise. For instance, Safari keeps track of the web sites you've visited in the past, and when you type in a web address, Safari offers addresses that start with the letters you've typed. If you see what you want in the resulting list, you can tap the suggestion to go there. You can also add icons for web pages you visit often right on a Home screen. You may want to add an icon (called a *web clip*) for Facebook, MySpace, CNN, or any other page you visit regularly.

Safari is available from the Home screen by default, and is one of the four icons across the Dock at the bottom of the screen. It's ready to use, so there's no muss and no fuss!

Get to Know Safari

Before you can use Safari to surf the web, you have to be somewhere that offers Internet access. You can access the Internet with any iPad model, and in Chapter 2 you learned how to connect to the Internet from a Wi-Fi hotspot, using your own home wireless network, or using a 3G connection from a provider like AT&T. If you aren't sure what model you have or how to get connected to the Internet, refer to that chapter before continuing here. When you're ready to get started and are sure you are in a location where you can connect to the Internet, touch the Safari icon, shown here.

Tip If you're sure you're within range of a free Wi-Fi hotspot but can't access the Internet, verify that Wi-Fi is enabled via Settings | Wi-Fi.

Understand the Safari Interface

Everything you need to know about Safari's interface is located in the top part of the browser, called the navigation bar. As shown in Figure 3-1, there are several buttons and areas to explore.

The Back and Forward buttons let you move among previously viewed web pages easily.

The Add Bookmark icon lets you save web page references so you can access them easily later.

The Address window is where you type a web page address.

The Search window is used to search for anything on the Internet.

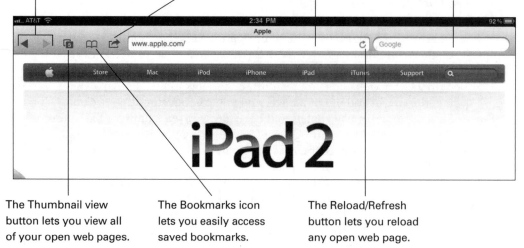

The Thumbnail view button lets you view all of your open web pages.

The Bookmarks icon lets you easily access saved bookmarks.

The Reload/Refresh button lets you reload any open web page.

FIGURE 3-1 Safari's navigation bar contains icons, an address bar, and a search window, among other things.

FIGURE 3-2 You can view all open web pages in thumbnail view, open a new page, or close an unwanted open page.

The icons on Safari's navigation bar are detailed in order from left to right here.

- **Back and Forward buttons** To return to the previously visited web page. The Back button will only be available if you've clicked a link in one page to go to another. After you click the Back button, the Forward button will become available. If you've visited lots of pages, you can click the Back and Forward buttons as many times as necessary to return to pages you've recently visited.
- **Thumbnail view** To turn the page you're currently viewing into a thumbnail, and to have access to a new blank page in Safari, as well as any other open web pages. See Figure 3-2.

Tip You can have up to nine web pages open at a time.

- **Bookmarks** To view bookmarks included with your iPad, including Apple's web site and the link to the iPad User Guide. You can tap any item in the list to go to the bookmarked page, or view your History (web sites you've recently visited), or to view the Bookmarks Bar (a place to organize some of the bookmarks you keep), which is shown in this illustration.

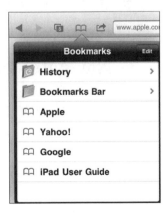

The Keyboard That Appears May Have Keys Unique to the Task at Hand

The virtual keyboards take many forms, but the one that usually pops up when you click the address window in Safari has a shortcut button that lets you enter ".com" with a single tap.

- **Add bookmark**   To add a bookmark for the current page so that you can access the same page later from a list of bookmarks. You can also add a web clip (icon) to your Home screen or email a link for this page to a friend.
- **Address window**   To type a web address and navigate to it. The keyboard appears when you tap inside this window, and an X allows you to delete what's already there quickly.
- **Reload/Refresh (the circular arrow in the address bar)**   To refresh and reload the current web page. Generally you reload a page when you want to view changes to the page, for instance, to read the latest headlines or get the most recent weather forecast. This icon is replaced with an X when you're typing in the address bar.
- **Search box**   To type keywords and search criteria to locate data on the Internet. Searches can be composed of a few words, a short question, or a complete sentence. By default, the search engine is Google. You can choose another if you desire, from Settings | Safari.

From any web page, feel free to explore these buttons and menus. Since you're probably already familiar with web surfing, type a few keywords in the Search window, or touch the preconfigured bookmarks to navigate to their pages. Don't worry, you can't hurt anything, and you can easily reset your iPad's settings should you ever wish to.

 Tip   If you're holding the iPad in Portrait view, hold it in Landscape view. If you're in Landscape view, try Portrait.

Navigate with Multi-Touch

You interact with Safari using your finger. You can scroll, pinch, tap, flip, and flick. You can also type with the virtual keyboard anytime you tap inside a window or form that requires it. While connected to Apple.com (or any other web page), try these moves to navigate to and through a web page:

- To move from page to page, touch any link in any page. The Back button will become available the first time you do this in a new page.

- To return to a previous page, touch the Back button. After you've used the Back button once, the Forward button becomes available.
- Tap the Bookmarks icon and tap any existing bookmark to navigate there.
- Tap inside the address bar, Search window, or Internet form to access the keyboard. You can then type a new web address, query, keywords, or other information.
- Tap the Thumbnail View icon (the two stacked squares). Tap the last page in the list, which is black, to create a new page. Now, type a keyword into the Search window to obtain results.
- If you're on a page that runs longer than the length of the screen, use a flick to scroll up or down.
- To zoom in on a page, use a reverse pinching motion with a finger and thumb. Pinch to zoom back out.
- To zoom in or out of a web page without pinching, tap the screen twice to zoom in. Tap twice again to zoom back out.
- To show a web page to someone sitting across from you, flip the entire iPad upside down. (Of course, the screen orientation can't be locked when you do this.)

View History

You can view web sites you've recently visited but did not bookmark, using the History option. You can access your History from the Bookmarks icon. Click History to see where you've been, and use the arrows offered to dive deeper into a specific date.

 Click Clear History to remove all items listed.

To access, view, use, and clear History data:

1. Touch the Bookmarks icon on the Safari navigation bar.
2. Tap History. (Notice that when you tap History, a new option appears on the header bar in the History window. Click it to return to the Bookmarks list.)
3. Tap any item in the History list, or touch the desired day in the History list. You can also tap Clear History.
4. After you tap a link, the History list will disappear back into the navigation bar.

Tip In the Bookmarks list and others, when you tap to access a subfolder, a button appears that will let you return to the previous list or menu. Tap that to return to the previous category.

Personalize Safari

There aren't as many personalization options as you might expect in Safari, and certainly not as many as you're used to in Safari on a Mac or PC. There's no "Action" or "Tools" menu where you can change the default font size, view additional toolbars, or change the color and appearance of web pages. However, there are a few things you can do, including saving web clips for your favorite pages on any Home screen and configuring web sites to log you in automatically. You can even personalize web sites to suit your own needs, such as inputting your zip code for weather and news, or changing the layout of content shown on a web page. These personalization options are offered by web sites, though, and differ from site to site. Options like the latter are not created by Safari or your iPad.

Note If you can't view Safari because of a visual impairment, refer to Chapter 16.

Save a Web Site as a Home Screen Icon

If there's a web site you visit often, you can put an icon for that page on your Home screen. This is called a "web clip." Doing this gives you one-tap access to the page. If you use a web-based mail program, or have a customized web page from a provider like Time Warner or Verizon, this may be just what you need. This is also a great option if you use a specific social network site regularly, or if you have a blog you write to daily.

To save a web page as a Home screen icon:

1. Open Safari and navigate to your favorite web page.
2. Tap the Add Bookmark icon. Click Add to Home Screen.

3. If desired, change the name offered, and then click Add.
4. Safari will close and the new web clip will appear on your Home screen.

Set Web Pages to Log You in Automatically

If you protect your iPad with a password (detailed at the end of this chapter), it's probably okay to configure web sites to log you in automatically and to keep you logged in. If you don't want to input a password each time you unlock your iPad, you may want to reconsider this. If you let web sites log you in automatically and keep you logged in for two weeks (a common option), then anyone with access to your iPad will also have access to your favorite sites. If these sites include Facebook or a page where you access your email, someone could do quite a bit of damage to your reputation and online activities if they gained unauthorized access.

Options to keep you logged in to a site for a long period of time or to remember your password are specific to a web page. Not all web sites offer this, and of course, this does not apply to web sites you don't log in to. However, for web sites you log in to often, here's how it works:

1. Open Safari and navigate to the site.
2. Log in, and look for an option to stay logged in or for the site to remember your password.
3. Tick the appropriate box to enable this feature on this web page.

 If you type something incorrectly, tap and hold your finger on the area of the misspelling. When the magnifying glass appears, drag it to the area to retype.

Personalize a Web Page You Visit Often

Some web pages allow you to personalize them with content, select a font color or apply a theme, change what part of the page you want to view and what part you want to hide, set your zip code for local information like weather and news, and more. For instance, you can create your own "iGoogle" page to personalize what content you see, the font used for text and hyperlinks, and more. Google's customization page for themes is shown in Figure 3-3. Beyond Google, you can configure Weather.com with your zip code, Facebook with friends you want to view and hide, and personalize Yahoo! with content and themes.

Note Not all web sites are compatible with the iPad, since it doesn't currently run Adobe Flash, a popular web program for adding interactivity to web pages. However, you can do quite a bit. It's fun to experiment with it anyway!

Here's an example of how you can configure Google with colors, themes, fonts, content, and more:

1. Open Safari and visit www.google.com.
2. Tap the Settings icon in the top right corner, and tap iGoogle.
3. Tap the content you'd like to see on your page. There are lots of options to choose from including News, Entertainment, Sports, Weather, and Technology.

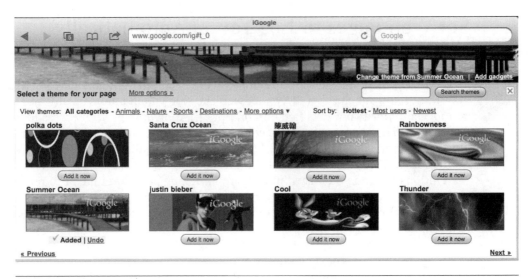

FIGURE 3-3 Personalize web pages using the tools offered by the entity that offers the page.

4. Select a theme from the available options.
5. Continue until finished and click I'm Done.
6. You can now save this page to your Home screen if desired.

Tip Some web sites require you to create a user name and password to configure and save a page. When creating user names and passwords, avoid the _ (underscore) character. It takes three taps on the keyboard to get to that symbol. As an alternative, use a period (only one tap), or the – (two taps).

View Web Media

You can't view all of the media on the web, because you can't view media that plays with Adobe Flash. However, you can view lots and lots of media, and it looks good on the iPad. To see how good it looks, watch a video about Safari from the Apple web site:

1. Open Safari and navigate to www.apple.com.
2. Click the iPad tab at the top of the page.
3. In the iPad web page, click Guided Tours.
4. Scroll down, and tap Safari. See Figure 3-4.
5. To stop or pause the video, tap the video. Controls will appear that you can use to stop, pause, play, or replay the video.

FIGURE 3-4 You can view lots of kinds of web videos on your iPad.

Work with Bookmarks

You've heard a little about bookmarks already in this chapter, and have likely surmised that a Bookmark offers a quick link to a web site you visit or plan to visit often. You already know how to add a web clip, which is a sort of bookmark available from a Home screen, but the bookmarks we'll talk about here appear in lists, and can be organized into folders. You can save bookmarks in two places, the Bookmarks list and the Bookmarks Bar.

Add Bookmarks

There are some bookmarks already in place, including Apple, Google, and Yahoo!. These bookmarks appear in the Bookmarks list, available with a single tap after you tap the Bookmarks icon. The Bookmarks list includes the iPad User Guide too, along with any bookmarks you've added already. You'll notice two other options too, History (sites you've recently visited but did not bookmark) and Bookmarks Bar.

You can save bookmarks to the Bookmarks list or the Bookmarks Bar, which is a kind of folder. All bookmarks stored in the Bookmarks list appear in the Bookmarks window. All bookmarks saved in the Bookmarks Bar folder are saved to the Bookmarks Bar folder, requiring a second tap to access. Bookmarks saved to the Bookmarks Bar are also revealed beneath the Navigation bar when you tap either the Search field or Address window within the Navigation bar. You can change this in the Settings app (select Safari), to make the Bookmarks Bar permanent, instead of appearing only when you touch the URL or search fields.

To add a bookmark to the Bookmarks list:

1. Open Safari and navigate to the page for which you'd like to add a bookmark to the Bookmarks list.
2. Click the Add Bookmark icon and click Add Bookmark. (This menu was shown earlier when you learned about adding a web clip to the Home screen.)
3. If you like the name of the bookmark given by Safari, that's great; if you'd like to change the name, simply use the back key on the keyboard to erase what's there and type in something more favorable. Alternatively, you can tap the X at the end of the title to erase what's there before typing your own entry.

4. Verify that Bookmarks is selected underneath that. If it shows Bookmarks Bar instead, click Bookmarks Bar and then select Bookmarks.
5. Click Save.

Tip If you're an avid Internet Explorer user, a Bookmark is the same as a Favorite.

To add a bookmark to the Bookmarks Bar:

1. Open Safari and navigate to the page for which you'd like to add a bookmark to the Bookmarks Bar.
2. Click the Add Bookmark icon and click Add Bookmark.
3. If you like the name of the bookmark given by Safari, that's great; if you'd like to change the name, simply use the back key on the keyboard to erase what's there and type in something more favorable. (Alternatively, you can tap the X to erase what's there instead of using the back key.)
4. Verify that Bookmarks Bar is selected underneath that. If it shows Bookmarks instead, click Bookmarks and then select Bookmarks Bar.
5. Click Save.
6. To view this new bookmark in the Bookmarks Bar, shown in the illustration here, tap the Address window.

Organize Bookmarks

The Bookmarks Library holds your bookmarks. With it, you can organize your bookmarks by saving them in a long list, or by creating folders to hold similar bookmarks. You could create a folder named, Travel, say, and put links to all of your favorite web sites that offer information about travel there. You could create additional folders named Help Pages, Apple, Job Hunting, Real Estate, or any other topic, to organize other bookmarks you want to keep.

To create a new bookmark folder on the Bookmarks list:

1. Tap the Bookmarks icon on the toolbar.
2. Tap Edit.
3. Tap New Folder.
4. Type a name for the folder.
5. Verify that Bookmarks is showing. If Bookmarks Bar is showing instead, tap it and then tap Bookmarks.
6. Tap Bookmarks.
7. Tap Done.
8. Note the new folder in the Bookmarks list.

To create a new bookmark folder on the Bookmarks Bar:

1. Tap the Bookmarks icon on the toolbar.
2. Tap Edit.
3. Tap New Folder.
4. Type a name for the folder.
5. Verify that Bookmarks Bar is showing. If Bookmarks is showing instead, tap it and then tap Bookmarks Bar.
6. Tap Bookmarks.
7. Tap Done.
8. In the Bookmarks list, tap Bookmarks Bar.
9. Note the new folder in the Bookmarks list.

To move a bookmark into a folder:

1. Tap the Bookmarks icon.
2. Locate the screen that contains the bookmark to move. You may have to click Bookmarks Bar or a folder you've created.
3. Tap Edit.
4. Tap a bookmark you created that you'd like to move.
5. In the Edit Bookmark window, tap Bookmarks or Bookmarks Bar, or whatever appears at the bottom of that window.

Other

☑ Sync bookmarks with [Internet Explorer ▾]
☑ Sync notes with [Outlook ▾]

FIGURE 3-5 You can opt to sync or not to sync bookmarks in iTunes, after connecting your iPad to your computer.

6. Tap the folder to move the bookmark to.
7. Tap Bookmarks to return to the Bookmarks list.
8. Tap Done.

Sync Bookmarks

Depending on how you set up bookmark syncing in Chapter 1, you may or may not be set up to sync the bookmarks you create on your iPad with your computer. You may have decided now that you want to sync them, or you may want to keep the bookmarks you configure on your iPad on your iPad and not sync them.

To find out how your settings are configured and to make changes if desired, and to sync bookmarks if applicable:

1. Open iTunes on your computer.
2. Connect your iPad to your computer.
3. While iTunes backs up your iPad, in iTunes, click the iPad source pane.
4. In iTunes, click the Info tab.
5. Scroll down to Other. Change the sync options as desired. See Figure 3-5.
6. Click Apply.

Tweak Safari Settings and Preferences

You can change settings and preferences related to Safari for a better browsing experience from Settings on the Home screen. You can configure preferences, including what search engine to use, whether or not to automatically fill in web forms with your name, address, and the like, and whether or not you want to show the Bookmarks Bar permanently in Safari. Figure 3-6 shows what the Bookmarks Bar looks like when enabled. Notice that the folders that have been created previously for the Bookmarks Bar under the Bookmarks icon appear, as do the individual bookmarks you've created there.

Safari helps you maintain your safety and privacy while on the Internet too. Settings that Safari deems optimal are already set, but it's always a good idea to review them. You can also clear your History, Cookies, and Cache, among other things. Safari's settings are shown in Figure 3-7.

FIGURE 3-6   When you enable the Bookmarks Bar, it's always available, and you can tap a bookmark on it to access the web page.

FIGURE 3-7   From the Settings app, you can access settings for Safari.

The following security settings are enabled by default:

- **Fraud Warning**   To warn you when you visit a fraudulent site that may try to get you to input personal information or information about your bank or credit cards. Some fraudulent web sites also try to infect computers and devices with adware, spyware, and viruses.
- **Block Pop-ups**   To block pop-ups from web sites that initiate them. Pop-ups are generally advertisements, and open in a new window.
- **Accept Cookies**   To accept cookies from web sites you visit. Cookies are small text files that are stored on your iPad that tell a web site what you prefer when visiting. Cookies can include your name, browsing history on the site, and information about items you've purchased.

AutoFill is not enabled by default. When you enable AutoFill, you tell your iPad and Safari that you want it to populate web forms automatically. While this is a convenience, it can also create a security hole. If your iPad is stolen and is not protected by a passcode, the thief can access Safari and populate the forms themselves.

There are also a few things you can do to erase the information that Safari has thus far stored about your web browsing. With only a couple of taps you can clear the following information:

- **History**   A list of web sites you've recently visited.
- **Cookies**   Information about you regarding your preferences at specific web sites, like what you generally shop for, your name, and other information.
- **Cache**   What the iPad stores regarding the web pages you visit. The iPad and Safari store information about a web page the first time you load it, save some of that data, and reuse it the next time you visit. This helps pages you've previously visited load faster. You may want to clear the cache if the data on web pages is outdated, and new data isn't being loaded.

How to... ## Secure Your iPad with a Passcode

If you really want to secure Safari, create a passcode to unlock your iPad.
To create a passcode:

1. Tap Settings on the Home screen.
2. Tap General.
3. Tap Passcode Lock.
4. Tap Turn Passcode On.
5. Type a four-number passcode, and type it again when prompted.

4

Communicate with Mail

HOW TO...

- Configure a web-based email account
- Configure a POP3 email account
- Incorporate MobileMe
- Verify that all email accounts are configured properly
- Explore Mail's interface
- Compose an email and insert a photo
- Email a video
- Do more with cut, copy, and paste
- View incoming email and respond to it
- Open an attachment
- Use gestures to manage email
- Search email folders with Spotlight
- Explore Mail Settings

The iPad comes with Mail, an email management program already built in and ready to use, and available from the Home screen. You have to tell Mail about your email accounts before you can use it, though, including your email address, password, and associated settings, and you need to test the email accounts you configure to make sure they're working properly. It's notable that Mail integrates with several types of email almost seamlessly, including Yahoo! Mail, Gmail, AOL (America Online), and MobileMe, as well as Microsoft Exchange accounts, which are used in larger enterprises. This helps make the setup for these types of accounts a simple and generally flawless task. Mail also allows you to configure email accounts from Internet Service Providers (ISPs), such as Time Warner, Comcast, Verizon, and the like, as well as email accounts you've acquired from schools, businesses, and other various email providers, although setting up these accounts sometimes takes a little more effort than the supported email accounts previously mentioned.

Once your email addresses are configured, you're ready to use Mail. Of course, you'll need to be within range of a wireless hotspot or your home network, or you'll need a data plan from a service provider like AT&T or Verizon if you're out of Wi-Fi range to send and receive mail, but you knew that!

 You can't receive new email unless you can connect to the Internet.

So without further ado, let's get your email addresses configured, send a few test emails, and then focus on what you need to know to use Mail on your iPad.

Set Up Mail

As mentioned in the introduction, you need to tell Mail about your email addresses. If you're used to setting up email accounts on a computer, this is a little different. While you can set up your first email account in the Mail program easily, if you want to set up a second or third account, you'll want to do that in Settings.

 Mail knows the configuration settings for several types of accounts. So, it's generally best to type in the most basic information, and see if the iPad and Mail can do the rest. Before you start, make sure you're within range of and can connect to a Wi-Fi or 3G network.

Configure a Web-Based Email Account

A web-based email account is an account provided by an online entity, which is often a search provider as well, such as Google, AOL, or Yahoo!. With web-based email, your email data is stored on web servers and you can access that data using a web browser. Because of this, you can get your email from anywhere and any computer, as long as the computer offers Internet access. For instance, if you have a Gmail account from Google, you can go to www.google.com from any computer, sign in, and access your email easily.

You don't have to use the provider's web site, though. You can get email from web-based providers on your iPad with Mail. Additionally, Mail knows the settings and can automatically configure email accounts for these and other web-based email accounts, which makes setting up these types of email accounts a breeze.

If you're worried that you'll receive email on your iPad and won't receive it on your computer at home, have no fear. You can get email on your iPad and then retrieve the messages again at your home or office computer the next time you log on, even if you delete them in Mail.

 If you're in the market for a new email address, consider one from Google, Hotmail (also known as Windows Live), AOL, or Yahoo!. With it, you can easily configure your iPad and access mail from any computer you have access to (that also has access to the Internet).

To configure a web-based email account like Yahoo! Mail, Gmail, or MobileMe (MobileMe is a subscription service that we'll introduce later):

1. On the Home screen, tap Mail.
2. Tap the option that matches the type of account you want to configure. See Figure 4-1. If your web-based email account isn't listed (Windows Live, for example), click Other.

 Note   If you don't see this screen, open Settings and tap Mail, Contacts, Calendars to access the option to add a new account.

3. Fill out the required information:
   a. **Name**   Type your name as you'd like others to see it when you send them mail.
   b. **Address**   Type your email address.
   c. **Password**   Type your email account password, and remember that passwords are case-sensitive.
   d. **Description**   Type a description for the account (such as AOL, Hotmail, or Yahoo!).
4. Click Next. The Inbox for this account will appear.

FIGURE 4-1   Mail can configure various kinds of email accounts automatically.

Cancel	Test	Send

To: Joli Ballew

Cc/Bcc, From: joliballew@gmail.com

Subject: **Test**

Testing from my Gmail account.

Sent from my iPad

FIGURE 4-2 Test each email account you configure.

Now, send a test email to yourself to verify the account has been set up correctly:

1. Tap the New Mail icon in the top-right corner of the Mail interface; it looks like a pen and a piece of paper.
2. In the To line, type the email address for this account. For example, if you just set up an account for yourname@yahoo.com, type that.
3. Tap the Subject line.
4. Type **Test** or something like it. See Figure 4-2.
5. Tap the Send button in the upper-right corner. Wait a few seconds for the email to be sent and received.

 If you receive errors when testing your email account, from the Home screen, tap Settings. Tap Mail, Contacts, Calendars to access the account and edit it. If you do see errors, those errors are probably related to an incorrect email address or password.

Did You Know?

There Are Special Keys Available on Your iPad's Virtual Keyboard

If you have very little experience typing on a virtual keyboard, typing the information required to set up your email account may be a tad difficult. If you're having trouble inputting the required information, try these typing tips:

- If you need to capitalize a letter, touch the up arrow.
- If you need to locate an underscore, dash, or similar character, click the .?123 key. Note that you may have to touch the #+= key on the numeric keyboard to access additional characters.
- Look for special keys on some keyboards (such as .com) to complete your typing tasks more quickly.

Configure a POP3 Email Account

POP3 email accounts differ from web-based accounts in many ways. POP3 email accounts are commonly provided by companies that offer Internet service you pay for, such as Time Warner, Comcast, Verizon, and the like. You can also have a POP3 email account from a place where you work or go to school, or from a dedicated email host. These are often referred to as email providers, but can still be POP3 in nature. Email providers like these have their own mail servers, and unlike web-based servers, they often delete email after you've downloaded it to your computer. If you download email to your home or office PC before it can be downloaded to your iPad, then you won't get it on your iPad.

So, if you have your home or work PC configured to automatically download your messages from your provider's POP3 email server, and you have not changed the default settings on that computer to leave a copy of the messages on the server for a specified period of time, you won't get those same messages on your iPad. That's because those email messages, once downloaded to your home or work computer, are no longer available on your email provider's servers when you log on with your iPad. If you want to receive all of your email messages on your iPad as they arrive at the server, you'll have to change the settings on your home or work PC.

It's important to note that configuring your computer's email program to leave a copy of your email messages on the server differs depending on what email program you use and what type of computer you use at home and at work. This makes it difficult to give you specific instructions for making the change on your home or work PC. However, because it's important to configure your computer to leave a copy of your messages on the email provider's server, here are some generic instructions to do so:

1. On your home and/or work PC, and any laptop you use to obtain your email, open your email program. This may be Outlook Express, Apple Mail, Windows Mail, Windows Live Mail, Thunderbird, or something else.
2. Locate a Help menu or Help button. Here are some suggestions:
   a. If you don't see any menus, press the ALT key.
   b. If you don't see a Help menu, look for a question mark.
   c. If you don't see either, press F1.
3. Click the option to get help regarding your email program.
4. In the Help window, search for *read pop3 email messages on multiple computers*.
5. Follow the directions to leave a copy of the messages on the POP3 mail server. See Figure 4-3, which shows Microsoft Outlook.

> **Tip** While you must opt to leave messages on your email provider's POP3 server, you are often limited to how much data you can keep there. If you go over that limit, you will no longer be able to get email until you delete some data stored there. Consider leaving messages on the server for four days or less.

Once you're sure you've configured your computers correctly, you're ready to set up POP3 email accounts on your iPad. Luckily, the iPad and Mail know that you're using a handheld device, and the iPad is already configured to automatically leave a

FIGURE 4-3 If you want to get email from a POP3 email account on your iPad, configure the settings required to leave a copy of the messages on your provider's email server.

copy of your messages on the server for you. So, no worries; when you use your iPad to get your POP3 messages, they won't disappear from the provider's servers. This means that you can access your POP3 email messages (from Time Warner, Verizon, Comcast, and so on) on your iPad and retrieve them again when you log on to your account from your home or work PC.

The more difficult part comes in setting up your POP3 accounts. Not all accounts are supported at this time, and you may run into problems. Because of this we'll talk in detail here about how to set up POP3 accounts, and later you'll learn workarounds if a specific account doesn't work as you planned.

Did You Know?

You Can Use iTunes on Your Computer to Sync Mail Account Settings

If you use the POP3 email account you want to configure here on the computer you currently use to sync your iPad, you can sync the email settings instead of manually inputting them. Only the settings will sync, though, not the password, email messages, folders, or contacts. See the How To box for more information.

To create an email account in Mail for a POP3 email account on your iPad:

1. On the Home screen, tap Settings.
2. Tap Mail, Contacts, Calendars.
3. Tap Add Account.
4. Tap Other.
5. Tap Add Mail Account.
6. Type your email name, email address, password, and description of the account.
7. Click Save.
8. If prompted, type any required information for the server names, host names, user names, and so on. You can get this information from your email provider. Click Save. See Figure 4-4.
9. If you get all green check marks by each entry, the email account was properly set up. Send yourself a test email from this account to this account to be sure.
10. If you receive an error, you'll have to resolve it.

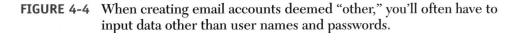

FIGURE 4-4 When creating email accounts deemed "other," you'll often have to input data other than user names and passwords.

To resolve errors:

1. Review the settings for incoming and outgoing servers. Make sure you've typed the names correctly. You can get the information you need from your email provider or the Internet if you're unsure.
2. If you're positive you've input all of this information correctly, click Save and go ahead and set up the email even if you receive a message that it may not work properly.
3. Then, in Settings, under Mail, Contacts, Calendars, click the problematic account.
4. In the resulting window, scroll down to Advanced (as shown in the illustration at right) and tap it.
5. Review the settings. You may need to enable SSL (which is a security setting) or type in a different server port. It's best to call your email provider and ask what the settings should be. If you still can't get it to work, refer to Appendix B, or choose to apply one of the workarounds detailed later in this chapter.

6. With errors resolved, your email will arrive immediately.

How to... ## Sync Mail with iTunes

You can use iTunes to transfer information about your email accounts, but it won't transfer your passwords or your messages. It won't transfer the folders you've created. In fact, it won't sync web-based email accounts in Outlook (like Hotmail) either. However, it is often easier to sync email account settings than it is to look up and type in the required information for POP3 and IMAP accounts (and it's a great way to avoid typing errors). Thus, in some instances, especially if you've encountered problems trying to set up the account manually, this is a better option:

1. Connect your iPad to your computer and wait while syncing completes.
2. In iTunes on your computer, select your iPad in the left pane.
3. Click the Info tab.
4. Click Sync Mail Accounts from_____, and select your email program.
5. Select the accounts to sync.
6. Click Apply.

 Tip

In this section we covered web-based email accounts and POP3 email accounts. The directions for setting up other accounts, such as IMAP or Microsoft Exchange, are similar.

How to... ## Configure One Account as the Default

If you set up more than one email account on your iPad, the first account you set up will be the default account. The default account is the account your iPad will use to send mail when you want to share a photo, a contact, or any other data. The account you use most should be set as the default account, though, and that isn't necessarily the first account you configured. (You can always choose a different account before sending an email data, but it's nice to have the correct account selected in most instances.) You should verify which account is the default and change it if you desire.

To configure an email account as your default account:

1. On the Home screen, tap Settings.
2. Tap Mail, Contacts, Calendars.
3. Scroll down and tap Default Account.
4. Tap the account to use for the default account.
5. Tap Mail, Contacts, Calendars to return to the Settings page.

Consider MobileMe

MobileMe is a service that "pushes" new email (and contacts, calendar events, and other data) over the air to all of your devices. The devices you can use include your iPad, iPhone, iPod Touch, Mac, and your PC. You can configure MobileMe on a single device and the rest will fall into place easily. Although you can get a free trial of MobileMe, it will only be free for 60 days. After that, it's $99 a year for you, or $149 for you and your family. If you're still interested, read on; if not, skip to the next section.

 Once you have a MobileMe account, you configure it on your iPad the same way you input web-based or POP3 accounts.

Here are a few reasons to consider MobileMe:

- MobileMe keeps all data "in the cloud" (on Internet servers), and pushes the information to your devices.
- The MobileMe Inbox offers spam and virus protection.
- Contacts and addresses are synced automatically between compatible devices without docking.
- Calendars and events are synced automatically between compatible devices without docking.
- Photos are stored on Internet servers and you can allow friends and family to view them, upload their own, make comments, and more.
- iDisk offers a place to store, access, and share files online.
- Find My iPad can help you find your iPad should it become lost or stolen.
- Me.com offers access to all of your data, from anywhere.

Verify Proper Configuration of All Accounts

If you haven't done so already, you should send a test email from your iPad for each account you've configured back to that account. So, if you created an account for Yahoo!, you'll want to send an email from that account back to that account. And if you've also created an account for Time Warner, you'll need to send an email from your Time Warner account back to that account too. This will allow you to see three things: first, whether the email accounts are properly configured on your new iPad; second, how long it takes to receive an email in your Inbox once it's been sent; and third, verification that the email also arrives at your home or work PC. There are instructions on how to do this in the section "Configure a Web-Based Email Account." For POP3 accounts, perform this test using a Wi-Fi network and a 3G network (if you have a Wi-Fi + 3G model and you've signed up for a data plan). If the test email arrives successfully, you'll see it in the appropriate Mail Inbox, shown in Figure 4-5.

After that's complete, turn off your iPad and perform the same email test from each of your other devices that receives email from the accounts you configured on your iPad, including Macs, PCs, iPod Touch, and/or smartphone devices. Allow those

| .ull. AT&T 🛜 | | 10:21 AM | | 72% 🔋 |
| Gmail Inbox (45) Edit | | | 📁 🔾 ↩ ✏️ | |

Q Search Inbox

Joli Ballew   9:50 AM
Test
Testing myGmail account. Sent from my iPad

From: (Joli Ballew)   Details

Test
April 6, 2011 9:50 AM

FIGURE 4-5   You should see your test email in the appropriate Inbox in Mail.

emails to arrive at each of your devices, and then, turn on your iPad and verify that they come in there also. (If they don't, refer to the POP3 section earlier in this chapter to learn how to leave a copy of those email messages on the server for each device you own.) It's important to do this testing because you may encounter odd bugs in the setup of your email accounts. For instance, you may be able to send and receive just fine while connected to Wi-Fi, but only be able to receive (and not send) while connected to 3G. If this occurs, you'll likely have to call your email provider to help you resolve the problem, which generally involves changing some of the advanced settings (or choosing a new outgoing server or enabling the provider's outgoing server). The solution depends on the problem, the situation, and the provider.

In a worst-case scenario, if you can't use Mail with your POP3 email address, you can always open Safari and navigate to the email provider's webmail page; you can send and receive email there while connected to Wi-Fi or 3G. For added convenience, you could create a web clip. You can then access the webmail page from your iPad's Home screen. For more information about web clips, refer to Chapter 3.

Tip   We really like Gmail from Google because you can create labels for your email at Google's web site (mail.google.com), and those labels will appear as folders within Mail on your iPad, allowing you to organize mail you want to keep.

Learn Mail Fundamentals

We're sure you know how to email. You can send and receive messages, and you can probably even create folders on your computer and manage email you keep effectively. You can forward and reply, you can likely attach a picture, and you can browse folders like Sent and Deleted Items (or Trash). That said, in this section we won't bore you with anything too basic, but it is important to cover all of our bases to get every reader up to speed with emailing on the iPad. In this section you'll learn the following:

- How to find what you want and need by familiarizing yourself with Mail's interface
- How to send email and insert pictures, video, and other data
- How to get the most from the available views
- How to view and respond to incoming email
- How to open and view an attachment

Explore Mail's Interface

When you first access Mail after creating your email accounts, the first thing you'll see is the Accounts page. Note that there are options to view what's in any Inbox, or to view *All Inboxes* at once. When you tap any of these, you only see the Inbox(es) and the mail in it (them).

You can also tap an email account in the Accounts section, which offers access to the Inbox, and in many instances, Drafts, Sent, and Trash. If you have a Gmail account and have configured labels (folders), in this view you'll have access to those as well. What you see here depends on what the email account provider offers access to. Figure 4-6 shows what Gmail looks like with several labels (folders) created and synced.

> **Tip** It's really best to view Mail in Landscape view for now. In Landscape view you have easier access to all of the features. Portrait view does not offer the same amenities.

In Landscape view, after you tap an Inbox for a specific account (vs. All Inboxes), you'll have access to the following options (from left to right):

- **Account Name** The email account name for the Inbox you've selected. (If you choose All Inboxes in the Accounts view, you'll see Mailboxes instead.) Click this name to return to the Accounts list. If you're unsure how juggling multiple email accounts works, refer to the next "Did You Know?" box.
- **Inbox (with a number)** Lets you know what folder you're in, in this case Inbox, and how many unread messages you have there.
- **Edit** Tap to delete or move selected emails.
- **Move** Tap to move an email.
- **Trash** Tap once to move the current email to the Trash folder.
- **Reply/Reply All/Forward/Print** Tap to have the option to reply to or forward the current email, or to print it.
- **Compose** Tap to create a new email.
- **Details** Tap to view information about the sender and recipient(s) of the email. Tap Hide to hide details.

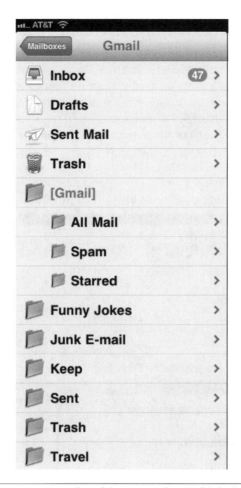

FIGURE 4-6   If you're using Gmail and have configured labels, you'll see them in Mail.

Did You Know?

Mail Has a Built-in Hierarchy of Folders

The icon that appears in the top-left corner of the Mail interface while you're in Landscape view is ultimately a "back" button. Mail is laid out such that Accounts is the starting place for Mail, or the "home" page, if you will. In Accounts, all email accounts are listed, and you tap to access them. Once you're in an account, you have access to the account's Inbox and Trash folders. To return to previous tiers, click this "back" button. The name of the button will change depending on where you are in the hierarchy.

Compose an Email and Insert a Photo

You know how to compose an email if you've sent out test emails to verify your email accounts are working properly. You may have also noticed that the Compose icon appears across the top of the Mail screen no matter where you are in the app. While it may be easy to compose and send an email, there are a lot of hidden features you may not have uncovered. For instance, when composing a new mail message, you can click the + sign to add contacts from your Contacts list. Here are two more things you can do.

1. Tap the Cc/Bcc, From line to view the Cc and Bcc lines in the message and/or to choose a different account to send from.

2. Tap and hold a word briefly to select it, select everything, or paste something you've already copied. (Once you select a word or Select All, you'll see options to cut, copy, paste, or replace.)

You might be surprised to learn that you can't attach a photo to an email from within the Mail app. You can paste a photo you've copied, and you can send a photo from the Photos app, but there's no option to attach a photo in a new mail message as you're used to in Outlook, Apple's Mail, or other computer email programs. However, you can copy and paste a photo, and the photo will appear in the body of the email.

To compose an email and insert a photo:

1. Open Mail.
2. Tap the Compose button.

3. Fill in the To: line using one of the following methods:
   a. Type an email address, or, begin typing and tap any result offered.
   b. Tap the + sign and select a contact from the resulting Contacts list (see the following illustration) by searching, scrolling, or tapping.

4. Tap and hold the Cc/Bcc, From line to view those lines and add additional recipients or to choose a different account from which to send.
5. Tap the Subject line and type a subject.
6. Tap inside the body of the email and type a message.
7. To insert a picture:
   a. Press the Home button on the iPad to view the Home screen. (Don't worry, Mail will remember where you left off.)
   b. Tap Photos.
   c. Locate the photo to insert, and tap and hold it briefly until the Copy option appears. Tap Copy. Alternatively, you can tap the button in the top-right corner (the one with the arrow on it) to see the options Email Photo, Assign to Contact, Use as Wallpaper, or Copy Photo.
   d. Double-tap the Home button.
   e. Tap Mail.
   f. Tap and hold briefly inside the message body, lift your finger, and tap Paste when it appears.
   g. To see the entire message without the keyboard, click the keyboard icon on the virtual keyboard to hide it (bottom-right corner).
   h. Repeat as desired, completing the message and adding more pictures. When finished, click Send.

How to... Save an Email for Completion Later

To save an email for completing later, tap the Cancel button. Tap Save when prompted. (You need to have typed some words in the body of the email for this to work.) After you tap Save, the email will sit in the Drafts folder until you're ready to complete it. The Drafts folder will only be available when unfinished email is in there. Otherwise, it's hidden.

Email Multiple Photos

You can email multiple photos at once. This is quite a convenience, especially if you have a dozen or so pictures to send. You'll have to be in an album of photos to select multiple photos.

To select multiple photos to email:

1. In Photos, tap any album that contains multiple photos.
2. Tap the icon in the top-right corner, the one with the arrow on it.
3. Tap each photo to send. Each time you tap a photo, checkmark will appear on it.

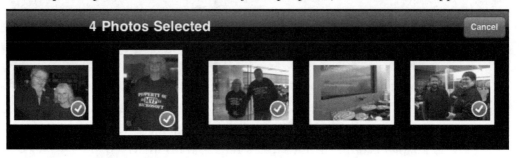

4. When your photos are selected, tap Email in the top-left corner. (Note you can also tap Copy.) See Figure 4-7.

Email a Video

You can email video as well as pictures. You may want to email a short video you shot with the Camera app, for instance. Keep in mind when emailing video that it must be very short, because you can only attach so much data to an email, and video is quite large. To email a video:

1. From the Home screen, tap Photos.
2. Locate the video to send. If you've taken a video with the Camera app, tap Albums, and tap Camera Roll.
3. Tap the video.
4. Tap the Forward button (the arrow).

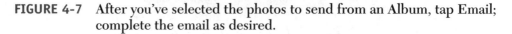

FIGURE 4-7   After you've selected the photos to send from an Album, tap Email; complete the email as desired.

5. Tap Email Video.
6. Complete the email and send when ready.

Work with Cut, Copy, and Paste

In the last section you learned how to copy and paste a picture. You can use this same technique in other apps and for other uses. For instance, when composing an email, you can cut, copy, or paste text or other data in lieu of retyping information you already have. While this is a bit more complex than simply copying a picture, it's still pretty easy. The technique is to first make a selection by inserting a cursor in the appropriate area of the text that you want to copy. Then decide if you'd like to select the word, select everything, or select only a specific part of the data.

To cut or copy text and paste it into an email:

1. Compose an email as detailed earlier.
2. To copy text from another app, click the Home screen button and locate the data. (You can copy the data before composing the email, if you find that you can't access the data to copy easily during email composition. Text can be copied from apps such as Safari, Notes, Calendar, and Contacts, as well as from other emails.)
3. Touch and hold on the text you wish to copy until you see the magnifying glass.
4. Use the magnifying glass to drag the cursor to the position where you'd like to begin cutting or copying.
5. Release your finger to display the selection buttons.
6. Select the text:
   a. Tap Select to select the adjacent word.
   b. Tap Select All to select all of the text.
   c. Drag the blue "grab points" to select more or less text.
7. With the text selected, tap Cut or Copy.
8. Return to the Mail app, and tap and hold again in your email message where you'd like to paste the text. Release your finger and tap Paste to insert the text. Note that you can also replace text.

 Shake the iPad to undo the last edit. (We had to shake ours pretty hard, and you may not be comfortable with this.)

View Incoming Email and Respond to It

There's likely no need to rehash how to view email that's arrived; you simply drill into the email account you want to view, using the Accounts button and the Inbox.

Once in the desired account's Inbox, you can preview any email in the Inbox list, and tap it to view it.

To reply to or forward an email:

1. With the email selected and open, click the arrow above the email. You can then opt to reply or forward.
2. Tap Reply, Reply All, or Forward (see the illustration at right). (You won't see Reply All if there aren't multiple people to reply to.)
3. Complete the email as desired.

Open an Attachment

Attachments are add-ons to emails, and can be pictures, spreadsheets, videos, documents, or even presentations. You can open many types of attachments on your iPad, although not quite as many as you can on a Mac or a PC. As you'd expect, in the preview of the email, you'll notice an icon of a paper clip and an attachment; to open the attachment, open the email, scroll down to locate the attachment, and touch the attachment icon. You can view the attachment on your iPad, and if you have the iWork apps (see Chapter 7), you can edit many document types and save them.

Pictures behave a little differently than other attached data. You don't have to open pictures separately. Pictures will automatically appear in the body of an email, and a momentary tap and hold on the image gives you the option to save it or copy it.

This list includes some of the types of email attachments you can view on your iPad:

- .doc and .docx (Microsoft Word)
- .htm and .html (web pages)
- .jpg, .tiff, .gif, .png (images)
- .key (Keynote)
- .numbers (Numbers)
- .pages (Pages)
- .pdf (Preview and Adobe Acrobat)
- .ppt and .pptx (Microsoft PowerPoint)
- .txt (text); .rtf (rich text format)
- .vcf (contact information)
- .xls and .xlsx (Microsoft Excel)

To view an attachment represented by a paper clip:

1. Open Mail and tap the email that contains the attachment.
2. In the body of the email, scroll down to locate the attachment icon.
3. Click the attachment to view it, noting that Mail only supports the attachment types listed here, so clicking an attachment is no guarantee it'll open.
4. To stop viewing the attachment, if it's taking the entire screen, tap at the top of the document, presentation, or spreadsheet, and click Done.

To save an image in an email to your iPad:

1. Open an email that contains pictures.
2. Tap and hold briefly on the picture and then select one of the following options (see the following illustration):
   a. Save Image
   b. Save # Images (this option appears only if there are multiple images)

Manage Your Email

The best way to manage email is to read it and respond to it when it arrives, and then delete it. This keeps you up to date and keeps your Inbox from getting cluttered. Responding to an email can be as simple as reading and deleting it, sending a reply or forwarding the email to someone else, or it may be a bit more complex and involve saving the data in the email in the appropriate app (saving photos to the Photos app, for instance). Unfortunately, the world is not a perfect place. You'll have email you can't respond to right away, email you need to file so you can reference it later, email you're not sure what to do with, and other scenarios that don't allow you to deal with specific email as promptly as you'd like.

At the present time, there aren't many options for managing the email you acquire on your iPad. You can't create your own organizational folders just yet. So, the best way to stay organized is to delete items once you know you won't need them, or forward them to a different email account to store them, away from your default account's Inbox.

Beyond managing what you want to keep, you'll also use shortcuts for dealing with email, like using a flick to bring up the option to delete. You'll learn about that in this section too.

> **Tip**   Remember, the email you receive on your iPad will also arrive at your home and/or work computer if you've configured them as detailed in this chapter. This means you can delete anything you don't actually need to deal with on your iPad, and deal with it when you're back at your home or work computer.

Use Gestures to Manage Email

When you manage your email on your home or work PC, or on a laptop, you can't generally touch the screen to perform tasks. You can on an iPad. Therefore, there are new ways to interact with email, including using gestures like swiping to delete email or flicking to scroll through a long email. As you already know, you can tap and hold to select data in an email, or tap to open an attachment. To perform these gestures and learn how to manage your email with them, try the following:

- **Delete a message**   Tap the Trash icon to delete the email that is currently open, or swipe left or right over the message title in the message list, then tap Delete.

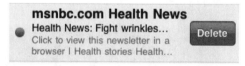

How to... **Create Your Own Organizational System in Mail**

If you want an organizational system complete with folders in Mail, you can do it with Gmail. It's not a perfect solution, but it might work for you. You'll have to create a new email account at Google (Gmail), create email labels at the Google web site that match how you'd like to organize your mail, and then, forward email you want to keep to it. Then, you can use that account's Inbox to store data you want to keep.

FIGURE 4-8   Tap a contact to add them to your Contact list.

- **Delete multiple messages**   Tap Edit, select the messages you want to delete, then tap Delete.
- **Move a message to a different mailbox or folder**   Tap the Folder icon (Move icon) and then choose a mailbox or folder.
- **Move multiple messages**   Tap Edit, select the messages you want to move, and tap Move.
- **Zoom in on a message**   Pinch your fingers outward.
- **Follow a link**   Tap the link.
- **See all recipients of a message**   Tap Details.
- **Add a sender to your Contacts**   Tap Details, and then tap the contact to add. Click Create New Contact or Add to Existing Contact. See Figure 4-8.
- **Mark a message as unread**   Tap the blue dot next to the subject line in the preview pane when Details is selected.

Search Email Folders with Spotlight

Sometimes you need to locate an email but can't remember where it is or who it was from, but you do remember what the email was in reference to. Perhaps you need to locate an email that outlined the rules of the game bocce, for instance. You can use Search to look through all of your emails for you, using a specific keyword (like bocce). Of course, the more unique the word, the more likely you'll find what you're looking for; performing a search for a less unique word would result in a longer list of search results.

To search for a specific email by keyword using the Search window:

1. Open Mail and navigate to the desired account area to search, perhaps in Inbox.
2. Type a keyword into the Search window.
3. Review the results (see the following illustration).
4. To open any result, tap it.

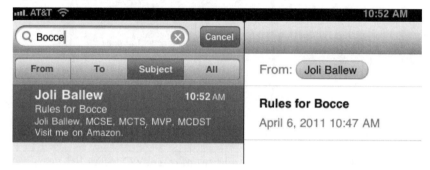

Tip   Remember, Mail on the iPad is best navigated in Landscape view.

Explore Mail Settings

As you know, you can configure settings for Mail in the Settings app on the Home screen. You'll find the information under Mail, Contacts, Calendars. We've already discussed the Accounts section at length, but there are plenty of other options to explore, shown in Figure 4-9.

The first option under Accounts is Fetch New Data. As you can see in Figure 4-9, it's set to Push. Push is a technology that allows Internet servers to send information to your iPad as soon as the message is received by your email provider on their email servers. Some email servers will push email to you, while others won't. Email providers that support Push include MobileMe, Microsoft Exchange, and Yahoo!. Be aware that using Push will use battery power to obtain the updates and also because of the data it transfers, so it can minimize battery life. Transfers while connected via 3G are counted towards your monthly data usage as well. This could become a problem if you have a limited data plan.

Other email accounts such as POP, IMAP, AOL, and Gmail aren't Push-compatible on the iPad. This means that no email will arrive at your Inbox in Mail until you open Mail and access the Inbox. At that time, Mail will check for email and obtain mail from your email servers. If this is inconvenient and you'd rather have Mail check for email automatically, even when you aren't using it, you can configure your iPad to *fetch* your email on a schedule, such as every 15, 30, or 60 minutes. You can also set Fetch settings to Manually so that no fetch occurs by default. As with Push, Fetch will drain your battery more quickly on than off. To maximize battery life, fetch less often

FIGURE 4-9   The Settings app offers a Mail, Contacts, Calendars category.

or fetch manually. Fetch also kicks in for Push email accounts if Push is turned off, so if you're watching your data usage you may need to turn off Push and set Fetch to Manually.

Under Mail, you can configure various options for showing and previewing mail including:

- **Show**   To configure how many recent messages appear in your Inbox.
- **Preview**   To configure how many lines are available in an email shown in the Message list.
- **Minimum font size**   To set how large or small text should appear in emails.
- **Show To/CC label**   To show or hide the To/CC label when composing a new email.
- **Ask before deleting**   To confirm or not confirm the deletion of emails.
- **Load remote images**   To load images at the same time you load an email, or not to.
- **Organize by thread**   To identify and group the email messages that comprise a series of emails and replies between a sender and recipient.
- **Always Bcc myself**   To always send a copy of the email to yourself, or not to.

- **Signature** To add and/or configure a signature for all outgoing emails. A signature appears at the bottom of the email. By default, the included signature is "Sent from my iPad."
- **Default account** To set which account will be used by default when sending photos from the Photo app and when sending data from other apps.

Under Contacts, you can change:

- **Sort order** To set if contacts are sorted by first name, last name or last name, first name.
- **Display order** To set if contacts are displayed by first name, last name or last name, first name.

Under Calendars you can change:

- **New invitation alerts** To set to on or off.
- **Sync** To select how far back you want to sync calendar events. The shortest is two weeks back.
- **Time zone support** To select a time zone.
- **Default calendar** To set the default calendar if multiple calendars are available.

PART III

News and
Entertainment

5

Go Digital with iBooks

HOW TO...

- Install iBooks and browse the iBooks library
- Read reviews and preview books
- Buy and download a book
- Open and read a book
- Create, locate, and delete a bookmark
- Adjust text size, font, and screen brightness
- Copy and paste text
- Search for and look up the meaning of a word
- Highlight text and make notes
- Sort and reposition books
- Delete a book
- Create your own collection

iBooks is a free app you can obtain from the App Store that enables you to browse, download, and read digital books you obtain from the iBookstore. It's an easy way to turn your iPad into a fully functional e-book reader. If you're already somewhat familiar with Amazon's Kindle, this is similar. iBooks offers some really innovative features too, including touch screen control and support for color images, among other things.

iBooks lets you do much more than download and read digital versions of books on your iPad, though. With iBooks you can personalize a book in a way you never thought imaginable with printed books, such as changing the font size and font type. You can purchase a book without ever setting foot in a physical store. You can even set an electronic bookmark so you can come back to a page and read it again if desired, or highlight text or make notes about passages. And if you're worried about not being able to preview the book before buying it, have no fear. You can view a sample of the book before you purchase it. Beyond all that, though, you can search a book for a specific word or phrase, look up the definition of a word, locate a specific word in the book, and use iBooks' available controls to navigate a book. Once you've acquired several books, you can even organize them into your own personal collections.

 Tip   iBooks is a free app, and there are lots of free books to choose from. Don't worry if money is tight; you can enjoy iBooks without spending a dime.

Get Started with iBooks

iBooks isn't installed by default; you have to get it from the App Store. It's free, though, and since you have the option of reading free books too, you don't have to lay out any money to enjoy iBooks. Figure 5-1 shows some of the books we've acquired, most of which are free.

iBooks has some pretty tight rules, though. You can't shop for books online at your computer; you have to go through the iBooks app on your iPad. iBooks aren't available in the iTunes Store either. So, if you want to purchase, download, and read iBooks, there's no way around installing the iBooks app and shopping at the iBookstore. The iBookstore and the iBooks app are for obtaining and reading electronic books, and nothing else. (The iBookstore does not offer audiobooks or podcasts, for instance.)

 Tip   If you're in the market for audiobooks, look to the iTunes Store. If you're looking for digital books from other sources, like Amazon or Barnes & Noble, check out the App Store for the apps that will enable you to access those stores easily and read the digital content on your iPad that you acquire there.

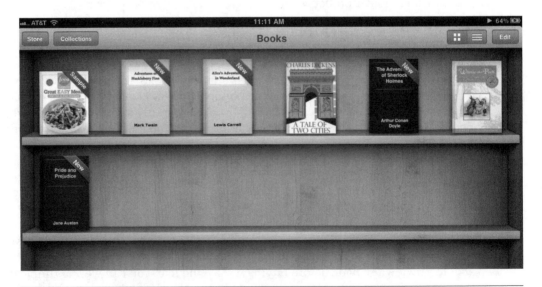

FIGURE 5-1   The classics, from authors like Mark Twain, Charles Dickens, and Lewis Carroll, are all free at the iBookstore, along with many others.

The iBooks you acquire on your iPad can be synced to your computer. However, even though you can see their titles in iTunes, you can't read iBooks on your computer (at least not yet). You can only read iBooks on your iPad, iPhone, or iPod Touch. You can play audiobooks you acquire from iTunes on your computer, though, and you can play videos you acquire from the iTunes Store, but iBooks doesn't work that way.

Install iBooks

There are two ways to get the iBooks app. One way is to download the iBooks app from the iTunes Store at your computer. The next time you sync your iPad with your computer, the iBooks app will be transferred to it. If you're like most people, though, you'll opt to install iBooks from your iPad, which is what we'll outline here.

Note   At your computer, the next time you connect your iPad to sync in iTunes, under the Books tab, verify that books are configured to sync automatically.

To install iBooks using your iPad:

1. Click the App Store icon on the Home screen.
2. Tap the Featured button at the bottom of the screen.
3. Tap in the Search window, and type **iBooks**. (You may actually be prompted to install iBooks, as shown here.)
4. Make sure you're in the iPad Apps section, locate iBooks, and tap Install.

5. Type your password and tap OK.
6. Wait while the app installs.

Note If iBooks is the first app you've installed, you'll notice that the app downloads to a secondary Home screen. To return to the Home screen with the Apple apps, flick right.

Browse for Books

The first step in browsing for books from the iBookstore is to get online. You have to be connected to the Internet to access the store. Once you're online, you'll need to locate the magic button in the iBooks app that transports you to it. That button is located in the top-left corner of the iBooks app and is labeled Store.

Tip The first time you open iBooks on your iPad, you'll be prompted to sync your bookmarks, notes, and collections between your devices (such as your iPhone or iPod Touch). Click Sync or Don't Sync, as desired.

Once in the store you can browse to your heart's content. You can peruse the *New York Times* bestseller list, look through a list of Featured books (those chosen by the people at iBooks), view the Top Paid and Top Free books, and even preview books you think you'll enjoy. Of course, you can browse by category as you'd expect, such as History, Nonfiction, Romance, or Sports & Outdoors. You can also search for a specific title or author.

To browse books in the iBookstore:

1. Touch the iBooks app on the Home screen.
2. Locate the button labeled Store in the top-left corner of the screen and tap it. (That button will change to Library after you tap it, to enable you to return to your own personal iBooks Library when you're finished browsing.)
3. Once in the store, touch Featured at the bottom of the page to view Featured books, NYTimes to see the current bestsellers, Top Charts to see what's hot, or Browse to search for books by title or author. Figure 5-2 shows the Top Charts category. Note all of the free books.
4. After you've obtained books (see the Tip here if you'd like to download a free book now), you can then tap Purchases at the bottom of the page to see the items you've purchased, including books you've downloaded that were free. (From here you can redownload books if you like.)

Tip To get a free book right now, tap Free, shown in Figure 5-2, then tap Get Book, and type your password (if prompted). Tap Store to return to the iBookstore.

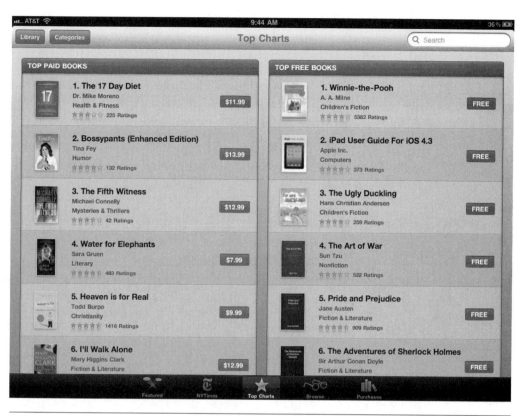

FIGURE 5-2   Some great free books are available from the iBookstore.

Read Reviews of Books

Although you'll often go directly to the book you want to buy in the iBookstore, sometimes you'll find an interesting-looking book while window shopping. Since you may not be familiar with the book or its author, you'll need a bit more information before you commit. That's where reader reviews come in. It's safe to say that most books will have reviews written for them by readers, but if not, at the very least, you'll be able to read a description of the book, find out a little about the author, and discover any special features included with the book.

Tip   Watch for readers who post reviews that spoil the book's ending, or those labeled "spoiler alert." You'll have to be careful to avoid reviews that may give away the ending of a book you're interested in.

To read the reviews for any book or to get more information about a book or its author:

1. Locate a book in the iBookstore.
2. Touch the book's cover to go to the book's information page.
3. In the information page you'll see a description of the book, publisher, publication date, and more. You can tap to go to the Author Page, and you'll have access to price information and book ratings. If there are any customer reviews, you'll see those also. See Figure 5-3.
4. Tap outside the information window to close it.

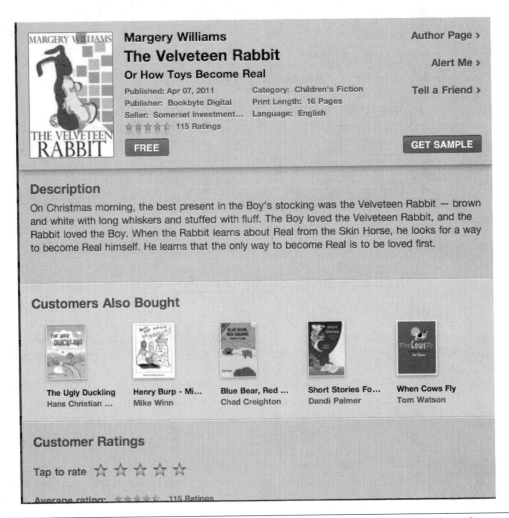

FIGURE 5-3 A book's information page offers various information including the price and description.

After reading a book, come back to the book's information page and write your own review.

Preview a Book

When you're in a "real" bookstore, you can open a book and flip through the pages. You can read the Table of Contents, front cover and back cover, and even the inside pages. Of course, you can sit down and read a chapter if the bookstore allows it. You can perform similar actions at the digital iBookstore, although you can only look at the parts of the book that iBooks allows you to see!

Some things you can preview include (as applicable to the book)

- Table of Contents
- Acknowledgments
- Foreword
- A sample chapter, sample chapters, or part of a single chapter

To preview a book, click the Get Sample button in the information page. The information page with this button was shown earlier in Figure 5-3. A sample will download and will appear in your Library. It will have a "Sample" banner across it.

While you're previewing the book, if you decide to purchase it, a Buy button is available. Just click Buy to get started. There are additional options in this window to help you make your decision, though, including the option to view the Table of Contents, and to skip to another chapter of the sample provided (as applicable). See Figure 5-4.

Access the Table of Contents, bookmarks, and Chapter titles.

Purchase the book.

Change the brightness.

Change font size and type.

| Library | ☰ | BUY | Joli Ballew | Microsoft® Windows® XP: Do Amazing Things ☀ ₐA 🔍 🔖 |

Microsoft®
Windows®

Copyright © 2009 Joli Ballew (Content)

Return to your Library of books.

Search for a word or phrase.

Insert a bookmark.

FIGURE 5-4   When the Contents icon is available, you'll see these options.

FIGURE 5-5 When Resume is available, you'll see these options.

When you tap the Contents button, it becomes Resume. From there you can tap what's available to you, and view any bookmarks you applied in the previous view. What's available in this view depends on the book. Additionally, in this view you can tap any item in the Table of Contents to jump to it. Figure 5-5 shows these icons.

When in this view:

- Tap Library to return to the library.
- Tap Resume to return to the previous view.
- Tap Buy, if available, to purchase the book.
- Tap Table of Contents to see chapter titles and skip to a page quickly.
- Tap Bookmarks to see bookmarks you've previously saved.

Purchase and Download a Book

If you've ever used the App Store on an iPhone or purchased music from your computer using iTunes, you will see lots of similarities between what you've seen there and what you see in the new iBookstore. Even the "Buy" and "Free" buttons look the same. Once you've located a book to buy, it's a very simple process to purchase and download the book:

1. Tap Library if applicable to return to the iBooks Library view.
2. Tap Store if applicable to enter the iBookstore.
3. Locate a book to purchase or download for free, and tap its icon to see the Details page.
4. Tap the book's price or tap Free, as applicable.
5. Tap Buy Book or Get Book, as applicable.
6. iBooks may prompt you to enter your iTunes account password. When you buy a book, your iTunes account will be charged.
7. Wait while the book downloads to your Library, which should only take a minute or less.

iBookstore Password Prompts

In the iBookstore, you'll be prompted for your password the first time you try to purchase a book. Subsequent purchases will not require you to input your password, as long as you purchase something within 15 minutes of the previous purchase. After that time, you'll have to enter your password again. It's a way to protect you in case someone else uses your iPad, while at the same time remaining unobtrusive if you feel inspired to load up on books in one sitting.

Read a Digital Book

When you're ready to read a book, simply open iBooks and tap the book you'd like to read. All of the books you've downloaded are on the virtual bookshelf. You can view the books as thumbnails, the default view, or as a list.

To open and read a book:

1. Open iBooks.
2. If you're in the iBookstore, tap Library.
3. Tap any book on your bookshelf to read it.
4. Hold the iPad in Portrait or Landscape orientation to view as a single page or facing pages.

With a book open, there are several ways to navigate through it:

- To turn a page, tap or flick near the right or left margin of a page to access the previous page and the next page. By default, tapping the left margin takes you to the previous page; however, in Settings under iBooks, you can change this behavior so that tapping the left margin takes you to the next page instead.
- To go to a specific page, tap near the center of the current page to show the slider at the bottom of the page (see the following illustration). Drag the slider to the desired page. Let go to jump to that page in the book.

- To return to or go to the Table of Contents of a book, tap the Contents button at the top of the page next to the Library button. If you can't see either button, tap in the center of a page to show them.

Library ☰   Charles Dickens

A Tale of Two Cities

- To locate the start of a specific chapter, tap the Contents button to access the Table of Contents, and then tap the desired chapter number to go there. To momentarily view the Table of Contents without losing your place, tap the Contents button to view the Table of Contents, then tap Resume to return to the current page.

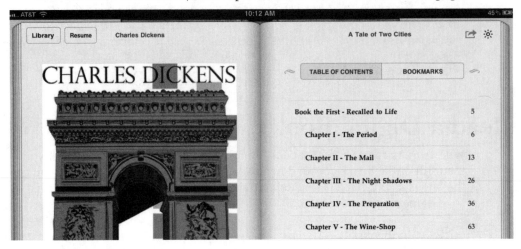

- Tap Library to return to the books in your Library to access a new book to read. If you can't see the Library button, tap in the middle of any page to access it.
- Tap the Home button to access another app or to stop reading. iBooks will remember the page you're on the next time you open the book.

To read a book while lying down or to keep the iPad from switching views when you reposition yourself in a chair, enable the Screen Rotation lock. The Screen Rotation lock is located on the outside of your iPad above the Volume buttons in Portrait view or in Landscape view. If this lock mutes the iPad instead, change its behavior in Settings, under General, or double-tap the Home button, swipe the bottom bar that appears from left to right, and tap the Screen Rotation icon.

Create, Locate, and Delete a Bookmark

You can tap Library or click the Home button to leave your iBook, and when you return, iBooks will remember where you last left off reading. This is true even if you are reading multiple books at the same time. You simply don't have to create a bookmark when you leave a book. However, there are times when you want to create a bookmark, perhaps to make a note of a specific plot twist, clue, definition, or picture. You may also want to highlight a phrase so you can come back to it later. Once you've created bookmarks you can access the bookmarks by tapping the Contents button. The Contents button offers two tabs: Table of Contents and Bookmarks, and is located next to the Library button while you're in a book.

To create (or delete) a bookmark:

1. Locate the page to bookmark.
2. Tap the Bookmark icon.

A Tale of Two Cities

To access bookmarks you've set:

1. Tap the Contents button. If you can't see it, tap in the center of any page to show it.
2. Note the two tabs, Table of Contents and Bookmarks. Tap Bookmarks. See Figure 5-6.
3. Tap the bookmark to access that page.

Adjust Text Size and Font

You can adjust the text size and the font used in any book you get from the iBookstore. If you have to wear reading glasses to see the text on the page, consider making the font larger. If you have trouble reading the font used in the book, choose another one. And if you don't have any problems at all reading what's on the page and want to flip pages less often, consider a smaller font size. Everything you need is available on the top-right corner of iBooks. (If you don't see anything there, tap in the center of any page to show these controls.)

TABLE OF CONTENTS   BOOKMARKS

BOOKMARKS

Chapter IV - The Preparation   62

Today, April 8, 2011

FIGURE 5-6 Access your bookmarks from the Bookmarks tab in the Contents page.

To increase or decrease the font size:

1. Tap the Fonts button. It consists of two capital letters, both A, one small and one large.
2. To increase the font size, tap the large A. Tap again to increase the font size more. Repeat as desired.

3. To decrease the font size, tap the small A. Tap again to decrease the font size more. Repeat as desired.

To change the font:

1. Tap the Fonts button. It consists of two capital letters, both A, one small and one large.
2. Tap Fonts.
3. Tap a font in the list.

Note At the present time you cannot install your own fonts. You have to choose one of the fonts listed.

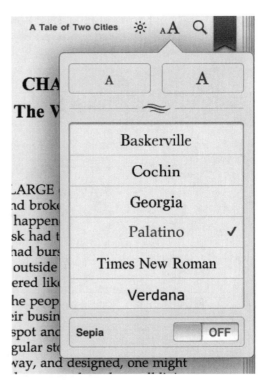

Adjust Brightness

By default, your iPad will adjust the screen's brightness automatically. There's a sensor in the iPad that ascertains how much light is available and uses that information to make the adjustments. You can disable Auto-Brightness in Settings, and Brightness & Wallpaper if you'd rather not have your iPad do this automatically. You can also change the brightness manually in iBooks while reading.

To change the brightness manually while reading a book in iBooks:

1. Tap the Brightness icon. It looks like a sun.
2. Drag to reposition the slider.

Explore Additional iBooks Features

You're not finished yet! There are still more features to discover. You can copy text, look up a word in the dictionary (included with your iPad), and search for a specific word or phrase to locate it in the book or on Google or Wikipedia. The search results offer results for the entire book too, allowing you to easily find all instances of the word. There are options that enable you to reorder books on your Library's bookshelf (and even create your own sub-libraries, called Collections), and delete books or samples of books you no longer want.

Copy and Paste Text

You can copy text in free, public domain books and then paste that text in another app, such as an email in Mail or a note in Notes. To access the Copy command:

1. Tap and hold briefly any word in the book. If the book is a free, public domain title (as most of the free books offered in the iBookstore are), the option to Copy will probably appear along with Dictionary, Highlight, Note, and Search. If the book is a copyrighted work, you will not have the option to copy text.
2. As when copying in any other app, you can drag from the "grab" points to select additional text.
3. After you've selected the text, click Copy, as shown in Figure 5-7.
4. You can now open any Apple (or other compatible) app on your iPad and paste that text.

Search For and Look Up the Meaning of a Word

If, while reading, you come across a word you don't recognize, a term you don't understand, medical terminology you'd like to learn more about, or a company name you've never heard of, select the word and click Dictionary or Search. See Figure 5-7. Tapping Dictionary will cause the Dictionary entry to open and will provide you with its definition. Figure 5-8 shows the word "billets" selected, and the definition the Dictionary provides.

If the Dictionary option doesn't provide the answers you're looking for, tap Search instead of Dictionary. The Search option looks for additional references in the book itself, which may provide the information you need. If that doesn't offer what you want, click Search Google or Search Wikipedia to learn more online (see Figure 5-9). When you click either of these, iBooks closes and Safari opens.

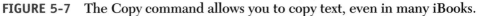

FIGURE 5-7   The Copy command allows you to copy text, even in many iBooks.

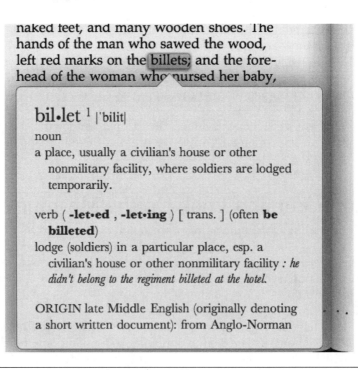

FIGURE 5-8   If you're not sure what a word means, search for a definition in the book or online.

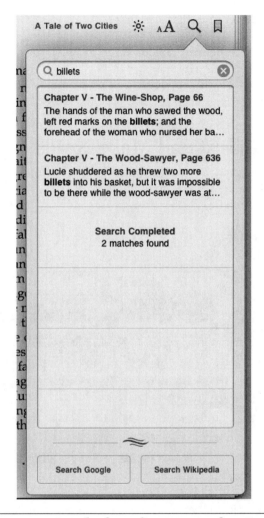

FIGURE 5-9   When you tap Search after selecting a word in iBooks, you'll see other references to that word in the book you're reading, and the options to get information from Google or Wikipedia.

To research a word in iBooks:

1. Tap to select the word and use the grab points if necessary to select words around it.
2. Tap Search.
3. Browse the other instances of the word in the book for a meaning, or click Search Google or Search Wikipedia.

 To select a word that contains a hyphen, try to tap at the beginning of the word and then drag the grab points to select the rest of it.

To look up a word in the Dictionary:

1. Tap to select the word to look up in the Dictionary.
2. Tap Dictionary.
3. The definition will appear in a pop-up window on the screen.
4. Tap anywhere outside the box to make it disappear.

Highlight Text and Make Notes

After you've selected text, as instructed in the previous sections, you also have options to highlight the text or make notes about it.

To highlight text:

1. Select the text.
2. Tap Highlight.

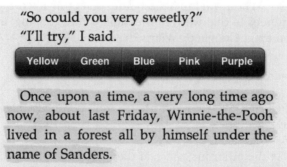

3. To change the color of the highlight, tap it again, tap Colors, and tap a new color.

To make a note about text:

1. Select the text.
2. Tap Note.
3. Type the desired note, as shown in Figure 5-10.
4. Tap outside the note to resume reading.

Sort and Manage Books

After you've used iBooks for a while, you may discover that you have too many books on your bookshelf and in your Library, and they are getting hard to manage. You may have books you've read, books you started but didn't like, or samples of books from the iBookstore that you'd like to delete. You may have so many books that you need to sort your books by their titles, authors, or by their category, or even put them in additional libraries you create. You may even want to reorder the books on your bookshelf, placing the books you want to read in the order you plan to read them. There are several options in the iBooks app that you can use to manage your books.

 If you're in a book now, tap Library.

FIGURE 5-10   Type a note as desired, and tap outside the note to return to the book.

To sort books by their titles, authors, or by their categories:

1. Tap the List icon in the Library. The list icon is to the left of the Edit button and consists of three horizontal lines.
2. At the bottom of the page, tap Titles, Authors, or Categories.

Store **Collections**	**Books**	**Edit**
Adventures of Huckleberry Finn Mark Twain		Fiction & Literature
The Adventures of Sherlock Holmes Sir Arthur Conan Doyle		Fiction & Literature
Alice's Adventures in Wonderland Lewis Carroll		Fiction & Literature
Food Network Magazine Great Easy Meals Food Network Magazine		Cookbooks, Food & Wine
Pride and Prejudice Jane Austen		Fiction & Literature
A Tale of Two Cities Charles Dickens		Classics
Winnie-the-Pooh A. A. Milne		Children's Fiction

Bookshelf | Titles | Authors | Categories

Note You can tap Edit to delete books in this view and others.

To reposition the books on your bookshelf:

1. Tap the thumbnail icon to return to the default thumbnail view, if applicable.
2. Tap and hold any book's icon.
3. When the icon enlarges, drag the book to a new position on the shelf.

To delete a book (and this only deletes the book from your iPad, not from your computer provided you've already synced it there):

1. In any view, tap Edit.
2. Tap a book to select it. You can also tap Select All or tap multiple books. (In List view, tap the circle next to the book.)

3. If you select a book you do not want to delete, tap it again to deselect it.

4. Tap Delete, and tap Delete when prompted to verify.
5. Repeat as desired, and then click Done.

 Deleted books remain in your iTunes Library on your computer provided you've previously opted to sync books (and have actually synced them). If you delete a book you purchased, you can sync it back to your iPad in iTunes.

View Collections and Create Your Own Collection

The Library offers a button called Collections. Tap it to see the two available collections, Books and PDFs. The default view is Books, and if you download and need to access PDFs, you'll find them in the PDF collection. You can also create your own "collection." Once you've created a collection, you can move books there to organize them.

1. In Library view, tap Collections.
2. Tap New.
3. Type the name for the new collection.

4. Tap Done.
5. Repeat as desired.
6. Tap outside the collections window when complete.

To move a book into a collection you've created:

1. In Library view, tap Edit.
2. Tap a book to select it, or select multiple books, or all books.
3. Tap Move.
4. Tap the collection to move the book to.
5. Note the new view with the book moved. Tap Collections to return to any other collection.

6

Read News and Commentary, and Use Social Networks

HOW TO...

- Find and read your local newspaper
- View an RSS feed
- Read the *New York Times*
- Explore free news apps
- Read an online magazine
- Follow friends on social networking sites
- Explore free social networking apps
- Send an SMS text
- Instant message with AIM
- Locate and read a blog
- Locate and listen to a podcast

With an iPad, you can stay up to date with everyone and everything. You can read newspapers, magazines, and blogs, and you can listen to and watch podcasts to stay in touch with the world. You can use social networking to stay in touch with friends. And with the right third-party apps, you can even exchange texts with friends who have cell phones, a feature not supported out of the box from Apple. You can even exchange instant messages through familiar instant messaging applications, like AIM. If you're looking for a way to stay in touch, this is the chapter for you.

Read Newspapers and Magazines

There are lots of printed newspapers that offer online versions for web users. Reading a newspaper online and on your iPad is generally a much more convenient experience than reading its printed counterpart. When reading a newspaper on an iPad, you'll never again elbow the person next to you on a bus when trying to turn a page. You won't have to fold up that paper when you arrive at your destination, and then look for a place to recycle it. And, if you see something interesting, you can email the article to a friend (versus clipping it and putting it in the mail, ugh)!

Besides newspaper publishers, several magazine publishers have made their content available online, and many have created an app version of their publications, designed specifically for the iPad. Check out the iPad versions of the magazines *Popular Science*, *GQ*, and *Time*. Open Safari and type **app.time.com** for a quick preview of the Time Magazine app. You can also browse the App Store for magazine apps.

Find and Read Your Local Newspaper

If you have a favorite local newspaper (or a hometown newspaper), you may be able to find an online version of that paper, and read it on your iPad. At the present time, many online newspapers are free, even though their printed versions have to be purchased, so there's good reason to check it out. Some larger newspapers require you to create a user account to view the paper online, and a few require you to subscribe and pay a fee to access them online. If you already subscribe to the print version of a paper, the online version will likely be free too, provided you create an account and sign in.

To locate the online version of your favorite newspaper:

1. Tap Safari and tap the Search window.
2. Type the name of your local paper.
3. Review the results and tap the official newspaper page.
4. You can almost always view the front page of a newspaper, so tap any link on that page to see if access is available to the rest of the site. See Figure 6-1.

 Tip Just because you can access your newspaper's front page doesn't mean you have full access to the paper. You may be able to read some articles but not have access to the classified ads, or you may be able to view only a few pages before being asked to create a user account.

5. If required, create a user name and password and/or set up a subscription to access the paper online. If you already know you want to subscribe, look for an icon for eEdition, Online Edition, or something similar.

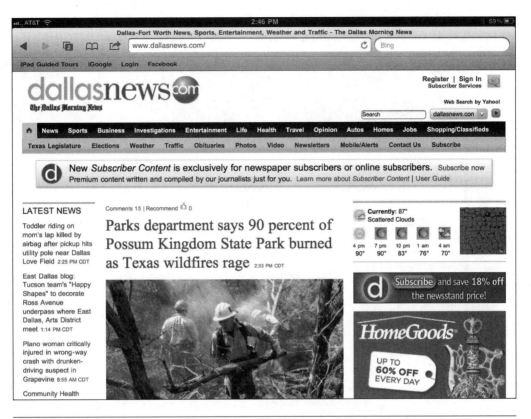

FIGURE 6-1 Your local newspaper may be available online, for free.

View an RSS Feed

Some newspapers, magazines, tech sites, and such also offer an RSS option. RSS stands for Really Simple Syndication, which is a way for you to get the latest information, data, and news in a list, also called a "feed," and forgo scanning the page for information you've yet to see. You'll see RSS icons when you visit web pages that offer them. The following illustration shows CNET Blogs (news.cnet.com/tech-blogs), where you'll find RSS feeds for all kinds of technical topics. If you find an RSS feed you'd like to follow, tap the RSS icon and then create a bookmark for the resulting page.

Read the *New York Times*

The *New York Times* seems to be the defining newspaper for many Americans, so a chapter on newspapers, magazines, blogs, and such wouldn't be complete without a trip to the *New York Times* online newspaper's front page! Once on the page, you can zoom in on any article to increase readability or tap any link to access the full article.

Did You Know?

You Can Manage Multiple Feeds with an RSS Reader from the App Store

There are lots of apps at the App Store that are RSS "readers." With these readers, you can pick and choose what feeds you want to follow, and add them as desired.

To access the *New York Times*:

1. Tap Safari to open it.
2. Tap inside the address window. If a web address is already there, tap the X to erase it. Now, type **nytimes** and tap the .com key. (Your iPad knows you want an http:// in front of that, so there's no need to type it.)
3. Explore both Portrait and Landscape view. Portrait view is shown in Figure 6-2.

While exploring the paper, tap each tab: Home Page, Today's Paper, Video, Most Popular, and Times Topics. From the Video page, tap any video to play it. To access controls while watching a video, tap the video once.

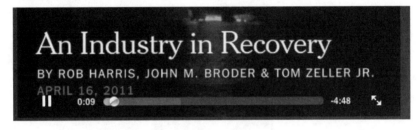

Explore Free News Apps

If you like news, you'll be amazed at the variety of free news apps you have access to from the App Store. There are apps from Reuters, BBC, AP, and *USA Today*. There are apps for NPR, Bloomberg, and other popular agencies.

To see the most popular news apps:

1. If Safari is open, tap the Home button to access the Home screen.
2. Tap App Store.
3. Tap Categories at the bottom of the page.
4. Tap News.
5. Tap Sort By and tap Most Popular.
6. Browse the available apps. Try USA Today for iPad, Flipboard, BBC News, NYTimes for iPad, and any others that interest you. See Figure 6-3.

Read an Online Magazine

If you subscribe to a lot of magazines, you know what a pile you can acquire in only a few months. It's difficult to read them all and even more difficult to throw them away. Moving from the printed version of a magazine to the online version can resolve these issues, by making your magazines available on your iPad. You can also take all of your magazines with you wherever you go, without all the weight and inconvenience.

FIGURE 6-2 The *New York Times* is available to everyone.

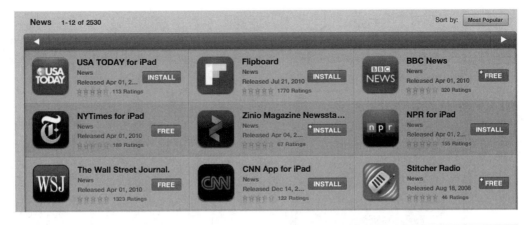

FIGURE 6-3   If you're into news, there are lots of news apps available.

There are several ways to locate an online magazine:

- Visit the home page for the magazine; for instance, *Time* can be found at www
  .Time.com and *Newsweek* is located at www.newsweek.com.
- Search for "online magazines," and visit a web site that offers access to them. For
  example, www.onlinenewspapers.com/magazines offers magazines from around
  the world. You'll be amazed at what you find. You may even find that a few of
  your favorite magazines can be accessed online, for free.
- Visit the App Store and look for your favorite magazine there, or search for
  "magazines." You'll find plenty! The problem is, though, that there aren't a lot
  of discounts; often you'll pay the same for the iPad version as you would the
  printed one.
- If you know you want to subscribe to a particular magazine, get the Zinio Magazine
  Newsstand app from the App Store. From there you can access just about any
  magazine imaginable, and subscribe to it or purchase the current issue. See
  Figure 6-4.

Facebook, Tweet, and Text

There are many ways to build and maintain your social contacts using your iPad. You
can post to Facebook and other social networking sites, you can tweet on Twitter, and
you can even text your friends on their cellular phones or hold instant messaging
conversations via familiar instant messaging applications, like AIM. None of these
things are available out of the box, though; no Facebook app is preinstalled, nor is
a Twitter app, and by default, you can't text or send instant messages on an iPad.
However, there are lots of free apps to help you do all of these things and more, and
they're all available from the App Store.

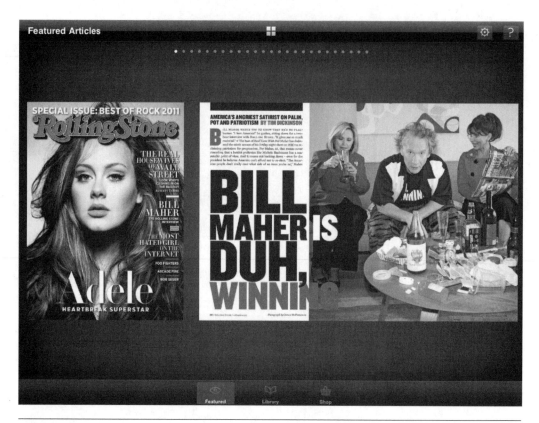

FIGURE 6-4 Zinio, a free app from the App Store, lets you easily subscribe to and read just about any digital magazine.

Follow Friends on Social Networking Sites

You may use Facebook, or you may use another social networking medium like MySpace to connect with friends online. You may belong to online groups. You may also host a personal blog with WordPress, or share your thoughts using other networking options. Whatever you do, you can likely find a way to do it on your iPad. Because Facebook seems to be the most popular social networking site at this time, we'll focus on Facebook here.

No matter what social networking option you use, open Safari and navigate to its home page. For Facebook, type **facebook.com**. When prompted, log in. You should be able to use the site in the same manner you're used to on your computer at home. You can

- Post status updates and view your friends' updates
- View videos friends have posted
- Join groups

- Post your own pictures via email
- Edit your personal information
- Invite people to join you or any group you create
- And lots more!

If you have a Facebook account (and if you don't, you can create one), search Groups for How To Do Everything: iPad. Our group is open to everyone, and you can easily post your own pictures and videos, write on our wall, and "talk" to other iPad fans online. Figure 6-5 shows our group. Once on the group's page, tap Add Bookmark (+) and tap Add to Home Screen, and you'll have one-tap access to the group! See Figure 6-5.

FIGURE 6-5   Log in to Facebook and search for How To Do Everything: iPad to join our group.

Explore Free Social Networking Apps

There are free social networking apps at the App Store, just as there are free news apps. There are apps you can purchase too. To find a social network app related to your social networking site, at the App Store search by the network name, like Facebook, or perform a more general search with a phrase like Social Networking. You'll find all kinds of related apps including those that allow you to chat with others, send and receive instant messages, and upload and share photos. Photobucket for iPad, for instance, allows you to upload media from your iPad directly to your Photobucket albums. You can share these albums with anyone you like.

To get started:

1. Tap the App Store icon on your Home screen.
2. Tap the Categories tab, and select Social Networking. (You may have to tap the "back" button to return to the list of all categories.)
3. Tap next to Sort By, and select an option. I suggest Most Popular.
4. Browse the available apps or search for a specific term, like Facebook or MySpace. Figure 6-6 shows some of the more popular apps.

Tweet with Twitter

If you tweet or if you want to, visit www.twitter.com on your iPad via Safari. Alternatively, you can install and use the Twitter social networking app shown in Figure 6-7. Sign up or sign in to get started. Depending on the medium you choose, you'll either type your tweet in the What's Happening box in Safari, or tap the Compose icon in the Twitter app. Tap Tweet to post your tweet in Safari.

FIGURE 6-6 You'll find plenty of social networking apps to choose from.

FIGURE 6-7   In the Twitter app, after tapping the Compose button, you can type tweets quickly.

Tip   To access Twitter quickly using Safari, add a web clip to Twitter on your Home screen (click the Add Bookmark icon and click Add to Home Screen).

Send an SMS Text

An SMS text is a short text message that's generally sent from a cell phone to another cell phone, and generally, the recipient of the text sends one back. This exchange of words via cell phones is called *texting* and is achieved over a cellular network like AT&T. You can send a text from your iPad to a cell phone, even if you don't have a cellular data plan, though, using a third-party app called Textfree. There are other texting apps, though, so don't assume you have to use this one. We're only discussing this one because it was the first one we tried and the texting app with the most reviews (implying it's quite popular).

>
> **Note** At the time this book was written, there were not many texting apps available for the iPad. By the time you read this, though, there may be many more. Try a search for SMS Text and see what you find in the App Store.

To get Textfree and send your first text:

1. Tap the App Store icon on your Home screen.
2. Search Textfree.
3. Locate the Textfree app. There are two versions: Textfree Unlimited and Textfree with Voice. Both are free apps.
4. Tap Free, and tap Install App.
5. Tap the icon for Textfree. You'll notice that the app only takes up half the screen, because it was originally designed for the iPhone and iPod Touch.
6. Create an account when prompted.
7. After signing in, tap the wrench icon. This is Settings. Next to Phone Number, tap Get one.
8. Fill out the required information and write down your new free number.
9. Tap the New Message icon.
10. Type the cell phone number to send the text to, tap Start Text, and type your message.
11. Tap Send. See Figure 6-8.

FIGURE 6-8 Texting apps let you send texts from your iPad to a cellular phone.

Your contacts will need to send texts to the number you received in Step 7 to send a text to your iPad, or simply click Reply on their phones after receiving a text from you.

Instant Message with AIM

Instant messaging is quite different from texting. Texting is done between two cell phones, generally; instant messaging is a common way to communicate between two computers. It is also possible to send and receive instant messages on iPads, iPhones, tablets, smartphones, or other mobile devices.

Instant messaging is often called chatting. There are lots of ways to exchange instant messages, including Windows Live Messenger, AIM, Facebook Chat, Google Talk, Skype Chat, and Jabber, to name a few. If you currently exchange instant messages on your computer, you may be able to continue to exchange instant messages in the same manner on your iPad.

One of the instant messaging options is AIM, created by AOL. With it, you can chat directly with Facebook friends; get updates from Facebook, MySpace, Twitter, and others; add a location to your status; and more. Figure 6-9 shows the AIM app's interface.

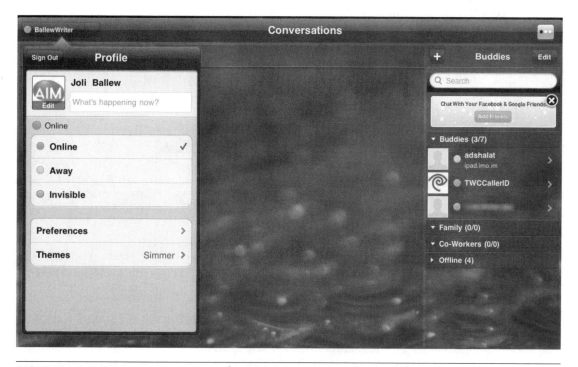

FIGURE 6-9 AIM is one way to exchange instant messages.

Explore Blogs, Podcasts, and Newsgroups

You can keep up with social commentary via the web from your iPad. You can read blogs, listen to podcasts, and join newsgroups, for instance, and have easy access to a wide range of opinions from just about every segment of the population. Often, these types of Internet communications and updates consist of personal views on politics and social issues, like health care, immigration, and a host of other hot (and sometimes volatile) topics, but can also encompass things like technology, breaking news, and simple personal observations.

Locate and Read a Blog

A blog is a "web log," and is often updated daily, sometimes hourly, and occasionally more often than that. A blog is written and posted to a web site, and the entries are listed most-recent-first. More often than not, a blog consists of observations made by a person about a specific thing, like their take on a new technology or what is going on in their business or company, but blogs also offer descriptions of events that allow others to access minute-by-minute details. (Some news correspondents offer blogs about a war or specific battle, for instance, or how quickly floodwaters are rising during a dangerous storm.) More often than not, though, blogs are simply social commentary and include how the person feels about specific things, sometimes on issues like health care, war, immigration, and the like.

You can search for blogs the same way you search for anything on the Internet, using keywords. If you know or have heard about a specific blog you want to read, perform a search for the person and his or her blog. You can search for "Apple iPad Blog" and you'll see plenty of results. Figure 6-10 shows the "Apple" blog from CNET News.

FIGURE 6-10 Blogs offer updated information on almost anything imaginable.

Locate and Listen to a Podcast

A podcast is a form of audio and video broadcasting over the Internet. It's kind of like a radio show (or lecture) on demand, if you can imagine that. Since we've talked quite a bit about news in this chapter, we'll take a look at podcasts available from news outlets.

One way to access podcasts is to open Safari on your iPad and navigate to a web site you know offers podcasts. If you like CNN, try cnn.com/services/podcasting. The following illustration shows an example, and we've zoomed in on it so that you can see the three buttons available (Subscribe, Listen, and iTunes).

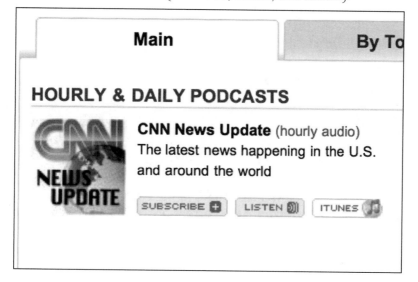

Subscribe lets you subscribe to the podcast series, Listen lets you access the podcast immediately, and iTunes opens the podcast series in iTunes so you can download this podcast or any other that's available from the series, as shown in Figure 6-11.

Podcasts can help you keep in touch with the latest news, sports, entertainment, technology, and more, without having to actually "tune in" to a show.

You can also access podcasts from the iTunes Store, right from your iPad's Home screen. Just tap the Podcasts tab. From there you can view a list of featured podcasts, or tap the Categories button in the upper-left corner to further sort by category. iTunes features the largest selection of audio and video podcasts on the web. The iTunes interface makes it easy to find what you're looking for. All podcasts are free and can be downloaded on demand. You'll learn all about iTunes in Chapter 9.

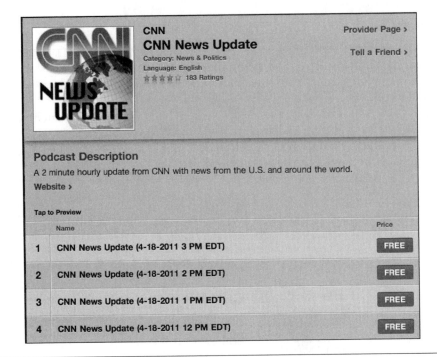

FIGURE 6-11 When you tap iTunes in the CNN options, iTunes opens on your iPad, where you can acquire the current podcast and previous ones.

7

Get and Use Apps
from the App Store,
and Incorporate Game Center

HOW TO...

- Open and explore the App Store
- Use the Search box to find an app
- Read reviews of apps before you buy them
- Purchase and download an app
- Download and install a free app
- Get app updates
- Start and use an app
- Find apps created specifically for the iPad
- Delete apps you don't use
- Consider iWork
- Consider iMovie and Garage Band
- Back up apps to your computer
- Explore Game Center

The App Store is available via an Internet connection and the App Store icon on the Home screen. The App Store is where you get "apps." Apps are programs you can run on your iPad (or iPhone or iPod Touch), and they run the gamut with regard to what they offer. If you can imagine doing it, there's probably an app for that!

For example, there are apps that let you keep track of your workouts, apps that tell you how many calories are in the food you're eating, apps that help you choose or follow your fantasy football team, apps that are games, and even apps that enable you to play a virtual instrument, like a guitar or piano. You can get apps for Solitaire or Tetris, apps that help you learn a new language, and apps that enable you to communicate via social networking, right from your iPad. The App Store offers them all, offering over a quarter of a million apps with more and more coming every week. On Saturday, January 22, 2011, the 10 billionth app was downloaded from the Apple App Store.

Once you're in the App Store, it's simple to browse listings of apps like "What's Hot" or "Top Charts." You can also browse by category, including (but not limited to) Social Networking, Education, or Games. You can even filter apps by which ones are free, which is a perfect place to start if you're unsure about what apps are or what they offer. Let's start off simple—let's browse the App Store for the most popular apps first. Once you've learned a bit about apps, and perhaps acquired some games, you'll explore the Game Center, where you can keep up with your game stats and see how other players are faring, among other things.

Explore the App Store

To use the App Store, you must be connected to the Internet. You'll also need an iTunes Store account, something you set up when you registered your iPad. To enter the store, simply tap the App Store icon on the Home screen. You can download and install any of the apps in the store, including apps designed for the iPhone and iPod Touch. When searching for apps, try to stick to apps created specifically for the iPad, at least for now. You know these apps will take advantage of the iPad's larger screen and Multi-Touch features, and will have been tested on an iPad. (Some apps created for the iPhone look distorted when you position them to take up the entire iPad screen, even though they work as they should.) You can also sync apps you have already purchased for your iPhone or iPod Touch using iTunes, if you want to try those apps on your iPad.

Open the App Store and Explore

The easiest way to get started with the App Store is to simply try it out. Touch the App Store icon while connected to the Internet and start browsing. Most of the time, that's all there is to it. On occasion you may find that you aren't connected to the Internet (when you thought you were), or you need to tap the "back" button in a view to return to a previous screen, but there's really not much that can go wrong here.

To open the App Store and explore the apps:

1. Position yourself within range of a free wireless network and connect to it, or use your provider's 3G network to connect to the Internet.

 To learn more about how to connect to the Internet, see Chapter 2.

2. Touch the App Store icon on your iPad. If you are within range of and connected to a Wi-Fi network or connected through 3G cellular paid services, you'll see the store and be connected. If you aren't connected to the Internet, you'll receive a message stating that you can't access the store until you are.
3. Note the five options across the bottom of the App Store: Featured, Genius, Top Charts, Categories, and Updates. Tap to switch views.

Find the Most Popular Apps

If you want to browse the most popular apps in the App Store, you can do so easily. There's an option at the top of the *Featured* page entitled What's Hot. What's Hot shows what's "trending" at the moment. This doesn't mean the apps in this list have outsold all others or are more popular in the long term; it just means that at this moment, they're hot.

To browse What's Hot:

1. Touch the App Store icon on the Home screen.
2. Touch Featured at the bottom of the App Store interface.
3. Touch What's Hot at the top of the App Store interface. See Figure 7-1. There are lots of browsing options:
   a. Scroll up and down to see additional categories.
   b. Tap the left and right arrows in a category to view more.
   c. Tap See All to see everything in a category.

There are free apps too, and the fact that they're free often makes them popular. There are free versions of games like Solitaire, free practical apps like calculators, and apps that let you play air guitar or a virtual piano. There are media apps from companies like Netflix, Time Warner, and ABC, and newspapers, including *USA Today*.

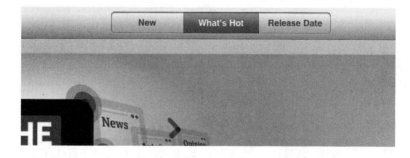

FIGURE 7-1   Find out what's trending by looking at What's Hot.

To find popular and free apps for your iPad:

1. Touch the App Store icon on the Home screen.
2. Tap Top Charts at the bottom of the page.
3. In the right pane, scroll to browse the Top Free iPad apps.

TOP FREE iPad APPS

1. MyPad - Facebook for iPad (Facepad)
Social Networking
Released Dec 29, 2010
★★★★☆ 152 Ratings
FREE

2. Angry Birds Rio HD Free
Games: Puzzle
Released Mar 22, 2011
★★★★☆ 4455 Ratings
INSTALLED

3. iheartradio for iPad
Music
Released Mar 10, 2011
★★★★★ 177 Ratings
FREE

4. Friendly for Facebook
Social Networking
Released Nov 03, 2010
★★★★☆ 9096 Ratings
FREE

5. Simply Find It
Games: Trivia
Released Apr 05, 2011
★★★★★ 2576 Ratings
INSTALLED

 Tip Although we'll discuss purchasing apps later in this chapter, if you find a free app you want, click Free, and click Install App. (You may also see Install or Installed if you've downloaded the app before.)

Did You Know? ## Why Some Apps Have a + Sign by Them?

That + sign you see on some of the Free or price buttons means that there is a single version of the app that's designed both for the iPad and the iPhone.

Find Apps by Category or Search

You may not care about what's hot, and you may not even care whether the app you're looking for is free or if you have to buy it. What you care about is finding an app that will do a specific thing, such as enable you to play Tetris on your iPad, or keep track of certain data such as calories eaten or miles driven, or an app that has a specific keyword in its description such as Facebook or Netflix. In these instances you need to browse apps by their category, or search for them by their name.

There are lots of categories of apps, and you can browse them from the App Store. Just click the Categories button at the bottom of the page. Here are some descriptions of a few of the available categories and what you can expect to find in them:

- **Games**   As you'd expect, you'll find games here. There are all kinds of games to choose from including action, adventure, arcade, board, card, casino, dice, and so on. Try a free version of Angry Birds; it's all the rage and it's easy to play.
- **Entertainment**   Generally apps under the Entertainment category are meant to "entertain." These apps don't usually have anything to do with entertainers, although they can. For the most part, you'll find jokes, quizzes, aquariums, and games like Truth or Dare.

 If you tap an app icon to learn more, touch the Back button to return to the previous screen.

- **Utilities**   For the most part, apps in the Utilities category are things like alarm clocks, messaging programs, web browsers, spell checkers, and system activity monitors. They're "utile."
- **Social Networking**   This is where you'll find programs for communicating with others via Facebook, AIM, GPS tracking, and instant messaging. Look for Facebook, Skype, Yahoo! Messenger, and Google Chat, to name a few.
- **Music**   You won't find songs here; instead look for apps that teach you how to learn to play the guitar; apps that let you listen to radio stations, play finger pianos, and tap on virtual drum sets; and apps that offer the lyrics to your favorite songs.
- **Productivity**   These apps are meant to help you be productive, in terms of getting things done. There are PDF readers, apps that help you find the lowest gas prices in your area, apps that convert measures and money, and even apps to help you redecorate your house.
- **Lifestyle**   Lifestyle apps help you cook, mix drinks, give a toast, or spout a great quotation. You'll find diary apps, find-a-restaurant apps, and even apps to help you grill the perfect steak or find the perfect bottle of wine. Not all of the lifestyle apps are Rated G, though—but the titles usually give that away!
- **Reference**   This category contains dictionaries, grammar guides, math apps, and similar reference materials.
- **Travel**   Here you'll find apps for tracking flights, sharing trip information, keeping travel journals, and even apps to help you pack.
- **Sports**   Sports apps offer just what you'd expect. Keep track of your favorite teams and players here. Learn the rules of the game, where to fish, and how to hit the perfect golf shot.

There are more categories, but we're sure you're getting the idea. App makers put their apps in the category that best relates to what they offer. Other categories include Navigation, Healthcare and Fitness, Photography, Finance, Business, Education, Weather, Books, and Medical.

To browse apps by category:

1. Touch the App Store icon to enter the store.
2. At the bottom of the page, touch Categories, as shown in the following illustration.
3. Touch any category to view the available apps.

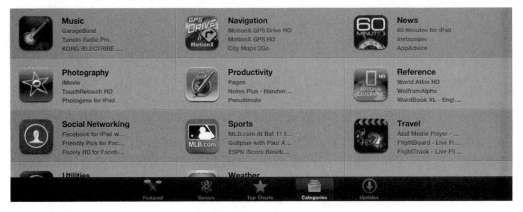

If you've searched for an app by What's Hot or Top Free, and you've looked for an app in the appropriate category but still haven't found what you want, consider searching for it by keyword. There's a Search box in each of the App Store's windows (except Updates), and all you have to do is touch and type. Search the App Store using keywords that describe what you're looking for, and try to use only one or two unique keywords for best results.

Here's an example. Say you want to locate an app that can help you decide what plants would be best for your climate, when to plant them, and how to take care of them. Touch Search and type plants. You'll get lots of results and can browse them and read the reviews to find one you want. Later, if you decide on roses, you can search for an app that tells you about growing roses. This time, you'll look for an app that tells you where and when to plant roses, how much to water, how to fertilize, how to trim, and so on. Although a search for "roses" will produce results that don't include what you're looking for, there's a good chance you'll find a gardening app that just deals with the rose.

To use the Search box to find an app:

1. Touch the App Store icon on the Home screen.
2. Touch inside the Search window. If you've searched before, you may see the keyword you typed last time. If this is the case, use the X to erase what's there.
3. Use the keyboard to type in a keyword. It's best to search using one keyword first, and if there are too many results, try typing two.

FIGURE 7-2   You'll see apps for the iPad and the iPhone. If given a choice, see if an iPad app suits your needs.

4. Touch Search on the keyboard to show the results. See Figure 7-2.
5. If you see iPad apps and iPhone apps, see if one of the iPad apps will work for you before opting for an app made for the iPhone.
6. Tap the icon for the app to learn more about it.

Read Reviews of Apps

You should always read the reviews of apps before you purchase them. While an app may look good on an iPhone and have many excellent reviews, it may lose its luster on an iPad. Additionally, app reviews can reveal bugs with an app, problems contacting the manufacturer, or information regarding the value of the app in comparison to its price. Finally, reviews can help uncover any problems with the app, such as it being too violent or sexual (like a game), or not including information required to make it useful (which is often the case with reference apps).

Just about every app has a few reviews. Some have a ton. To find and read reviews for apps:

1. In the App Store, locate an app that you would like to learn more about.
2. Touch the app's icon. You won't have to buy the app right now; touching the app here takes you to the app's information page.
3. Scroll down to the bottom of the information page, as shown in the following illustration to access the ratings and other customer feedback.

4. Read any app review on the page, and if there are more than will fit on one page, touch More.

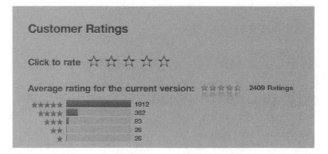

5. Click the Back button (which should show Search) to return to the list of matches found for your keyword(s).

Purchase, Download, and Install an App

We'll assume that you've found an app you like, and you're ready to purchase, download, and install it. Since we want to be thorough here, we'll detail each of these: how to purchase an app from the iTunes Store, download, and install it; how to download and install a free app from the iTunes Store; and how to keep your apps up to date by downloading and installing updates.

 On the fence about apps? Try a free app. You can always delete it if you don't like it. No harm, no foul.

Purchase and Download an App

If you've read the reviews and are ready to purchase an app, you're in the right place. Get your iTunes password handy; you'll be asked for it. Remember that you'll have to be connected to the Internet too.

To purchase and download an app:

1. Locate the app you want to purchase in the App Store.
2. Touch the app to go to its information page, if desired.
3. Touch the price of the app.
4. Touch Buy App.
5. Type your iTunes password, if prompted. (If you've already made a purchase within the last 15 minutes, you won't be asked for your password again.)

Note iTunes passwords are case-sensitive.

6. Watch the download process on your Home screen. Once the download is complete, tap the app to start it.

Download and Install a Free App

If you're on the fence about apps, or simply aren't ready to shell out any money for one, try a free app. If you're a fan of Facebook, try one of the available Facebook apps. Not into social networking? Look for Fruit Ninja, The Weather Channel Max for iPad, Flipboard, Netflix, or Bing for iPad. If you want to really step out, try the ABC Player. With it you can watch the latest episodes of many of your favorite ABC shows from Desperate Housewives to Castle to Private Practice.

To download and install a free app:

1. Locate the free app you want in the App Store.
2. Touch the app to go to its information page, if desired.
3. Touch Free.
4. Touch Install App.
5. Type your iTunes password, if prompted.
6. Watch the download process on your Home screen. Once the download is complete, tap the app to start it.

Install App Updates

Manufacturers may offer updates to their apps to enhance their quality, offer more features, or add more data. You'll know when these updates are available because a number will appear on the App Store icon, and you'll see a number on the Updates tab of the App Store once it's opened. It's up to you whether or not to install updates. If it's an app you use, you likely have nothing to lose. If it's an app you never use, it's probably better to delete the app altogether and get it off your iPad (why waste the space?). Whatever the case, you should always read the information offered about the update before installing it. To check for update information, review it, and install app updates from your iPad:

1. Touch the App Store icon.
2. Touch the Updates tab. It will have a number on it if updates are available.

Agree to Terms of Service

The first time you use the App Store, you may be prompted to agree to Terms of Service. If so, click OK to continue. Read and review the terms, and click Agree. Note that you may have to touch Agree again. If prompted to "try your purchase again," start over with Step 1. Agreeing to the Terms of Service is a one-time inconvenience, and you should not be prompted again unless the terms change.

3. If more than one update is available, don't immediately click Update All. You should go through each update individually to verify that you really want to download and install the update. That said, touch any item in the list to view update information.
4. Decide if you want to install this update or not.
   a. To install a single item, click the Free button on the app update information page (or the price icon) and click Install.
   b. If prompted, enter your iTunes password.
   c. To install all updates, click Update All.

You can also check for updates any time and install them, using your computer:

1. Connect your iPad to your computer.
2. Under Library in the source pane, click Apps.
3. Check the bottom-right corner to see if updates are available.
4. If updates are available, click the arrow button next to the description of how many updates are available.
5. You can view updates, or opt to download all free updates at once.
6. When all desired updates are installed, scroll to the bottom of the page and click Done.

 To make sure you have the most recent version of iTunes, click Help, and click Check for Updates. To make sure you've downloaded everything you've paid for, click Store and click Check for Downloads.

Use Apps

You're probably surprised that we've dedicated this many pages to apps and we haven't even shown you how to use an app yet! The wait is over. To start any app, simply touch it on the Home screen to which it was downloaded.

The first time you start an app, you'll probably see an introductory screen that either tells you how to use the app or offers a button for getting directions. If it's a social app, it'll ask you to log in with your username and password. After getting through these screens, you may then see a menu screen that offers options for the app, like entering data, inputting a zip code or city, adding a player, or continuing where you left off the last time you used it. Because all apps are different, the best we can do is generalize the options you'll see when you start an app, and what you'll need to do to use it.

To start an app and use it:

1. Locate the icon for the app on the Home screen.
2. Touch the icon to start the app.
3. Read the introductory statements, and read any directions supplied.

4. Click Start, Play, Begin, or another option. Once you've started an app, you may be prompted with instructions for play or use, or you may be presented with a screen for playing multiplayer games or viewing achievements.

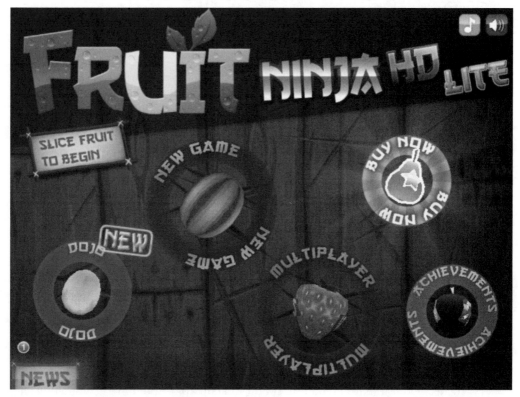

Note If you like an app and want to move it to another Home screen for easier access, tap and hold the icon for a second until all icons start to "wiggle," and then drag the app to its new location. Press the Home button to apply.

Find the Perfect App

By now you know that there are a ton of apps! And if you've downloaded your fair share, you've likely seen the good, the bad, and the ugly. You probably also know that good reviews don't always mean great apps. Even apps with excellent reviews can be less than optimal on the larger iPad if created for the iPhone; they may fail to offer what you're looking for or do what they're supposed to do, or they might not entertain the way you expected. And by now, you know that just because an app is "hot" doesn't guarantee it's a great app, and free apps won't always meet your expectations.

There are apps that have been specifically designed for, or redesigned for, the iPad. These apps are optimized for the iPad's larger screen, compared to the iPhone or iPod Touch. You'll find these apps in a special section of the App Store, as detailed here:

1. Enter the App Store on your iPad.
2. Tap Top Charts at the bottom of the page.
3. View the top apps for iPad.
4. Scroll down to view the Top Grossing iPad apps.

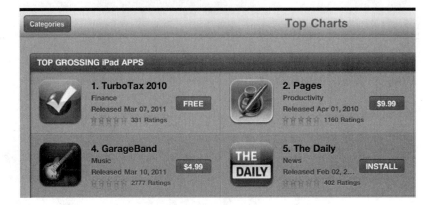

Delete Apps You Don't Use

We don't know what model iPad you purchased—if it was the 16GB, 32GB, or 64GB model—but no matter, you don't want to keep apps you don't use on your iPad. You only have so much space, and there's no need to fill up that space with apps you'll never use. Therefore, you should delete apps you know you don't like.

Depending on how the app arrived on your iPad (either directly or via your computer), permanently deleting an app from your iPad may take up to two steps. If you've downloaded an app directly to your iPad through the App Store and haven't synced the iPad back to your computer since, you can delete the app from the iPad immediately and permanently. When you delete an app from your iPad, it's not there any more, and it isn't taking up any space.

If the app arrived on your iPad via your computer or has been synced back to iTunes after obtaining it on your iPad, a copy of the app will remain on your computer even after you've deleted it from the iPad. So, if you really want to delete all traces of an app, you'll have to delete it from your iTunes library on your computer too. If you like, though, you can leave the app on your computer, and if you ever change your mind about it, you'll have the option to sync it back to your iPad. You can also download it again from the App Store, if desired.

FIGURE 7-3   To delete an app from your iPad, tap the X.

To remove an app from your iPad:

1. Locate the app to delete on the iPad.
2. Touch and hold the icon for the app until all of the icons start to "wiggle."
3. Click the X that appears on the app, as shown in Figure 7-3.
4. Click Delete to verify you want to delete the app.
5. Click No Thanks or Rate if prompted to rate the app before deleting it.
6. Press the Home button to stop the icons from "wiggling."

To remove the app from your computer:

1. Connect your iPad to your computer.
2. Under Library in the left pane, click Apps.
3. Right-click the app to delete. In the drop-down list that appears, click Delete. See Figure 7-4.
4. Click Remove.
5. Click Move to Recycle Bin. Note that the app will be removed from your iTunes library on your computer and will also be removed from your iPad and other devices, if you have not removed them manually.

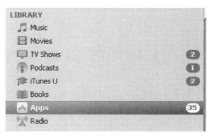

Consider iWork

The iWork suite of applications includes Keynote, Pages, and Numbers. You can use the apps to be productive while away from your home or work computer. Unlike other productivity apps you may have encountered, the iWork apps are extensive, and you

FIGURE 7-4 To completely delete an app, you must also remove it from your iTunes library on your computer.

can do much more than just open and lightly edit documents, presentations, and spreadsheets. Unlike many apps designed for other mobile devices, these apps actually enable you to create things; you can create a slideshow presentation; a newsletter, brochure, or report; and even a spreadsheet, all from scratch or using the templates provided. Every app in the iWork suite of apps is surprisingly substantial, and offers much more than you probably expect.

There are three apps available in the iWork app suite: Keynote, Pages, and Numbers, and each app costs $9.99. Each app has a specific function, and you can use an app to edit existing documents, presentations, and spreadsheets, or create new ones. You may not need every app in the iWork suite, though, so before you buy, make sure you know what you want and need. As an aside, the iWork apps are compatible with Microsoft Office file formats.

Understand Keynote

Keynote is a presentation app. It's the iPad's version of the larger Keynote application originally designed for Apple computers. If you're familiar with Microsoft Office products, it's Apple's answer to PowerPoint. With Keynote, you can create stunning presentations that include pictures, animated charts, transitions between slides, playback of presentations you create, and more. You can use the Media Browser to easily add your own images too. You can even add shadows, reflections, and picture frames with a simple touch. As with other iWork apps, you can add tables and charts.

There are lots of great things about Keynote:

- A dozen themes to help you easily build your presentation
- The ability to drag objects like pictures and text to move them around on a slide
- Options for animating slides and transitioning between them
- A media browser for locating pictures, tables, charts, and other data quickly
- A navigator to help you reorder slides and add new ones

You Can Present with Your iPad

When you're ready to share your presentation, you can connect your iPad to a projector, TV, or monitor using an optional adapter. You can also email your presentation or use iTunes to copy the presentation to your computer if you need additional options.

Changes are saved each time you make a change, automatically, and you can always "undo" your work even after you've left the app and returned to it later.

Understand Pages

Pages is a word processing app. It's the iPad's version of the larger Pages application originally designed for Apple computers. If you're familiar with Microsoft Office products, it's Apple's answer to Word. With Pages, you can create just about any type of document you can imagine, from newsletters to reports to flyers. As with Keynote and Numbers, you can use the included templates to create documents quickly. Pages also offers spelling and punctuation tools, and options for adding bulleted and numbered lists. You can even set margins and tabs! As with other iWork apps, you can drag the data around in the document to move it. This makes placing text and images a breeze.

Here are a few other reasons to consider Pages:

- Sixteen templates for easy document creation.
- A page navigator that lets you access parts of your document quickly.
- The option to type with a dock and wireless keyboard for more efficient document creation.
- Formatting tools to make any document pop.
- Easy photo-editing options like twisting photos, rotating them, or resizing them, with a touch of your finger.
- You can print from Pages. Click the wrench on the toolbar and it will look for Airplay-compatible printers on your network.
- Various options for sharing files including via email and iTunes, but also by exporting as a PDF or a Microsoft Word file.

Understand Numbers

Numbers is a spreadsheet app. It's the iPad's version of the larger Numbers application originally designed for Apple computers. If you're familiar with Microsoft Office products, it's Apple's answer to Excel. With Numbers, you can enter and edit data and create tables and charts from it. You can add almost anything, from the miles you drive to the money you spend. You can manage your household budget or keep track of soccer team members, goals, and assists. As with the other iWork apps, you can drag and drop data anywhere you want. It's much more flexible than other spreadsheet apps, and was redesigned from the ground up just for the iPad.

Numbers includes lots of features you wouldn't expect in a portable spreadsheet app:

- Sixteen predesigned templates for easy spreadsheet creation
- Drag-and-drop technology for moving and calculating data in tables
- Forms that look like recipe cards for keeping data organized
- The ability to create stunning and useful charts of data you've entered
- An intelligent keyboard for entering data and a full calculation engine for calculating data
- The ability to import and edit files from Microsoft Excel and export them as a Numbers document or PDF

If you think you can benefit from any of these apps, they're all available from the app store.

Consider iMovie and Garage Band

iMovie and Garage Band are two apps Apple is really promoting. Both iMovie and Garage Band are $4.99. If you want to make your own movies from video you shoot with your iPad, consider iMovie. If you want to create music using your iPad, consider Garage Band.

iMovie

iMovie helps you turn your HD video you shoot from your iPad into professional-looking movies. To use it, you shoot the video with the camera, and then tap iMovie. You can select a theme, add music, insert photos, narrate the movie, and share your completed project with others in various ways. iMovie is compatible with the iPad 2, iPhone 4, and iPod Touch (fourth generation).

Garage Band

Garage Band offers virtual digital musical instruments you can play and record, including guitars, basses, amps, drum sets, keyboards, and synthesizers. You "play" these devices and record what you create, and then you use the virtual music studio to blend them all together to mix them. This is an eight-track studio that enables you to create professional-sounding music tracks. As with iMovie, once you've completed a project, you can share the music you create in various ways, including email and exporting to your iTunes library. Garage Band is compatible with the original iPad and the iPad 2.

Tip Visit Apple.com, tap the iPad link, and tap From the App Store. From that page you can view a video about using iMovie and Garage Band, if you'd like more information.

Back Up Apps on Your Computer

When you sync your iPad to your computer, your apps will automatically be backed up. You should sync and verify that a backup is taking place, though, especially if you've recently purchased an expensive app. Alternatively, if you don't want to wait until you have time to do a sync, you can just open up iTunes on your computer, navigate to the app, and click to purchase the app. iTunes will think about it for a minute and say that you have already purchased the app and ask if you want to download it again for free.

To back up your apps on your computer:

1. Connect your iPad to your computer.
2. Click your iPad in the source pane of iTunes.
3. Click the Apps tab.
4. Tick Sync Apps, if it is not ticked already. See Figure 7-5.
5. Verify that your new apps are selected in the list.
6. Click Apply.
7. Do not disconnect your iPad from your computer until the backup and sync process is complete.

FIGURE 7-5 Make sure to sync apps you like and to always sync new apps you acquire.

Explore Game Center

The Game Center offers access to an online gaming network. Basically, it's an Apple-designed alternative to third-party matchmaking, leaderboard, and achievement-tracking services, which will only mean something to you if you're a big fan of gaming! In layman's terms, Game Center's purpose is to match up users who choose to play games against each other online, or to enable players to invite people they know or have previously met to play a game, and to let those players keep track of their scores and achievements.

You can also use the Game Center to download games, review the status of the gaming friends you make, and see friend requests, among other things. You'll have to sign in with your Apple ID to get started, and download games you want to play. After that, you're ready to compete!

 Game Center isn't available in all countries and regions, and the games may vary by region as well.

 Get some games from the App Store before continuing here, and look for games that are "Game Center" or "multiplayer" compatible.

The game you're playing also uses Game Center.

Sign In to the Game Center

Tap the Game Center icon and input your Apple ID and password to get started. Tap Sign In. You will have to input your country and your date of birth, agree to some terms of service, create a secret word or question, input the answer, create a nickname, and decide if you'd like to allow game invites and other communications (you'll need to allow game invitations to play multiplayer online games). Once you've done all that, you're ready to play! See Figure 7-6.

Understand the Interface

You'll notice, after signing in, that there are four options across the bottom of the Game Center interface. They include:

- **Me**   This view shows your name, nickname, friends, games, achievements, and other information. You can type your status. You can also tap any game's icon here to go to the App Store to get the game.

FIGURE 7-6   Open the Game Center and sign in to get started.

- **Friends**   This view shows your friends, their status and other information, and offers a way to add more friends.

- **Games**   This view offers access to games you've recently played, your achievements, leaderboards, and a place to share news about a game with friends.

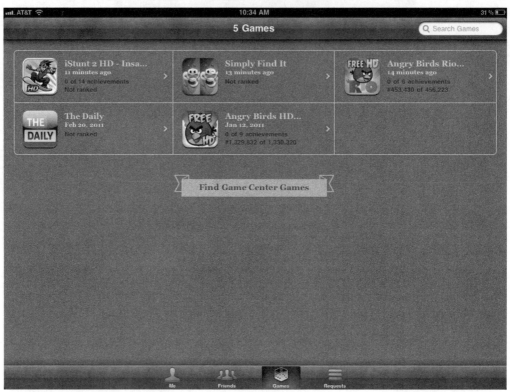

- **Requests**   This view offers information about friend requests, and gives you the option to ignore, accept, or report a problem.

Get and Play a Game

There are several ways to find games, but one of the easiest is to open Game Center, tap Games, and tap Find Game Center Games. This will take you to the App Store where you can search for and download games as desired. Alternatively, you can tap the Me button, and tap an icon for a game you recognize, to go directly to that page in the App Store. Once you've downloaded a game, tap it on the appropriate iPad screen to start it, and work through any setup pages. You may see, during setup, that a game is Game Center compatible.

   It's important to note that a game must be "Game Center compatible" to be used effectively in the Game Center.

FIGURE 7-7   Some games offer the ability to be matched with others to play online.

Most Game Center compatible games offer multiplayer modes, which bring up a Game Center matchmaking screen. This enables you to invite friends to play games with you. If you don't have enough friends to play against in a given game, Game Center includes Auto-Match, which will match you up against another player who's also interested in playing right now. When all players are ready, you can start playing together.

As an example, in Pool Bar - Online Hustle, the first screen asks if you'd like to incorporate Game Center, then offers the option to play the game online. To be automatically matched with another player, you can tap Play, or you can opt to invite a friend, as shown in Figure 7-7.

Once you've been matched up, you're ready to play.

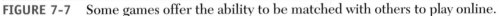

8

Use Your iPod App

HOW TO...

- Learn sync options and supported file formats
- Sync music from your computer to your iPad
- Browse your iPad's music collection
- Play a song and adjust the volume
- Pause and restart a song or skip to the next song
- View album art or the track list
- Create a Genius playlist
- Create a Genius Mix
- Create a Standard playlist
- Edit a playlist
- Play a playlist
- Sync playlists
- Shuffle songs in any list and use the Repeat button
- Use the Search box to find a song
- Explore audiobooks, podcasts, music videos, and iPod settings
- Stream music over your home Wi-Fi network

The iPod icon is positioned at the bottom of your iPad on the Dock (unless you've moved it), and when touched, allows you to access the music on your iPad, play it, and view album art and track information. While playing music, you'll have access to familiar controls, like pause, skip, and repeat, and some that you may not be so familiar with, like shuffle and Genius. You can use the iPod app to create playlists, sort your music, and search for specific music by its attributes too. The iPod app can easily run in the background while you do other things on your iPad. You can even use the volume controls on the outside of your iPad when your iPad is locked and the screen is dark.

For the most part, in this chapter we'll focus on music. However, you can listen to and control audiobooks, podcasts, and music videos in the same manner and using the same controls.

Get Music onto Your iPad

There are two main ways to get music onto your iPad. You can use iTunes and your computer to copy (sync) music you already own to your iPad (including music you purchase from the iTunes Store from your computer), or you can purchase music directly from the iTunes Store using your iPad. When syncing with your computer, you can opt to sync your entire Music library or just specific playlists, artists, and/or genres. Each time you acquire music, either from your iPad or your computer, it can be synced too, so your music libraries will always be up to date.

Note Currently, you can't drag and drop music from your computer to your iPad; you have to transfer music using iTunes. Copying someone else's music or sharing yours with someone else is probably a copyright violation.

Copy Options

If you haven't synced any music yet, it's time! You need to get some music onto your iPad. As you know, there are a few ways to do this, and you'll probably apply a combination of these techniques to populate your iPad with music. Here are the most common copy options, spelled out in more detail:

- You can connect your iPad to your computer and use iTunes to transfer your music. You should choose this option *using the computer you used to set up your iPad*. With this option you can
  - Use iTunes on your computer to manage your Music library.
  - Tell iTunes to look for shared music in other libraries on your home network.
  - Tell iTunes to share your Music library with other computers on your home network.
  - Transfer previously purchased music to your iPad.
  - Keep your Music library automatically synced between the computer and your iPad.
  - Keep only specific music that you hand-select in your library automatically synced between your computer and your iPad.
  - Disable automatic syncing with iTunes, if desired.
- You can get music "over the air" and without connecting to any computer. You should choose this option if
  - You don't have any music on any computer, and thus, have nothing to transfer.
  - You plan to get all of your music from the integrated iTunes Store on the iPad and do not want to sync that music with your computer because you don't have access to a computer.
  - You do not have your own computer (and you set up your iPad on a friend's or family member's computer).

> **Note** iTunes is covered in Chapter 9.

Your iPad only supports the following audio formats:

- **AAC** Advanced Audio Coding, a common audio format. You may have AAC music files on your computer already as it is the default standard for ripping CDs into iTunes. There are various versions of AAC that are supported, including HE-AAC V1 and V2, AAC (8 to 320 Kbps), and Protected AAC (from the iTunes Store).
- **MP3** MPEG-1 Audio Layer 3 is a common audio format for consumer audio storage, and is the de facto standard for digital music players (also called MP3 players). You probably have MP3 files on your computer, and those files can be played (as can the others in this list) on your iPad (and iPod, and iPod Touch, and almost any other digital music player). Two MP3 formats are supported including MP3 (8 to 320 Kbps) and MP3 VBR.
- **Audible (Formats 2, 3, and 4)** Audible.com is an online audiobook seller. The file format they use is Audible. Formats 2, 3, and 4 are compatible formats for the iPad, iPod, and iPhone. Format 2 creates the smallest file size, and the quality of the audio is the poorest of the formats. Format 4 creates the largest file size and offers the best quality of these formats. (The larger the file size, the more space it takes up on your iPad.) Audible Advanced Audio (AAX) is also supported.
- **Apple Lossless** An audio codec developed by Apple for lossless compression of digital music. The data is stored as an MP4 file. You may have these types of files on your Mac, and these files do not utilize any "rights management" schemes like the Protected AAC files you may have from iTunes.
- **AIFF** Audio Interchange File Format. The AIFF file is most commonly used on Apple computers and is a format for storing audio files. AIFF files are compatible on Windows PCs and Linux machines too, and of course, compatible with the iPad.
- **WAV** Waveform Audio file. WAV files have been around a long time, and were used way back when on Windows 3.1. Like AIFF files, they are compatible with Apple, Linux, and Windows, in addition to the iPad.

> **Note** If you don't have any music on your PC or Mac, you may want to skip over to Chapter 9, and purchase some music from iTunes. Then, come back to this chapter when you're ready.

Sync with iPad

If you want to copy music from your main computer to your iPad, you can do so using iTunes. The very best scenario is to put all of your music on one computer (the computer you used to activate your iPad), and use that computer to copy, manage, and ultimately sync music between the two. The main advantage to using iTunes to copy music from your computer to your iPad is that once it's copied, any changes made to either music library (iPad or computer) can be automatically synced each time you connect the two devices.

How to... **Find Out the Format of a File**

You can find out what format any audio file is by right-clicking the file on your computer and choosing Properties on a PC or Get Info on a Mac. For the most part, we'll bet that the audio files you have are compatible. You probably have some Protected AAC files from an older iPhone or iPod Touch, MP3 or MP4 files from CDs you've ripped from your own CD collection, and maybe even a few books from Audible (which you can sync directly to your iPad using the free Audible app). Don't worry too much about compatibility, though; iTunes will inform you of any problems.

If you plan to set up syncing, it's important to note that you should choose one computer, put your music on it, and then use that computer each time you want to back up, update, or sync your iPad. You should not use multiple computers when syncing your iPad. You can use your iTunes account and play your iTunes music on multiple computers, though, and you can even stream music to other devices using your iPad and home Wi-Fi network; that's not the issue. The issue is picking one computer, and using that one computer to sync your iPad, every time.

To sync music from your PC to your iPad using iTunes (performing this on a Mac is similar):

1. On your PC, connect your iPad. iTunes will open automatically.
2. The backup and sync process will likely start, but you can continue with the tasks here, even while the sync is in progress.
3. In the source pane in iTunes, on your computer, click the icon for your iPad.
4. Click the Music tab. See Figure 8-1.
5. As shown in Figure 8-1, you can opt to sync music (or not), sync your entire Music library, or sync only specific playlists, artists, genres, and/or albums. You can also include music videos and voice notes. Make your selections now. You might opt not to sync your entire library if
   a. Your library is larger than the space available on your iPad, or you do not want to take up the space you have with only music.
   b. You don't want all of the music in your library on your iPad because you don't like it all.
   c. Some of your music is protected by another music program and can't be played on your iPad.

| Summary | Info | Apps | Music | Movies | TV Shows | Podcasts | iTunes U | Books | Photos |

☑ **Sync Music**   243 songs

   ○ Entire music library
   ◉ Selected playlists, artists, albums, and genres

   ☑ Include music videos
   ☑ Include voice memos
   ☐ Automatically fill free space with songs

Playlists   **Artists**

☑ ♪ Purchased   ☑ Adrian Legg
☑ ♪ Purchased on Joli's iPad   ☑ The Allman Brothers Band
▼ ☐ ▦ Genius Mixes   ☑ Arlo Guthrie
   ☐ ▦ Contemporary Folk Mix   ☐ Astrud Gilberto, Joao Gilberto
   ☐ ▦ Blues, Boogie & Southern Rock Mix   ☐ Bob Acri
☑ ✿ Music Videos   ☑ Bob Dylan
☑ ♪ Favorite Songs   ☑ Bob Marley
☑ ♪ My Music   ☑ Bonnie Raitt
☑ ♪ Sleepy Time Music   ☑ Buddy Guy & Tracy Chapman
☐ ♪ Star Trek Mosaic   ☐ C. S. Lewis
☐ ♪ Test   ☑ Carrie Underwood
☐ ♪ Word of Promise   ☑ Chris Spheeris
                                                                ☑ Christina Perri
                                                                ☑ Dean Martin
                                                                ☑ The Drifters
                                                                ☑ Edie Brickell

Genres   **Albums**

☐ Alternative   ☑ ABBA - ABBA - Gold - Greatest Hits

| Capacity 14 GB | ☐ Audio 1.37 GB | ☐ Video 2.5 GB | ☐ Photos 0.63 GB | ☐ Apps 0.45 GB | ☐ Books 0.04 GB | ☐ Other 0.39 GB | ☐ Free 8.8 GB |

FIGURE 8-1   In iTunes, on your computer, and with your iPad connected, click the Music tab to see your syncing options.

6. If you opt to sync your entire Music library, you're finished, and can click Sync if you like. If you opt to sync only specific playlists, artists, or genres:
   a. Select the desired options, shown in Figure 8-1.
   b. If you like, tick Automatically Fill Free Space with Songs.
   c. Click Sync.

Once syncing is set up, syncing will occur automatically each time you connect your iPad to your computer.

Configure iTunes Preferences on Your Computer

There are several preferences you can set in iTunes on your computer to help you get more out of iTunes, and thus more from your iPad. To view the Preferences options, click Edit, and click Preferences. (It's important to note that we're using iTunes on a Windows-based computer, so if you're using a Mac, your screen will look a little different.)

Although we won't detail every option in the Preferences window, here are a few that might interest you (click OK when you're finished making your selections):

- **From the General tab** On this tab, there are options regarding what happens when you insert a CD into your computer's CD drive. If you know you're going to be ripping an entire CD collection (so that you can sync that collection to your iPad), change the setting for When You Insert a CD to Import CD and Eject. This will make ripping your large CD collection less time-consuming.

- **From the Sharing tab** If you want to share the music and media you've acquired on your iPad with your own home network, tick Share My Library on My Local Network. Note that you can share the entire library or only specific playlists.
- **From the Store tab** Tick Automatically Download Missing Artwork, and iTunes will look to the Internet for album artwork for songs you import when you rip CDs in your CD collection.

Locate and Play a Song on Your iPad

Now that you have some music on your iPad, it's time to play a song. That's the most basic thing of course, playing some music! If you copied single songs, entire albums, or even playlists from your computer to your iPad, you'll see those once you open the iPod app. You'll be able to tap a playlist you've transferred, and you'll see that playlist in the source pane. See Figure 8-2.

Note Because everyone's music collection is different from everyone else's, what you see in the images here will differ from what you see on your device when you browse it for music.

In this section you'll learn how to browse for a song by its title, and browse music by artist, album, genre, or composer. You will also learn how to play an existing playlist and what's in the default Libraries, like Music, Podcasts, Audiobooks, and more. You'll learn to play a song and adjust the volume, and how to switch from Album Art view to Track view. Of course, you'll use the controls, including pause, repeat, skip, and others.

A				
Ain't No Mountain...	Studio All-Stars	Music From Sister Act...	2:29	
Air of December	Edie Brickell & New Bo...	Shooting Rubberbands...	5:59	
Air of December	Edie Brickell & New Bo...	Shooting Rubberbands...	5:59	
Allura	Chris Spheeris	Culture	5:56	
Another Woman's...	Edie Brickell	Picture Perfect Morning	2:45	
Any Colour You Like	Pink Floyd	The Dark Side of the...	3:25	
Aria	Chris Spheeris	Culture	4:49	
Aria	Chris Spheeris	Culture	4:49	
B				
Bad	Michael Jackson		4:19	
Bad Love	Eric Clapton	Clapton Chronicles: Th...	5:14	

FIGURE 8-2 After you've synced, music and playlists will be transferred. "Sleepy Time Music" is a playlist transferred from my computer.

Browse Your Music Collection

Whatever music you copied from your computer will appear in your iPod app. Playlists, if you have them, will appear in the source pane along with the default categories. If you don't have any playlists, you'll see just the libraries that are already in place. Here are a few of the libraries you'll see:

- **Music** This is just music. All of your music is stored in this library. The default view is Songs, and the songs are listed alphabetically. See Figure 8-2 earlier. Note the other available views across the bottom: Songs, Artists, Albums, Genres, and Composers; there will be more on that later.
- **Podcasts** This library only holds media deemed by the iPod app to be podcasts. You may not have anything in here yet.
- **Audiobooks** This library only holds media deemed by the iPod app to be audiobooks. You may not have anything in here yet.

If you've obtained media from iTunes or synced playlists and the like from your computer, you will see additional entries including Purchased or Music Videos, among others.

Tap Music in the left pane and note the categories that run across the bottom of the screen. Tap any category title to change the results:

- **Songs** Click Songs to view all of the songs in your iPod app by title. Tap any letter on the right side of the page to go to the songs that start with that letter.
- **Artists** Click Artists to view your music by artist, as shown here. If you have multiple albums by the same artist, tap the artist's name to view the albums.

- **Albums** Click Albums to view your albums in alphabetical order. If you know what album you want to listen to, this is the best way to find it.
- **Genres** iTunes classifies your music automatically by genre. Genres can include Folk, Rock, Alternative, and Soundtrack, among others, as shown in the

following illustration. If you know you want to listen to a specific genre (say Folk, when your mom stops by), this is the place to go.

- **Composers** Click Composers to view your music by the composer of that music.

 Drill into any artist, album, or other folder to locate a song. Tap any song to play it.

Play a Song

Playing a song is one of the simplest things you can do with the iPod app. As you are aware, though, you have to find a song first. If you just want to experiment, touch Music in the iPod app, tap Songs across the bottom, and tap the first song to play it. If you're feeling a little more adventurous, try tapping the various titles within the Library pane to locate media (like Purchased or Podcasts).

Once a song is playing, there are a few things you'll want to do right away, including changing the volume.

To adjust the volume:

1. Locate the Volume buttons on the outside of the iPad.
2. In portrait view, click the top Volume button to make the music louder; click the bottom button to make the music softer.
3. Click and hold the bottom Volume button to mute the music. (Basically, doing this just reduces the volume to zero extremely quickly.) You can also use the Side Switch, if it's set to Mute.

Note While a song is playing, tap the screen to access the iPod controls. You can then move the volume slider on the screen to adjust the volume without using the Volume buttons.

To pause and restart a song:

1. While a song is playing, tap the screen. The iPod controls will appear. See Figure 8-3.
2. Touch the Pause button to pause the song (the Pause button consists of two horizontal lines). The icon will change to a Play button, which is a right-facing arrow. Click it again to play the song from the point where it was paused.
3. Tap the Back arrow to return to the default iPod view.
4. In the default iPod view, tap the album thumbnail to return to Album Art view.

Tip Purchase AirPlay-enabled speakers for your iPad and stream your music to them, without wires. Once you have the speakers set up, you'll see the AirPlay icon on the iPod app.

Connect Wired or Wireless Headphones

You won't always want to play your music for all the world to hear; in fact, most of the time you'll probably opt for headphones. There are two kinds of headphones you can install, wired and wireless (Bluetooth).

To install wired headphones, simply plug them into the headphone jack on the outside of the iPad. To install wireless stereo Bluetooth headphones, activate Bluetooth under Settings | General | Bluetooth and follow the manufacturer's instructions.

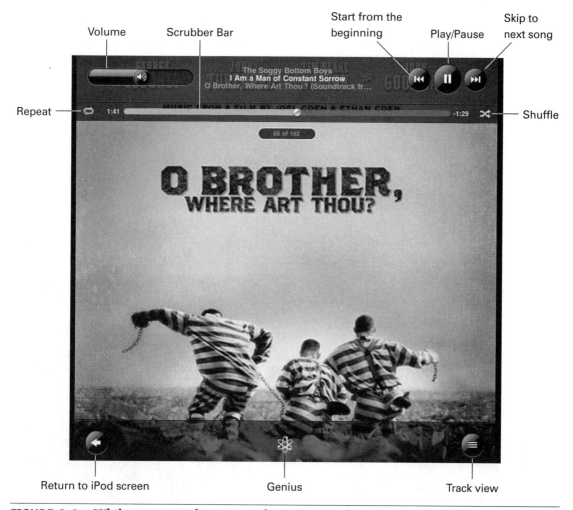

FIGURE 8-3   While a song is playing, tap the screen to show the controls.

To restart a song or move to the next song:

1. Depending on your view, tap to access the playback controls.
2. In Album Art view, tap the left-pointing arrow, located to the left of the Play/ Pause button, to restart the song (or press and hold to rewind it).
3. In the Album Art view, tap the back button shown here.
4. Tap the right-pointing arrow, located to the right of the Play/Pause button, to skip to the next song. Tap and hold to fast forward through the song that's currently playing.
5. You can also move the slider on the Scrubber Bar to quickly move to a particular place in a song.

View Album Art or the Track List

When you play a song, you have the option to view the iPod screen, album art, or information about the album or tracks on the playlist. You've already seen Album Art view, and you've seen the default iPod view. Track view shows the list of songs in an album, how long each song is, and more. Track view allows you to move among songs in an album or playlist easily, and is shown in Figure 8-4.

To switch between views:

1. Tap any item in the Library pane that has multiple songs in it.
2. Tap a song to play it.
3. If you're in the default iPod view, tap the album or song in Now Playing, at the bottom left of your iPod screen, to access Album Art view.

FIGURE 8-4 Track view offers information about what's next, how long each song is, and the song title and artist, among other things.

4. While in Album Art view, tap the screen to access the controls. Tap the icon located in the bottom-right corner to switch to Track view, as shown in the following illustration. (Alternatively, double-tap the screen.)
5. In Track view, tap the Album Art thumbnail in the bottom right of the screen, shown here. To return to the iPod screen, tap the left-pointing arrow located in the bottom-left corner of the screen.

 Any time you want to open or close a window or switch views in the iPod app, try a tap or a double-tap.

Incorporate Playlists

The list of songs on an album is called a *playlist*; it's a list of songs to be played. You can create your own playlists and add any songs you like to personalize your music experience. In a personalized playlist, you get to hand-pick the songs to include. There's built-in support for creating playlists in the iPod app. (Depending on your age, you may liken a playlist to an older type of music playlist of songs, the "mixed tape.")

You can also create "Genius" playlists. Genius analyzes your music library and draws conclusions about what type of list you'll like, based on a song you pick. There's also the option to create Genius "mixes," which are groups of songs that are alike in one way or another, too.

Get Started with Genius

You have to enable Genius on your computer before you can use it to create Genius playlists and mixes. You also have to sync your iPad to your computer to make sure all of the required information is copied. Once you've synced your iPad, you can easily create Genius playlists on your iPad and in iTunes at your computer. Also, after you've synced, the Genius playlists you create on your iPad will be available from iTunes on your computer. To enable Genius:

1. At your computer, in iTunes, click Store.
2. Click Turn on Genius, and when prompted, click Turn on Genius again.

3. Type your iTunes password and click Continue.
4. Agree to the terms and conditions, and click Continue.
5. For good measure, tap Store and tap Update Genius. Click OK when prompted.
6. Once that's complete, connect your iPad and sync it. This will ensure that Genius and your iPad's Music library are as up to date as possible.

Create a Genius Playlist

You can create a Genius playlist by tapping a song you want to base the list on, and tapping the Genius icon at the bottom of the screen:

1. Tap iPod to open the app.
2. Tap a song to be the basis for the playlist. It will begin to play.
3. With a song playing, and from any screen, tap the Genius icon.
4. If there is enough information for the iPod to draw from, a new Genius playlist will be created. You can access this playlist from the Genius tab in the iPod app's Songs view.
5. To save the playlist, press the Save button in the upper-right corner of the screen. Note that you can create a new Genius playlist here or refresh what's shown to get new results.

While creating a Genius playlist, you'll see Genius in the left pane, shown here. Once you save the playlist, this tab will disappear. As you can see, New is an option, as is Refresh.

Library	Genius Playlist			New Refresh Save
♫ Music	▶ How Much Did You...	The Pretenders	Get Close	3:47
Podcasts	Woman in Chains	Tears for Fears	The Seeds of Love	6:30
Audiobooks	Closer to Fine	Indigo Girls	Indigo Girls (Expanded...	3:00
Genius	What I Am	Edie Brickell & New Bo...	Shooting Rubberbands...	4:58
Favorite Songs	Dream a Little Drea...	The Mamas and the Pa...	The Mamas & The Papa...	3:00

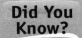

The Interface Changes Once You've Saved a Genius Playlist

Once you save a Genius playlist, Save will be gone as an option and Delete will appear.

Create a Genius Mix

A Genius Mix is something that iTunes creates, on your computer, per your command.
A mix contains songs that are similar in genre, artist, and other criteria. These mixes are
created automatically based on the music in your music library. You have to do a few
things to enable, create, and use Genius Mixes. In iTunes on your computer you must

- Enable Genius in iTunes on your computer (Store | Turn on Genius).
- Update Genius in iTunes on your computer (Store | Update Genius).
- Wait while iTunes generates the required information.
- With that done, you must connect your iPad, and opt to sync the new Genius
  Mixes to your iPad (Music tab under Playlists).

Playlists
- ☑ ♫ Purchased
- ☑ ♫ Purchased on Joli's iPad
- ▼ ☑ ▦ Genius Mixes
  - ☑ ▦ Contemporary Folk Mix
  - ☑ ▦ Blues, Boogie & Southern Rock Mix

Only then will you have access to Genius Mixes on your iPad, shown in Figure 8-5.

FIGURE 8-5   Genius Mixes combine like music in playlists based on the music in
your iTunes library.

Create a Standard Playlist

To create a standard playlist on your iPad's iPod app:

1. Tap the + sign at the bottom of the iPod interface. This is the Add Playlist button.
2. Type a name for the playlist and tap Save.

3. Tap each song to add. It will appear grayed out after you tap it.

4. Tap Done.
5. If desired, edit the playlist. You'll learn more about this in the next section.
6. Tap Done, or continue reading to edit the list.

Edit a Playlist You've Created

To edit a playlist:

1. Tap the playlist to edit and then tap Edit. (If you're working from the previous set of steps, skip to Step 2.)

2. To move a song up or down in the list, tap, hold, and drag the three gray bars at the far right of the song info to the desired location and then drop it there.
3. To delete any song, tap the red circle on the left side of the song name. (Deleting a song from a playlist doesn't delete it from your iPad.)
4. To add more songs, tap Add Songs, tap the songs to add, then tap Done.
5. Tap Done again.

Play a Playlist

You tap a playlist to access it, and tap a song in it to play it. When you play songs in any list, they play from top to bottom, or from start to finish, no matter what the source of the list. You may want to *shuffle* those songs so they play in random order (especially if this list is in alphabetical order or if the songs in the list are grouped by artist or album). Just tap Shuffle in any playlist.

Sleepy Time Music	
Shuffle ⤬	
Air of December	Edi·
► **Allura**	Chr

Shortcut To quickly shuffle all the songs in your collection, click the Music tab while in Songs view, and scroll to the top of the list, just above the A's. You'll see Shuffle there as an option.
1. Under Library, tap a playlist.
2. Tap any song in it to start playing it.

Sync Playlists

When you connect your iPad to your computer, playlists you've created on your iPad will sync to your iTunes Music Library on your computer. You'll see the playlist in two places in iTunes, in the source pane under Playlists, and when your iPad is selected, under the Music tab. You can select only specific playlists to sync by selecting them under the Music tab, as shown earlier with Genius Mixes. Additionally, you can create playlists in iTunes at your computer and include those too.

Tip Create a "smart playlist" in iTunes on your computer that contains your top-rated or favorite songs. You can also create playlists that contain the songs you play the most. Then, sync that playlist to your iPad. Smart playlists are just that; they're smart and update themselves as your tastes change and as criteria for the playlist are met.

Shuffle Songs in Any List and Use the Repeat Button

Songs always appear in some sort of list. The list may only include tracks from a specific album, or it can contain myriad songs or titles in a list for Genre, Composer, and other categories. It can be a list that Genius created for you, or a Standard playlist you created yourself. It may even be a smart playlist you created and synced with iTunes at your computer. When you play songs in any list, they play from top to bottom, or from start to finish, no matter what the source of the list. You may want to shuffle those songs so they play in random order (especially if this list is in alphabetical order, or if the songs in the list are grouped by artist or album). You may also want to repeat a song or the songs in a playlist.

Note You can tap Shuffle at the top of the Music library to set the iPod app to automatically shuffle all songs.

To shuffle songs in any list of music and thus play them in random order:

1. In the iPod app, locate any list of songs. Consider a Genius playlist, standard playlist, or simply the songs in the music library.
2. Start the playlist.
3. Tap the Now Playing icon in the left corner of the iPod screen.
4. Tap the Album Art icon to view the controls.
5. Click the Shuffle button. The Shuffle button is located to the right of the "time remaining" information on the Scrubber Bar, as shown in the following illustration:
   a. If the Shuffle button is blue, Shuffle is enabled.
   b. If the Shuffle button is gray, Shuffle is not enabled.

To repeat a song or playlist:

1. With a playlist playing, tap Repeat once to continually play the current playlist (the Repeat icon turns blue).
2. Tap a second time to continually play the song (the number "1" will be superimposed over the blue Repeat icon).
3. Tap a third time to turn off all repeat functions.

Search for Media

You may have discovered by now that there are lots of ways to view your music, including by song title, artist, genre, and composer, to name a few. While this may work for a while, you'll probably tire of all of the scrolling and tapping involved in finding that perfect song. In this section you'll learn how to search your media quickly for that perfect audio file, by searching by the artist's name, album name, song name, and other related data.

The iPod app contains a Search box that you can use to search for just about anything. If you're looking for a song, audiobook, podcast, or any other item that is in any of your iPod libraries, you can search for it here. When you type something in the Search box, the results will appear as you type. The more you type, the fewer the number of matching results, and thus, the shorter the list of results. The more precise you can be regarding what you want to find, the better results you'll have. So, try to type unique words, not common ones, specifically words that are related to the song in some way, for instance, a word in the title, a word in the album name, or a word in the name of the band.

To use the Search function of the iPod:

1. In the iPod app, click inside the Search window.
2. Type a word or two into the Search window.
3. Review the results, as shown in the following illustration. Click any result to play the song.

Bad Love	Eric Clapton	Clapton Chronicles: The...	5:14
Dedicated to the On...	The Mamas and the Pa...	The Mamas & The Papa...	3:00
A Deeper Love - (Tri...	Studio All-Stars	Music From Sister Act 1...	4:42
Famous Last Words	Tears for Fears	The Seeds of Love	4:31
(Love Is Like A) Heat...	Studio All-Stars	Music From Sister Act 1...	2:55

Explore Other Types of Media

We've focused on music in this chapter, but there are many other kinds of media you can listen to using the iPod app on your iPad. These include audiobooks, podcasts, and music videos.

Explore Audiobooks

You can get audiobooks from the iTunes Store, and this is detailed in Chapter 9. If you have an audiobook already, either one you've purchased or one you've synced from your computer, you can find it and listen to it using the iPod app on the iPad. For more information on purchasing and downloading audiobooks from iTunes, refer to Chapter 9.

Your iPad also supports Audible files, and Audible is one of the largest audiobook companies in the world. In addition to audiobooks, Audible.com offers magazines, radio shows, podcasts, stand-up comedy, and speeches from people who shape culture, politics, and business.

 Audiobooks are perfect for commuters, those who don't have time to read, or those who have difficulty reading due to a vision problem.

If you're interested in Audible, from your home computer navigate to www .audible.com. Browse the library to see what they have to offer, which currently stands at over 75,000 titles. If you see something you like, set up an account, purchase the book, and download it. With the plan you choose, whether it's simply one credit a month or 24 credits for an entire year, you'll also get access to the audio version of the *New York Times* or the *Wall Street Journal* (you choose). (For the most part, a credit equals one book.)

When you listen to an audiobook with the iPod app, the controls you're familiar with already are available, but they perform different things now. You'll still tap the audiobook in the Audiobooks library to get started, and you'll still click the book's icon in Now Playing to access the controls.

- There's now a speed control icon to the right of the Scrubber Bar. You can choose from ½×, 1×, and 2×. The ½× speed is the slowest and 2× is the fastest. See Figure 8-6. Changing this setting may distort the sound or upset the reader's flow.
- You can use the slider to move to a new position in the book.
- There's a 30-second repeat button at the bottom that lets you rewind 30 seconds, in case you miss something.
- When you click to see the Track view, you have access to the chapters in the book.

Explore Podcasts

Podcasts are digital media files, similar to audiobooks, which are released to the public and often downloaded through web syndication. They are recorded and then made available for download. They aren't live, although some are recorded live

---

FIGURE 8-6 There are controls for listening to audiobooks that include increasing or decreasing the speed at which it is read.

and uploaded later. All podcasts offered through iTunes are free, although you can sign up for services that offer podcasts for a price. You can listen to a podcast of the latest news at www.cnn.com/services/podcasting using Safari, or you can download podcasts to your iPad and listen to them in your iPod app.

 You can find a long list of podcasts at a podcast directory site such as www.podcastdirectory.com.

To listen to a podcast in Safari:

1. Open Safari on your iPad and navigate to www.cnn.com/services/podcasting.
2. Click the link for any podcast to listen to it.

To listen to podcasts using your iPod app, open iTunes, tap Podcasts, and download a podcast. Once it's downloaded, open the iPod app, tap Podcasts, and tap the name of the podcast to listen to, as shown here. Alternatively, you can sync podcasts from iTunes on your computer.

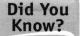

Music Videos Can Be Played in Another App

You can watch music videos in the Videos app as well as the iPod app. See Chapter 11 for more information.

Explore Music Videos

Music videos are just that, music and videos mixed together. From the time of MTV's introduction way back in the '80s, music videos have been all the rage. You can watch music videos on your iPad and save them to your Music library. You can get free music videos on the Web, from places like Download.com and of course, from iTunes and the iTunes Store.

To make sure you have access to music videos in the iPod app, make sure to tick Include Music Videos on the Music tab and tick the Music Video playlist, if you aren't syncing your entire library, when syncing music with iTunes at your computer.

To explore music videos in the iPod app:

1. Purchase or acquire a music video. iTunes sells music videos, and we acquired Michael Jackson's "Bad" for only $1.99.
2. Once you've purchased and downloaded the video, open the iPod app.
3. Tap Music Videos.
4. Tap the video to play it in. As with other media, you can tap the video to show the controls.

Configure iPod Settings

As with other iPad features, you can configure settings for your iPod app. Just tap Settings on the Home screen. You can turn on or off the following settings, as shown in Figure 8-7:

- **Sound Check**   To set your iPod app to play all songs at the same level. Sometimes sound from different sources can be louder or softer than the other songs in your library.
- **EQ**   To choose a specific equalizer sound, like Acoustic, Hip Hop, Latin, Spoken Word, and Treble Booster or Treble Reducer.

What's that Extra Icon You See?

AirPlay is a feature available on your iPad 2 only if you've purchased compatible AirPlay devices, such as AirPlay wireless speakers, AirPort Express, or an Apple TV. You'll see the AirPlay icon if you have compatible hardware.

FIGURE 8-7   Configure your iPod from Settings on your iPad.

- **Volume Limit**   To set a maximum volume limit and lock it.
- **Lyrics & Podcast Info**   To enable retrieval of lyrics and podcast information, when available.
- **Home Sharing**   To enable home sharing. Type your Apple ID and password, and then share (stream) your media to compatible devices using your home Wi-Fi network.

Stream Music over Your Home Wi-Fi Network

You can access music that's currently stored in your computer's iTunes library from your iPad over your home Wi-Fi network. This means that while you're at home and connected to your Wi-Fi network from your iPad, you'll be able to access the music in your library (the media stored on your computer) without having to actually put that media on your iPad. This will save space on your iPad, because you won't have to sync all of your music to have access to it.

To make this happen, you must first enable home sharing as outlined in the previous section from your iPad. Basically, you tap Settings, tap iPod, and type your Apple ID and password under Home Sharing.

Next, you must enable Home Sharing from iTunes at your computer. Click Advanced, and click Turn on Home Sharing, shown in Figure 8-8. Type your Apple ID and password, press ENTER, and click Done.

You can also select what to share. In iTunes, from your computer, click Edit and click Preferences. Click Sharing. Configure what you want to share, as shown here.

FIGURE 8-8 Enable Home Sharing from iTunes.

You'll notice that Pictures is not an option. However, music, podcasts, playlists, videos, and the like are options for sharing.

This is where you tap.

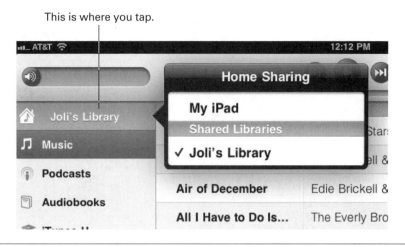

FIGURE 8-9   Tap your shared library to have access to the media in it from your iPad.

Now, in the iPod app on your iPad, tap Library in the left pane. Tap the new, shared library, shown in Figure 8-9. If you've opted to sync only specific music to your iPad and have not synced your entire music library, you'll notice the library grows larger immediately. This is because the music that has been made available in iTunes at your computer is now available from the iPad's iPod app. Tap any song to play it.

The more you experiment with Home Sharing, the more you'll uncover. As an example, in the Videos app, notice there's a new Shared tab here (provided you opted to share this media). Tapping the tab offers access to the shared video media on the computer.

Note   Your computer will have to be turned on, with iTunes active, for sharing to work properly.

9

Shop the iTunes Store

HOW TO...

- Explore the iTunes interface
- Browse and buy music
- Browse, rent, and buy movies
- Browse and watch TV shows
- Browse and listen to podcasts
- Browse and listen to audiobooks
- Browse and listen to media from iTunes U
- Explore art, classical music, museums, cultural exhibits
- Explore Genius

The iTunes Store is a one-stop shop for music, movies, TV shows, podcasts, audiobooks, and even college lectures from universities all over the country. You can preview and buy just about any kind of media imaginable. And, as with other iPad media, it's easy to sync your newly acquired media to your desktop computer.

The iTunes app, which is what you use to access the iTunes Store, is already on your iPad and ready to use. There's no need to download and install it, or do anything special at all. And, because you created an account when you set up your iPad, you already have an account configured too. All you need to do is tap the iTunes icon on your iPad to get started.

Once you've acquired media from the iTunes Store, you'll use other apps to view it or listen to it. You listen to music, podcasts, and audiobooks with the iPod. You can watch movies and TV shows with the Videos app. You can watch music videos and listen to media from iTunes U from both the iPod and the Videos apps.

Note For more information on watching, listening to, and managing media on your iPad, refer to Chapter 8 for more information about the iPod app and Chapter 11 for more information about the Videos app. Here, we're really just concerned with the iTunes Store.

Get Started with the iTunes Store

The iTunes Store is a media outlet complete with music, movies, TV, videos, and more. To get started, simply tap the iTunes app on the Home screen. The iTunes Store is shown in Figure 9-1, with Music selected.

The iTunes Store looks pretty similar to the App Store you learned about in Chapter 7. There are eight buttons that run across the bottom and various buttons and a Search window across the top. In order to effectively navigate the iTunes Store, you need to familiarize yourself with these buttons and features as quickly as possible. You'll use the buttons across the bottom to navigate iTunes by media type, by tapping the button that matches the media you'd like to browse. Once you're in the proper category, the items across the top will help you find exactly what you want.

The eight buttons that run across the bottom of the iTunes Store are

- **Music**   Touch to go to the music part of the store. You'll find music from just about every artist imaginable, and have easy access to music videos and what's free on iTunes.
- **Movies**   Touch the Movies icon to go to the Movies part of the store. Here you can buy or rent movies, see recent arrivals, and access free movie previews.

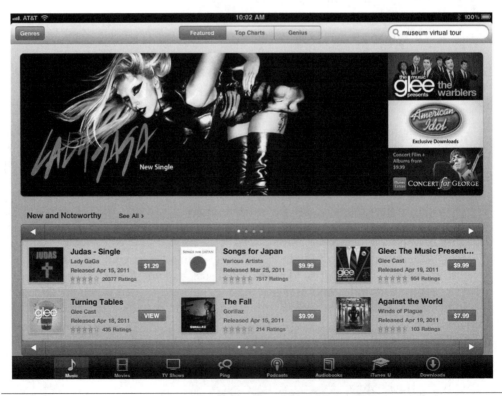

FIGURE 9-1   The Music part of the iTunes Store is only a small part of what's available. There are other categories including Movies, TV Shows, and Audiobooks.

You Can Stream the Media on Your iPad to Your TV

If you have an Apple TV, you can opt to stream your media through it, and watch it on your larger HDTV or similar device. You can also use the Apple Digital AV Adapter and an HDMI cable to attach the iPad to your HDTV. Everything you are doing on the iPad—watching a movie, playing a game—will be mirrored on the HDTV's screen.

- **TV Shows**   Touch TV Shows to view everything related to TV. You can purchase entire seasons of shows or simply a single show. Once purchased, those shows belong to you and are stored on your iPad. You can watch them on your iPad anytime you want. As with other media, you can sync them to your computer, too. So if you want to watch one of these shows on a larger screen, you can.
- **Ping**   Touch Ping to find people to follow by searching for a name, inviting friends, or choosing people that Ping recommends. This enables you to see what others are watching and listening to, and to receive recommendations from them. Tap Profile in Ping to view your own profile; mine is shown in Figure 9-2. (Feel free to "follow" me.)
- **Podcasts**   Touch Podcasts to browse podcasts that are available from the iTunes Store. You will find free items here, and you can browse both audio and video podcasts, among other things.

FIGURE 9-2   You may already have a Ping profile.

- **Audiobooks**   Touch Audiobooks to see what the iTunes Store offers in the way of audiobooks. As you know from the last chapter, though, you can also purchase and sync audiobooks from Audible.com, and in this chapter you'll learn how to get free audiobooks with iTunes U. So before you go crazy and spend a lot of money here, check out the other sources.
- **iTunes U**   Touch iTunes U to visit the intellectual side of iTunes. Browse college lectures from Yale or Berkeley, browse K-12 offerings, and even watch virtual museum tours. You may even find free audiobooks. Figure 9-3 shows the iTunes U category, with Top Charts selected.
- **Downloads**   Touch Downloads to see items related to media you're currently downloading. Once the media has been downloaded, the list will be empty, and data will be available in its associated app (music in iPod, movies in Videos, and so on).

Once you're in the proper category, explore the media in it using the buttons that run across the top of the iTunes Store, or use the Search window to search for something specific. Here are the buttons you may encounter:

- **Genres**   Tap this button to show the available genres at the iTunes Store when in the Music, Movies, or TV Shows categories. The genres listed change depending on what you've selected across the bottom of the screen. For instance, if you're browsing TV Shows, then the Genres button produces All, Animation, Classic, Comedy, Drama, Kids, Nonfiction, Reality TV, Sci-Fi & Fantasy, and Sports. If you're in Movies, Genres include some of those and others like Thriller and Documentary. (Tap Genres again to hide the list or tap outside of it.)
- **Featured**   Tap Featured, available in almost every category, to view media that Apple thinks is noteworthy. The items listed here are handpicked by Apple. Depending on the category you're in (TV Shows, Movies, Music, and the like), you'll see options under Featured including New to Rent or Own (Movies), What's Hot (Music), Latest TV Episodes (TV Shows), New in Fiction (Audiobooks), and

FIGURE 9-3   In any category, explore the options across the top; here is Top Charts in iTunes U.

the like. You'll see arrows that allow you to move left and right among the listings, and a button with a price for each one you see. There's also an option to "See All."

- **Top Charts**   Tap Top Charts to see the most popular media at the moment for a specific category. This list will change often as the top sellers change. What's hot today may not be hot tomorrow!
- **Genius**   Tap Genius (when available) to see if iTunes has any Genius suggestions for you. Genius will compile information about your preferences as you download media, and then offer recommendations for other media you might like. Genius bases its recommendations on what you've previously purchased or sampled. If you purchase a specific genre from the Top Charts listings in the music category, Genius will suggest similar songs in that genre as they are released. If you prefer show tunes, Genius may well suggest movie soundtracks and Broadway releases.

Browse Music

The best way to become familiar with the iTunes Store is to browse music. Touch Music to get started. You'll see several panes, boxes, and lists, most of which were detailed previously. Notice the arrows by New and Noteworthy under Featured, and note the See All option (see Figure 9-4). Tap these to explore more.

Now, scroll to the bottom of the music's Featured page to see Quick Links, where you can access Music Videos, Free on iTunes, and more. Remember to tap Featured, Top Charts, and Genius at the top of that page too.

FIGURE 9-4   It's easy to miss the arrows and the See All option.

In any music-related page, tap Genres to cull down the media to a specific type for that page. For instance, if you're in the Top Charts category of music and you only want to see songs that are considered "country," click Genres and choose Country, as shown in Figure 9-5. The list will change and only supply the top songs in that category. Continue to experiment with Featured, New and Noteworthy, and other categories, and sort by Rock, Pop, or Reggae, for instance.

Sometimes you know exactly what you want. You can use Search inside the iTunes Store to search for a specific song or album:

1. Tap inside the Search box in the top-right corner.
2. Type the artist's name, a song name, or other identifying information.
3. Tap Search on the keyboard or, if the result appears in the list (shown in the following illustration), tap that to locate the song.

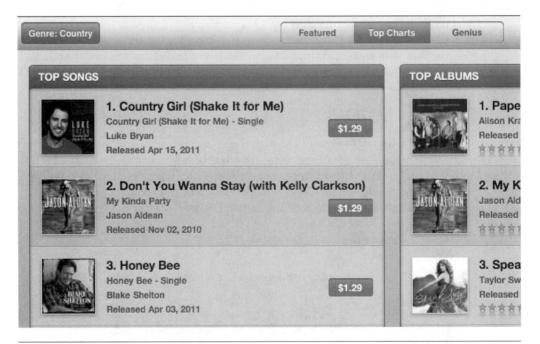

FIGURE 9-5   You can sort any music page by genre. Sorting by Genre is available in other categories too, including Movies and TV Shows.

As you browse for music, note that you can tap the album artwork to open a window that details the media, just as you can obtain information about an app by tapping its icon in the App Store. From the information page you'll find related information such as a list of tracks on an album, user reviews and ratings, the option to view the Artist page or tell a friend (via email), the option to "like" the media, and more. To close the information window, tap anywhere outside of it.

Buy Music

Once you've found a song you like, you can purchase it. You'll see the price in a button beside the song. Tap once to start the purchasing process. It will be an easy process, even the first time through, because you already set up an account with the store when you activated your iPad. You'll be prompted to input your password and to verify that you want to make the purchase, but it doesn't take more than a few seconds to get what you want.

To purchase a song:

1. Locate the song to purchase and locate the price button beside it. Note that you can also purchase albums, music videos, movies, and podcasts, if available.
2. Touch the price button.
3. Tap Buy Song, Buy Album, or other prompt.

GENIUS SONG RECOMMENDATIONS

You bought music by The TV Theme Players

Sopranos: Woke Up This Morning
Your Favourite TV Themes
Soundtrack & Theme Orchestra
Released Apr 07, 2008

BUY SONG

You bought music by Daniel Powter

Trust Me
How to Save a Life
The Fray
Released Sep 13, 2005

$0.99

4. Input your password if required.
5. Wait while the song downloads. If you want to watch the download process, tap the Downloads button on the bottom of the page.
6. You'll find the song, music video, or album in the iPod app.

Explore Movies, TV Shows, Podcasts, and Audiobooks

You may not be aware of all of the media that's available to you. You know you can buy movies from the iTunes Store, but you may not know that you can also rent them. You can purchase entire seasons of your favorite TV shows, or you can purchase a single episode. You can even purchase the latest episode of a show you missed, if the production company makes it available. There are podcasts and audiobooks too; there's so much media that we don't think you could ever watch or hear it all! As you know, you access the media options from the bottom of the screen. Let's continue to look at each of these in more depth, starting with Movies.

Browse and Obtain Movies

Your new iPad can play HD movies as well as Standard Definition movies, and you can rent or buy them from the iTunes Store. New movies are a little pricey, though, and can run you $20.00 or so apiece, which is about what you'd pay to buy them on DVD.

Renting is a little steep too; a new movie often rents for about $5.00, about the same as what it would cost at a movie rental store, or using an "on demand" service from your cable company. However, if you want to be the first on the block to watch a movie after it's been released to the public, and you want to watch it on your iPad, this is the way to go.

> **Note** The great thing about the iTunes Store with regard to movies is that it is possible to watch a newly released movie anytime and anywhere, right from your iPad.

You browse for, purchase (or rent), and download movies the same way you located and purchased music earlier, and you have the same access to ratings and reviews. Use the tabs across the top to locate the movie you want, and tap the appropriate icon to view and purchase the movie.

Here's an example if you'd like to walk through the process here:

1. In the iTunes Store, tap Movies.
2. In the Search window, type the name of any movie.
3. Tap Search.
4. In the results, scroll through the page to locate the Movies results. You may see Albums, TV Episodes, or Songs, for instance.
5. Tap View when you locate the movie. The movie's information page will open, shown in Figure 9-6.
6. Read any reviews, view ratings, read the movie summary, watch a preview, and use other tools to help you decide if this movie is the one you're looking for.
7. Tap Rent to rent the movie, or Buy to buy it. Note that both of these options may not be available; for instance, you may only be able to rent a movie, and not buy it. (Keep reading to learn more about buying versus renting.)
8. Wait while the movie downloads, and then open Videos to view it. For more information about the Videos app, refer to Chapter 11.

To Rent or To Buy?

You may already know you want to buy a movie, because you love it and want to have access to it all the time. You may be equally sure you want to rent it. However, if you're on the fence, here's a little more information about renting and buying from iTunes.

If you buy a movie, you own it, and can watch it as often as you like and on up to five authorized devices. "Authorized" devices can be PCs and Macs. You can authorize and unauthorize computers in iTunes from the Advanced tab. On a side note, you can sync the media you buy to an unlimited number of iDevices.

> **Tip** To learn more about authorized devices, visit http://support.apple.com and search for "authorize." Then, on the right side, click Learn More about iTunes (or something similar).

Tron: Legacy PG   Tell a Friend ›

Walt Disney Pictures
Genre: Action & Adventure
Released: 2010
☐ in English
★★★★☆ 2591 Ratings

PREVIEW

BUY $19.99   RENT $4.99   HD   Standard Def.

Learn About Rentals ›

Plot Summary
TRON: LEGACY is an action-packed adventure set in a digital world unlike anything captured on
the big screen. Sam Flynn (Garrett Hedlund), a rebellious 27-year-old, is haunted by the
mysterious disappearance of his father Kevin Flynn (Oscar®- and Golden Globe®-win... More ▼

Bonus Content:
If you purchase this movie, the next time you connect to the iTunes Store on your computer you will also receive:
📖 iTunes Extras - Tron: Legacy

Credits

Actors	Director	Screenwriters	Producers
Jeff Bridges ›	Joseph Kosinski ›	Edward Kitsis ›	Sean Bailey ›
Garrett Hedlund ›		Adam Horowitz ›	Steven Lisberger ›
Olivia Wilde ›			Jeffrey Silver ›
Bruce Boxleitner ›			

FIGURE 9-6   Most of the time you can rent or buy the movie.

Renting a movie is much different from owning one. When you rent a movie, you
only get to keep it for a short period of time. Here are the rules:

- When you rent a movie, you have 30 days to watch it.
- When you start a movie you've rented, you have 24 hours to finish watching it.

The rental expires when one or the other of these conditions has been met. So, if
you think you're going to want to watch the movie more than once, it may be in your
best interest to buy. (Before you commit to anything, read the section on Netflix later in
this chapter. You may find Netflix to be a good alternative to iTunes, and less expensive.)

Tip   To close a pop-up window that contains information about a movie, song, podcast,
or some other media, tap outside of it.

Netflix Offers Another Media Option

If your movie-watching ritual is relegated to new movies and you don't mind paying to buy or rent them individually, the iTunes Store may be all you need to satisfy your movie needs. If you enjoy watching older movies, and you watch a lot of them, you have additional options. One of the options is Netflix. For about $10 a month you can have a DVD or two at home and watch all you want on your iPad from the Netflix Instant Queue. Although many of the movies available from Netflix are older, Netflix is starting to offer a wider range of newer movies, as well as TV shows. We expect these new offerings to increase as time goes by. Whatever the case, unlimited on-demand movies, right from your iPad, for under $10 a month is a great deal.

To explore Netflix:

1. Open the App Store and browse for the free Netflix app.
2. Download and install it.
3. Browse the available free movies, sign up for a free trial, or just sign up!

Browse and Watch TV Shows

What we love most about the TV Shows portion of the iTunes Store is the Free TV Shows section. That's right; you can watch TV shows for free right from your iPad! Some are simply trailers or sneak peeks, but others are entire episodes. To access free TV episodes, from the Featured tab, scroll down and tap Free TV Episodes. The Free TV Episodes page is shown in Figure 9-7.

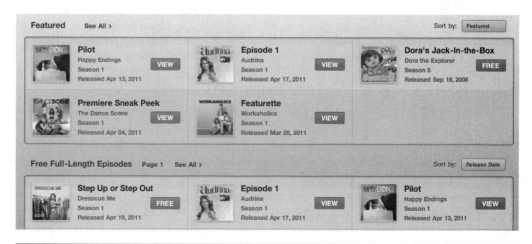

FIGURE 9-7   You can get free TV episodes at the iTunes Store.

Tip   Once you've downloaded a TV show (and it could take a while), open the Videos app and tap the show to watch it.

Beyond the free episodes, which may be just what the doctor ordered when you're waiting for a plane or commuting on a bus to work, there are episodes you can purchase. You can purchase shows like *House*, *Desperate Housewives*, and *Lost*, although prices differ. All you have to do is browse to locate the TV show you want, and click the price button to get it.

Tip   Remember that the "back" button is available to return to any previous screen in iTunes.

When browsing TV, note that there are various ways to browse. As with music and movies, you can tap Featured and Top Charts, and if you've previously purchased TV shows, tap Genius to get recommendations. There are other options to explore at the bottom of the Featured page. Explore these options as time allows.

Quick Links

Welcome Joli!   Your Apple ID has $25.00.

TV Rentals	Free TV Episodes	Latest TV Episodes
HD TV	Shows Just Added	Networks & Studios

Tip   As an alternative to purchasing an episode of a show aired on ABC, download and install the ABC Player from the App Store. You can watch quite a few of ABC's TV shows for free, including your favorites like *Dancing with the Stars*, *Castle*, *Brothers and Sisters*, and more.

Browse and Watch Podcasts

As you know by now, a podcast is an audio or video recording that has been made available to the public. Often podcasts are created by smaller entities than TV shows and movies makers. In the Podcasts section you may find "Indie" type subjects, offerings from NPR, newspapers, and news broadcasts, and even podcasts from ordinary people, stating opinions on sports, health, or other subjects. The best way to get a feel for podcasts is to click the Podcasts button, look for a free podcast, and play it. Podcasts, once downloaded, can be played in the iPod app. (This means you must exit iTunes and tap iPod to play it.)

Browse and Listen to Audiobooks

Audiobooks require quite a bit of input from actors, producers, directors, and writers. Because of this, audiobooks tend to be rather expensive, and you don't usually find too many free ones. In our opinion, though, the price of the audiobook isn't generally an issue, especially for those who don't have time to read but want to keep up with the latest fiction, nonfiction, biographies, and top sellers in books, or for those who are sight-impaired.

Tip Before you purchase a book from anyone, check out the iTunes Store's iTunes U. The Audiobooks section has some audiobooks you can listen to, without putting out any money at all!

If you have never listed to an audiobook, you really should give it a try. Audiobooks are perfect for commuters, great on airplanes, and ideal for those who have difficulty reading due to a vision problem (or too much sunlight on their iPads). To get started, click the Audiobooks button in the iTunes Store interface.

As with other categories, you can access quick links to various subcategories in the Audiobooks section. Tap Audiobooks, tap Features, and then scroll to the bottom of the Featured page to view the following categories:

- **Staff Favorites**   To browse favorites picked by the people at Apple and iTunes.
- **New in Fiction**   To browse the newest audiobooks in the Fiction category.
- **New in Nonfiction**   To browse the newest audiobooks in the Nonfiction category.
- **Top Fiction**   To browse the audiobooks in the Top Fiction category. These aren't what's new, necessarily, but what's the most popular overall.
- **Books made into films**   To access audiobooks for books that have been made into films, like *Precious*, *Angels & Demons*, *Twilight*, and *Frost/Nixon*.
- **My Alerts**   To access recent releases from artists whose work you've previously downloaded from iTunes, and any other artists you've specifically chosen to add to your list of alerts. (Tap Manage My Alerts to learn more and to configure alerts.)

You can also search the store for a title or author. A search will produce results that are categorized, and in this case, you'll look at the audiobooks results. Tap any book to learn more about it, including how many hours of entertainment you'll be getting if you purchase it.

To purchase, download, and begin listening to an audiobook:

1. In the iTunes Store app, click Audiobooks.
2. Tap the audiobook to purchase (or to learn more about).

3. Tap the price, and then tap Buy Audiobook.

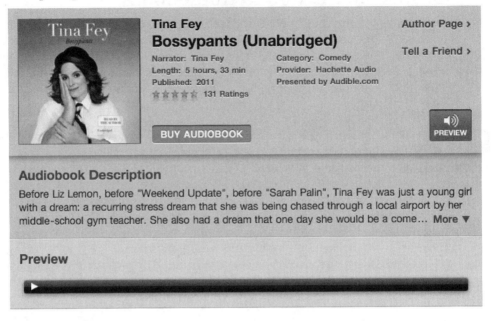

4. Input your password and wait while the download completes.
5. Once the download is complete, close the iTunes Store and open the iPod. You'll find the book there.

Get Smart with iTunes U

iTunes U, presumably short for iTunes University, offers audio and video related to learning and higher education. Here you can obtain media to help you learn a new language or a new skill, or even listen to lectures given previously at Yale, Stanford, Berkeley and other universities. You can browse museums without ever setting foot in them, listen and watch experts detail and describe an artifact in a museum, and explore information stored in the Library of Congress, among other things.

Browse and Listen to iTunes U

iTunes U offers a host of information, and it's all free. Open the iTunes Store and touch the iTunes U button to get started. Check out the following categories and features, listed next. Here are a few things to watch for, noting that media available here changes often:

- Tap Universities and Colleges on the Featured page to access media from colleges ranging from Aberdeen College to Zeppelin Universität. Tap any college name to see what's available from that college, as shown in the following illustration. (Tap outside the list to hide it.)

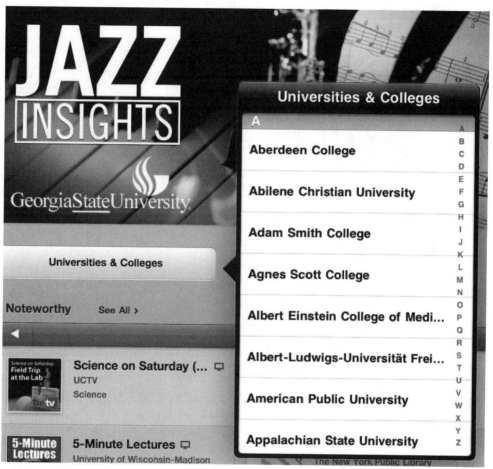

- Tap Beyond Campus on the Featured page to access educational offerings from off-campus institutions like museums and opera houses.
- Tap K-12 on the Featured page to access media from various K-12 institutions.
- Tap See All next to Noteworthy from the Featured page to see what Apple deems noteworthy. You might find offers from the Library of Congress, Stanford, and other highly notable institutions.

 After you've browsed the categories, perform a search in the Search window for specific media from a college, museum, or other entity.

To listen to free media you find in iTunes U:

1. Browse and tap the media to obtain.
2. Tap Free and tap Get Episode.

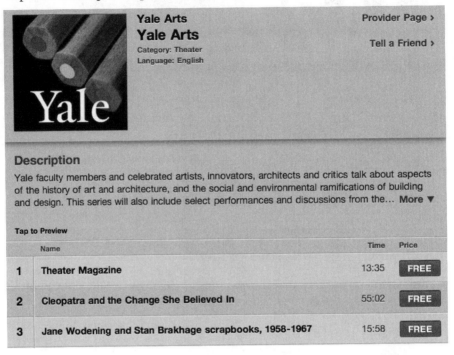

3. Wait while the media downloads. You can follow the progress in the Download link on the right side of the iTunes Store interface.
4. Once the download is complete, close iTunes and open your iPod. If the media is an audiobook or podcast, you can listen to it here in iTunes U. If you don't see it, look in the Videos app, under iTunes U. You may see it in both, as shown here.

Explore Art, Classical Music, Museums, and Cultural Exhibits

The Beyond Campus option in the iTunes U section, under Featured, is where you'll go to obtain educational media outside of college campuses, such as museums, opera houses, the Smithsonian, and others. Check out the following (noting that this list can change as time passes):

1. **Library of Congress**   Explore films and webcasts, podcasts, and classes for librarians, including entire classes on cataloging.
2. **Higher Education Channel Television**   Explore movies and shows related to higher education categorized into topics including I Love Jazz, Impact, Global Thinking, and Leaders and Legends.
3. **Metropolitan Museum of Art**   Browse the museum by subject, from African Art to Medieval Art to Photographs. You can also explore featured exhibits, and learn more about the museum itself.
4. **Washington National Opera**   Listen to opera from the latest opera seasons as well as archived media. Some of the archived media include *A Streetcar Named Desire, Das Rheingold, Madama Butterfly*, and *Tosca*.

To listen to any item in these categories:

1. Browse to and tap the media to obtain.
2. Tap Free, and then Get Episode.
3. Wait while the media downloads. You can follow the progress in the Download link on the right side of the iTunes Store interface.

As with other downloaded media, you'll find it in the Videos app or the iPod app.

Let the iTunes Store Lead the Way

You can let iTunes help you decide what media to browse and/or buy. In any category (Music, Movies, TV Shows, and so on), just click Genius, and let the recommendations begin. iTunes will analyze what you've purchased and/or downloaded and then offer suggestions regarding what other media you might enjoy. For instance, if you like the Red Hot Chili Peppers and you purchased their latest album on iTunes, Genius may suggest that you might also like the Dave Matthews Band.

 Genius has to be enabled in iTunes on your computer (the one you sync your iPad to) before you can use it on your iPad. See Chapter 8 for more information on enabling Genius.

To use Genius:

1. Tap any category button across the bottom of iTunes, making sure to tap a button for a category you've previously made purchases or downloaded media from.
2. Tap the Genius button at the top of the page.
3. Review the recommendations, and if you wish, tap the thumbs-up or thumbs-down icon to improve your recommendations next time. See Figure 9-8.

 The songs and media you obtain while using your iPad can be synced to your computer via iTunes. You can choose what to sync and when. Syncing is detailed in Chapter 1.

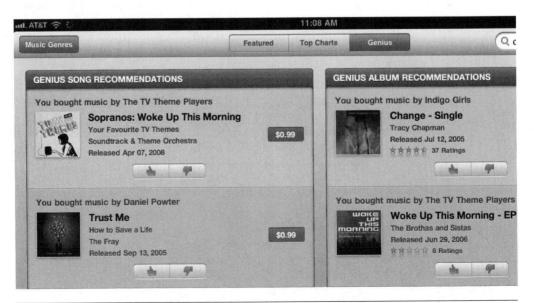

FIGURE 9-8 Genius helps you find new media you may like by making suggestions based on your previous purchases.

PART IV

Photos and Video

10

Take, View, Obtain, Manage, and Share Photos

HOW TO...

- Take a picture with the Camera
- Take a picture with Photo Booth
- Explore the Photos app
- Sync photo folders using iTunes
- Import photos with the optional Camera Connection Kit
- Explore Photos app views and use gestures
- Copy or delete a photo
- Share photos in an email
- Send a photo to Facebook
- Assign a photo to a contact
- Set a photo as wallpaper
- Create a slideshow of pictures with transitions
- Use Picture Frame
- Add music to a slideshow

Your iPad 2 comes with a camera that you can use to take pictures and shoot videos, and there's a lens on the front and one on the back. The Photos app complements the camera, and enables you to view the photos and videos you've taken. You can also upload photos and videos from a camera or SD camera card (with an optional adapter), share photos and videos via email, and even print photos if you have a compatible printer.

In this chapter you'll learn how to use the camera to take photos (you'll learn about taking video in Chapter 11), use the Photos app to view those photos, get pictures from other sources, and view photos in a slideshow. The Photos app offers features that allow you to share photos too, including the ability to send any photo in an email (or send multiple photos), assign a photo to a contact, or use a photo as wallpaper. You'll learn a little more about syncing too, because syncing all of the photos you keep on your computer can fill up your iPad (or at least make it difficult to find the pictures you want on it); you need to know how to sync only data that you need to help manage what's on your iPad at any given time.

 Tip iPad supports several common image formats including JPEG, TIFF, GIF, and PNG.

Take a Picture with the Camera

You're probably eager to take a picture, so we'll introduce that first. You take pictures using the Camera app, available from the default Home screen, provided you haven't moved it. The Camera app is shown in Figure 10-1. There are only a few things to notice: the icon for the last picture taken, the option to switch between photo mode and video mode, and the option to switch from the back-facing lens to the front, or vice versa.

Switch from the front- to rear-facing
camera lens and vice versa.

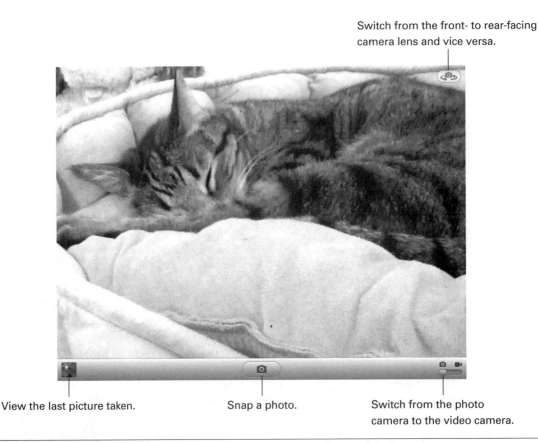

View the last picture taken.   Snap a photo.   Switch from the photo
camera to the video camera.

FIGURE 10-1 There are only four items to familiarize yourself with in the Camera.

Taking a picture is very easy. Just tap the Camera icon on the Home screen, choose which camera you want to use, and tap the Camera icon inside the Camera window to snap your shot. It's important to practice this so you can do it quickly; you never know when the perfect shot is going to present itself!

 Tap anywhere on the screen to cause the camera to adjust the lighting based on your subject and to set the focus. This tap will also provide an option to zoom in on a subject if you're using the rear-facing digital camera. Just move the slider to zoom in or out. (The zoom slider won't appear in video mode.)

1. Tap the Camera icon on the Home screen.
2. If applicable, tap the Camera icon in the top-right corner to switch to the front- or rear-facing camera.
3. If applicable, tap the Camera icon in the bottom-right corner to select the photo camera.
4. Aim, and if desired, tap the screen once to let the iPad adjust the exposure and focus.
5. Aim again, and then tap the Camera icon in the middle of the bottom of the screen to take the picture.
6. To view the picture in the Photos app, tap the thumbnail in the bottom-left corner. You'll learn more about the Photos app shortly.
7. Tap the screen and tap Done when you're finished viewing the picture. Later, you'll learn how to email a photo, view a slideshow, and more.

 If, while in the Photos app, you don't see Done, tap once on the photo. The controls disappear after a second or two of idle time.

Take a Picture with Photo Booth

The Photo Booth app lets you apply effects to a subject and manipulate them prior to taking a picture. There are nine effects in total, including but not limited to X-Ray, Twirl, Thermal Camera, and Kaleidoscope. To use the Photo Booth app, you simply select the effect you like, use your finger to drag and manipulate the effect as desired, and snap the picture. Once you've taken a few photos, you can view them in full-screen mode and delete them easily, as well as email and copy them.

Note Tapping once on the screen to set the exposure and focus does not work with Photo Booth (as it did with the digital camera), and the zoom slider is not available either.

1. Tap Photo Booth.
2. Tap the effect you like.

3. The Camera opens. In this window, drag your finger across the screen to apply additional effects. (This won't work if you chose Normal in Step 2.)
4. Tap the Camera icon to take the picture.
5. To return to Photo Booth to choose a different effect, tap the effect icon in the bottom-left corner; to switch camera lenses, tap the camera rotation icon in the bottom-right corner; to view the pictures you've taken, tap any thumbnail. See Figure 10-2.
6. In the view shown in Figure 10-2 (and you can tap the screen to make the controls reappear if they've gone missing), flick left and right to view the photos you've taken.

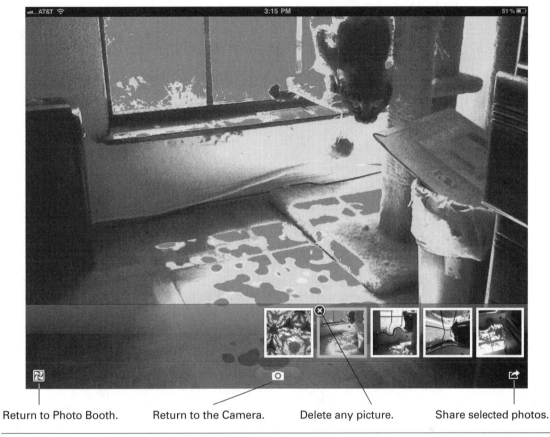

Return to Photo Booth.   Return to the Camera.   Delete any picture.   Share selected photos.

FIGURE 10-2   After you take a picture you'll have options.

7. Tap the screen again to bring up the controls and thumbnails.
8. Tap any thumbnail and tap the X by it to delete it.
9. Tap any other thumbnail to view it. Tap the screen to make the controls reappear if they disappear.
10. To stop viewing photos and return to the Camera, tap the Camera icon in the middle of the bottom of the screen.
11. To email a photo you've taken:
    a. Tap a photo to send.
    b. Tap the arrow that appears in the bottom right of the screen when in thumbnail view.
    c. Tap any additional thumbnails to add photos. See Figure 10-3.
    d. Tap Email. (Note you can also copy the photos to paste them somewhere else, or cancel the operation.)
    e. Complete the email as desired.

FIGURE 10-3 Select multiple photos and then tap Email to share them with someone quickly.

Explore the Photos Interface

You may have experimented a little with the Photos app after taking your first few pictures with the camera. If you didn't, that's okay; we're starting from scratch here, so you won't miss anything. The Photos app enables you to view and share photos with others easily. That's what you'll use it for first, most likely. The pictures are brilliant and bright, and are positioned to fill the entire screen, making sharing fun and effective. You can flick from left to right to change photos, flip the entire device to share a photo with someone sitting across from you, and tap and pinch to open an image in full-screen mode or zoom in on one. You can easily change views from Portrait to Landscape by simply turning the device 90 degrees left or right. You can even use your iPad as a digital photo frame and create your own slideshows of pictures with music!

To open the Photos app, just tap Photos on the Home screen. Photos will open, and you'll immediately notice at least two tabs across the top of the page: Photos and Albums. You may also see tabs for Events, Faces, and Places if your photos have been synced from programs such as iPhoto or Aperture on a Mac, or perhaps embedded with relevant information from a camera phone. (And you'll see Camera if you have a camera or camera card connected with the optional Camera Connection Kit.) If it isn't already selected, tap Photos. Here you can see all of your photos shown singly, and you can scroll through them by "flicking" your finger up or down the screen.

Tip Don't see any photos? Read and work through the next section to copy photos to your iPad from your computer.

Note what's available in the Photos interface. Specifically, note which of the five tabs are available to you:

- **Photos** You'll have this tab. Use this tab to view thumbnails of all of your photos individually and to scroll through those thumbnails by flicking. Tap any photo to view it in full-screen mode.
- **Albums** You'll have this tab too. Use this tab to view your photos by albums. Some albums are created by default by Photos, like Camera Roll and Photos. If you purchase the optional Camera Connection Kit and upload photos using it, you'll see Last Import and All Imported as well. You'll see other folders too, because an album can also be something you create on your computer to organize your

FIGURE 10-4   Albums offers pictures in related folders, called Albums.

own photos. When you sync the pictures you have in folders from your computer, you sync their respective folders to your iPad too. Figure 10-4 shows Albums.

- **Events**   If you use a Mac and iPhoto or Aperture to organize and manage your photos, you'll see an Events tab. You may also see an Events tab even if you don't sync your iPad with a Mac, provided you've somehow acquired photos on your iPad that it can classify as an event. Events are photos you organize by their dates and event names when you import them.
- **Faces**   If you use a Mac and iPhoto or Aperture to organize and manage your photos using the built-in face-recognition feature, you'll see a Faces tab. If you don't use a Mac, you won't. Faces lets you mark a person's face with a name, and then Photos can sort photos by the person's name, based on the information about their face.
- **Places**   When you acquire photos on your iPad, they may be categorized into "Places" if the iPad can figure out where they were taken. If you've uploaded or synced photos taken with a GPS-enabled camera or iPhone, you may see results in the Places tab, as shown in the following illustration.

You'll see additional options when you view a photo, although what you'll see depends on several factors, detailed in the Note that follows. To view any photo and these additional options, tap it. It will open in full-screen mode, and the additional options will appear at the top of the page. You can use the Share button to share the photo with others via email, send the picture to a social networking site like Facebook, or assign to a contact or as wallpaper. You can also print and copy the photo. If you subscribe to MobileMe, you can also opt to send the picture via MobileMe to ultimately sync at your computer (without actually connecting to it). You may even be able to rotate the photo or delete it. Tap the Share button to view the options you have for the specific photo you're viewing (that's the icon with the right-facing arrow).

 You'll have the Slideshow button and the Share button when viewing pictures synced from your computer. You'll see the Trash icon if you took the picture with the iPad or if it's an iPad screen capture. You can rotate pictures you've imported with the optional Camera Connection Kit, but you won't see this option when viewing photos you've synced from your computer or taken with the iPad's camera.

Tip You can easily capture what's on your screen by holding down the Sleep/Wake button and the Home button at the same time.

Get Photos on Your iPad

There are multiple ways to get photos onto your iPad, including syncing with iTunes on a PC or Mac, sending photos to yourself in an email, or using the optional Camera Connection Kit from Apple. If you don't yet have any photos on your iPad or have been too nervous to fully sync your iPad with your computer for fear of how much you'll actually put on it, don't worry—we'll show you how to add only what you want here. You'll also learn how to use the optional components you can purchase to import pictures from a camera or media card.

Copy Photos from Your Computer Using iTunes

We covered syncing in Chapter 1, but you may not have been ready to commit at that time to putting data on your iPad. You can refer to that chapter for the full explanation, but here's what you'll need to do if you just want to copy a folder or for the purpose of working through this chapter:

1. Connect your iPad to your computer. iTunes will open.
2. In iTunes, click your iPad in the source pane.

FIGURE 10-5   You don't have to commit to syncing all of your photos; just pick a couple of folders for now, if you want.

3. Click the Photos tab.
4. Click Sync Photos From.
5. Note the default picture folder. In Windows, it's the Pictures folder, but you can select a different folder using the arrows if your pictures are located in another folder.
6. To select only certain picture folders, tick Selected Folders. You'll see something similar to what's shown in Figure 10-5.
7. Select the folders to sync (copy) to your iPad.
8. Click Apply. A sync will occur immediately and you'll have photos on your iPad when it's complete.

Import Photos with the Optional Camera Connection Kit

If you purchased the optional Camera Connection Kit, you have two options for importing media. You can use the USB adapter and connect your camera, or you can use the SD card reader to use your SD card.

To use the USB adapter from the Camera Connection Kit, simply connect one end to your iPad and the other to the USB cable you connect to your digital camera. The adapter connects to the iPad via the 30-pin port at the bottom. Turn on your digital camera and position any settings for playback on that camera, as warranted.

FIGURE 10-6   Select the photos to import by tapping them.

Once the camera has been connected:

1. Wait while the iPad reads the picture information on the card or camera.
2. Green check marks on photos indicate that they've already been uploaded to your iPad. You may or may not see this.
3. Tap once on each photo to copy to your iPad (shown in Figure 10-6) and click Import (not shown). You can also tap any videos you see.
4. Tap Import Selected. Alternatively, you can click Import All.
5. After the import process has finished, click Delete to remove the files from your media card, or click Keep to keep them.

Using the Media Card Reader is even easier than using the USB adapter. Just remove the media card from your digital camera, and insert it into the Media Card Adapter. Then, insert the Media Card Reader into the proper port on your iPad.

Once the camera has been connected:

1. Wait while the iPad reads the picture information on the card.
2. Green check marks on photos indicate that they've already been uploaded to your iPad. You may or may not see this.
3. Tap once on each photo to copy to your iPad and click Import. Tap Import Selected. Alternatively, you can click Import All.
4. After the import process has finished, click Delete to remove the files from your media card, or click Keep to keep them.

View Photos

Now that you know a little about the Photos interface and have some photos on your iPad, you're ready to view some photos. As you are aware by now, you can view photos in lots of ways by clicking the tabs at the top of the Photos interface. For now, we'll focus on the Photos and Albums tabs.

 As with other apps, the Photos app offers a "back" button when you drill into folders. You may have to tap this button to return to the default screen that offers Photos, Albums, Events, Places, and the like.

View All Your Photos

To view all of your photos in a list, with each photo shown one at a time (rather than categorized in Albums), click the Photos tab. You can use various gestures to view them, including using a tap, flick, or pinch, and by physically repositioning the iPad. If you're not sure what some of those words mean, here's all you need to know:

- **Tap (on a thumbnail)**   A single, light touch on the screen, on any thumbnail for a photo. When you tap a thumbnail of a photo in the Photos tab, the photo will open in full-screen mode.
- **Tap (on a picture)**   Tap briefly anywhere on the screen when in full-screen mode. This will bring up the title bar where you can return to the previous page, among other things. Tap again to hide these controls.
- **Pinch**   A motion you make with your thumb and forefinger. To zoom in on a photo, put these two fingers together on the screen and pull them apart while touching the screen. To zoom back out, pull your thumb and forefinger back together while touching the screen. You can also reverse-pinch on a thumbnail to see it in full-screen mode.
- **Flick**   A quick motion you make across the screen, right to left, left to right, top to bottom, or bottom to top, generally with your forefinger. You can use a flick to move around in a screen that is longer than one page or to move from photo to photo when viewing pictures in full-screen mode.
- **Double-tap**   Two taps in quick succession are used to zoom in on and then zoom out of a photo.

To understand how the gestures are used, perform the following steps. You can use these motions in Photos and while viewing photos from the Photos tab:

1. In Photos, click the Photos tab.
2. Tap the thumbnail for any photo to view it in full-screen mode.
   a. Once in full-screen mode, pinch the photo to zoom in and out.
   b. Flick the photo to the left to see the next photo in the list. Flick right to return to the previous photo.
   c. Pinch inward on any photo to return to the Photos page.

3. Tap another thumbnail to open the picture in full-screen mode. Then you can
   a. Turn the iPad left or right 90 degrees to change view modes.
   b. Flip the iPad as you would to show a photo to someone sitting across from you. Flip again to return.
4. From the Photos tab showing thumbnails:
   a. Flick to scroll through thumbnails of photos if there are more than can be shown in a single screen.
   b. Rotate the iPad 90 degrees left or right to change from Portrait to Landscape.
   c. Tap any photo in the Photos tab. Drag your finger across the bar that appears at the bottom of the page to skim through all of your photos quickly. If you don't see this bar, which is shown in the illustration at right, tap the bottom of the page to view the controls.

View Photo Albums

In the preceding section, we focused mostly on how to navigate and view photos from the Photos tab in the Photos app. In this section, you'll explore the Albums tab. As you know, a physical photo album is a collection of photos that you put together yourself, for the purpose of easily accessing them when you wish. Like a physical photo album, albums in the Photos app also have multiple photos. But accessing the photos in these albums is much more convenient than accessing a physical album, especially since all of the albums fit nicely in a single unit—your iPad!

Note You can't create an album on your iPad. You have to create the album on a PC or Mac and sync the iPad to copy it.

The first thing you'll notice when you explore Albums is that each album has multiple images, and those images appear as a stack of photos, which represents the album itself. You can tap any album to view the photos in it, and (if necessary tap the screen and then) tap Albums to return to the Albums page. Additionally, you can use the same techniques you already know, like tap, pinch, and flick, to navigate the photos in your albums, although these movements will often produce different results. (Pinching outward on a stack of photos will allow you to "peek" at the photos, for instance, and if you continue pinching outward, the album will open. You can pinch inward to close the album too.)

To see how gestures work in Albums, perform the following steps:

1. Click the Albums tab. Note the stacks that designate the albums.
2. Tap any album to open it, and then browse the items in the album using tap, pinch, and flick in the manner described in the previous section.

3. When in full-screen mode, tap once to view the controls and tap the name of the album in the left corner to return to the albums. Then, click Albums in the top-left corner to return to the album page.
4. Back at the Albums tab, pinch an album by dragging your thumb and forefinger outward. Note this allows you to peek at the album. Continue pinching outward to open it.

Delete Photos

You may have photos on your iPad you don't want. You can delete photos that you've imported using a camera card, taken with the camera, saved from the Internet, or obtained via email. You can't delete photos you synced from your computer; you have to use iTunes for that.

To delete photos from your iPad that you've imported or taken with the camera, and not those that you've synced from your computer (and note that this is only one way to delete photos from your iPad):

 You can delete individual photos displayed in full-screen mode simply by tapping the Trash Can icon.

1. In the Photos app, tap the Albums tab.
2. Tap the album that contains photos you can delete. Consider Camera Roll, Last Import, or All Imported. Remember, you can't delete photos you've synced with iTunes on your computer.
3. Click the right-facing arrow next to Slideshow.

4. Tap the photos to delete.
5. Tap Delete.

6. Tap Delete Selected Photos.

How to... **Create a Photo Album**

Since you can't create a photo album on your iPad, you will have to create it on your computer. On a Mac, you'll probably use iPhoto to create albums, and on a PC, you'll create a new folder in an Explorer window. For both, once the folders are created, you'll move or copy photos into it.

If you use iPhoto on a Mac, click File, and click New Album to get started. Name your album, and then drag the photos you'd like to appear in the album from your library to the new album. If you use a PC, create a folder in the Pictures folder and copy or move pictures into it as follows:

1. On your PC, click Start, and click Pictures.
2. In the Pictures folder, right-click an empty area of that folder (in any white area in the right-side pane).
3. From the resulting menu, click New, and then Folder.
4. Name the folder.
5. Move pictures into this folder. You can cut and paste, or position this window with another window side by side, so that you can drag photos to it from other folders on your computer.

Once the album is created on your Mac, or a folder is created on your PC, you'll need to sync your iPad to the computer to get the new "album" on it.

Share Photos

It's easy to share photos with the people around you. The iPad has a large enough screen that people can view photos easily, and those photos can be viewed in Portrait view or in Landscape view. You can flip the iPad 180 degrees toward you or away from you to show a photo to a person sitting across from you. You can even pass the iPad around the room if you trust people not to drop it! And you may have even experimented with the dock or carrying case (optional components) for positioning your iPad as a digital photo frame and perhaps even placed it on your fireplace mantle for all to see.

The people you want to share your photos with aren't always in the same room with you, though. You may want to share your photos with a grandparent in another state or a son who's in college. You may want to share your photos with people you've never even met. You can share photos with others via email, MobileMe, Facebook, and various other ways.

You can also share photos (with yourself, perhaps) by assigning a photo to a contact or setting it as wallpaper. You can copy photos too, with a tap and a quick hold or by accessing the Copy command from the Photos interface. You can then paste any image you've copied into an email or other app. And finally, if you have a compatible printer, you can print the photo.

FIGURE 10-7   Tap the Share button to access the option to email the photo; if you don't see these controls, tap the screen one time.

Share a Photo in an Email

You'll have to have an email account set up on your iPad before you can email a photo, and setting up email is detailed in Chapter 4. If you haven't worked through that chapter yet, just come back to this section after you have. You don't ever have to email a photo if you don't want to; it's just one of the options for sharing.

To email a photo:

1. In Photos, locate the photo to email.
2. Tap it to open it in full-screen mode.
3. Position your finger in the top-right corner of the screen and look for the Share button, shown in Figure 10-7. Tap it.
4. Tap Email Photo.
5. Complete the email as desired.
6. When ready, click Send.

To select multiple photos to email:

1. From any album or list of photos, tap the Share button. That's the right-facing arrow in the top-right corner.
2. Tap up to five photos to select them. (You can't select photos from multiple albums.)
3. Tap Email.
4. Complete the email as desired.

Did You Know?

You Can View Videos Too!

If you have compatible videos in the Photos folder on your computer and you sync that folder to your iPad, those videos will appear in the Photos app on your iPad, alongside your still photos. (The same applies to videos you copy from the Camera Connection Kit, detailed earlier in this chapter.) Just tap any video to view it. Unlike other videos you watch on your iPad (which open in Videos), these videos will open in Photos. You'll learn more about videos in Chapter 11.

Send a Photo Using MobileMe

MobileMe is an add-on feature you have to subscribe to and pay for. MobileMe is the updated version of .Mac and iTools, if you're familiar with those, but includes many more features. MobileMe offers a free 30-day subscription, but the yearly rate is $99 and you'll be enrolled when the trial runs out unless you intervene. There's also a free MobileMe Gallery App that's a must-have for MobileMe users.

You can use MobileMe to send photos to your own personal MobileMe Gallery, an area on the web (or in the cloud, if you prefer) that you can use to store your photos and share them with others. People you allow access to can view pictures, download their favorites, and/or contribute their own pictures. Viewers can also skim albums to see what's inside, select an album, and choose viewing options such as Mosaic, Carousel, or Slideshow. MobileMe offers automatic resizing, so your photos adjust instantly to fit the viewer's browser window too, thus making it perfect for those with larger displays.

 MobileMe is a service that pushes email, contacts, and calendar events over the air to all your devices. This means that you can keep your iPhone, iPad, Mac, and PC in perfect sync. No docking required.

To send a photo to your personal MobileMe Gallery:

1. In Photos, locate the photo to share. Tap it. (Note you can select multiple photos, as detailed previously.)
2. Position your finger in the top-right corner of the screen and look for the Share button.
3. Click the Share button and click Send to MobileMe.
4. Complete any additional information as prompted.

Tip To learn more about MobileMe and to subscribe, visit www.apple.com/mobileme/.

Send a Photo to Facebook

There are so many Facebook users that we'd be lax if we left out how to send a photo to Facebook. If you're a Facebook user, read on. If not, feel free to skip this section! Before you can share a photo on Facebook from your iPad, you have to perform a few setup tasks:

• You have to get a personalized upload email address from Facebook. You'll use this email address to post pictures to your Facebook page.
• You have to have email set up on your iPad. You have to be able to send email in order to send a photo via email to Facebook.
• You have to be connected to the Internet when sending the photo.
• You have to send the photo to the personalized email address to post it to your Facebook page.

To get a personalized upload email address from Facebook, log in to Facebook, click Account, click Help Center, and click Photos. Click Mobile Photos. Follow the directions to get your personalized email address for uploading photos from your mobile device.

Now you're ready to send a photo from your iPad to your Facebook home page:

1. In Photos, locate the photo to send to Facebook. Tap it. If you like, select multiple photos, as detailed earlier.
2. Locate the Share button, and click Email.
3. Type the Facebook email address you received. (Learn how to save this email in the Contacts app so you don't have to type it in next time in Chapter 12.)
4. Type a subject in the subject line, and click the Mail icon to send the photo.

Tip   Currently when emailing photos to Facebook, what you write in the subject line is included with the picture. Anything you write in the body is not.

Assign a Photo to a Contact

You can assign any picture to any contact in the Contacts app. This picture will appear when you communicate with the contact. You can use a picture you already have on your iPad, or you can take a picture with the camera. However you want to do it, get the photo on your iPad prior to continuing here.

With the photo on your iPad, you can assign a photo to a contact:

1. In Photos, locate the picture to assign to a contact. For best results, choose a headshot. Tap it to open it in full-screen mode. (You may have to tap the "back" button to locate the correct folder that holds the picture.)
2. Click the Share button, and click Assign to Contact.

3. Choose the contact from the Contacts list.
4. If you wish, move and scale the image.
5. Tap Use, shown here.

Refer to Chapter 12 for more information about managing contacts and the Contacts app.

Set a Photo as Wallpaper

Wallpaper is what you see on both the Lock screen and the Home screen. You can set any photo as wallpaper for either or both of these, using the same techniques detailed earlier.

To set a photo as wallpaper:

1. In Photos, locate the picture to set as wallpaper. Tap it to view it in full-screen mode.
2. Click the Share button, and click Use as Wallpaper.
3. Tap Set Lock Screen, Set Home Screen, or Set Both, as shown in the following illustration.

Copy a Photo

There are many reasons why you would want to copy a photo, but you'll probably want to paste it into the body of an email. You may have apps that allow you to paste into them as well, like iWork apps including Pages, Numbers, and Keynote. Whatever you need to copy a photo for, it's easy to do.

To copy a photo:

1. In Photos, locate the picture to copy. Tap the photo to view it in full-screen mode.
2. Click the Share button, and click Copy. Alternatively, you can tap and hold the screen and tap Copy when it appears.
3. Open an app that supports the Paste command and can accept photos (Notes can't). For example, you can open a new Mail message.
4. Tap and hold, and tap Paste when applicable.

 You Can Save a Photo from a Web Page

To save a picture from a web page, touch and hold the photo, then tap Save Image. The same sequence works in an email.

Create a Slideshow

One of the best investments you can make to accessorize your iPad is an optional iPad dock. These docks enable you to display your iPad on a coffee table, mantle, or desk while you also charge or sync it. You can then do lots of things with one, like present a slideshow of pictures (or use a Bluetooth keyboard or watch a movie without having to hold your iPad in your hands or lap). If you intend to use your iPad as a digital photo frame in the long term, you can even connect the power cable and plug it in so it'll stay charged.

Another good investment is the Smart Cover, available from Apple. It makes a great stand for using the iPad for a frame, for watching movies, and even for typing in Landscape mode. You can position the Smart Cover so your hands are free to do other things too, like eat popcorn or pet the cats.

It's easy to create a slideshow of pictures anytime you want, and view it anywhere you want. To create a slideshow:

1. Open the Photos app and select an album you'd like to display in a slideshow. (You can tap the Photos tab to use all of your photos.) Tap a photo in the album to view it in full-screen mode.
2. Optional: Place the iPad on its dock. If you wish, connect the iPad to a power source to keep the battery from draining if you plan to show the slideshow for a while.
3. Tap Slideshow.
4. Choose a transition.

5. To play music with your slideshow:
   a. Move the Play Music slide to On.
   b. Tap Music and select a song. Tap Start Slideshow.

6. To change how long you'd like to play each slide for, or to repeat or shuffle photos, tap Settings on the Home screen, tap Photos, and make your changes as desired. You can opt to change slides every 2, 3, 5, 10, or 20 seconds.

7. Tap the screen to return to the Photos app or the Home button to exit to a Home screen.

Tip To stop playing the slideshow, tap the screen.

Use Picture Frame

Picture Frame is a feature kind of along the same lines as Slideshow. With Picture Frame, though, when your iPad is locked, you can display an album of photos. This is a great way to enjoy your iPad, while at the same time charging it in an iPad dock. You can also use Picture Frame with a Lock Screen password. Incorporating a Lock Screen password with Picture Frame enables you to pass your iPad around without worrying that someone will stop the slideshow and start looking at other data on your iPad.

You configure settings for Picture Frame in the Settings app; just tap Settings and Picture Frame. You can choose a transition, opt to zoom in on faces, or shuffle the pictures, to name a few. You can also opt to show all photos, only albums, or only events. With that done, it's easy to start or stop Picture Frame:

1. Press the Sleep/Wake button to lock the iPad.
2. Tap the Sleep/Wake button again or Home button to view the Lock screen.
3. Tap the Picture Frame icon next to the slider to start the show.
4. Tap anywhere on the iPad screen or press the Home button to access the Lock screen again, where you can tap the Picture Frame icon to stop the show and to unlock the iPad using the slider.

11

Take, View, Obtain, Manage, and Share Videos

HOW TO...

- Explore the Videos app
- Get movies and videos on to your iPad
- Play a video and explore video controls
- Watch media you've purchased from iTunes
- Show closed captions
- Take video with the Camera and view it
- Upload a video to YouTube
- Delete a video
- Open and navigate the YouTube app
- Search for, bookmark, like or dislike, comment on, and share a video
- Install the ABC Player for the iPad
- Watch a TV show from ABC
- Search for additional Internet TV programming
- Sign up for a free trial to Netflix
- Set up FaceTime
- Hold a FaceTime video chat
- Use Video Mirroring and the Digital AV Adapter

The Videos app, which comes preinstalled on all iPads, allows you to watch music videos, movies, and TV shows you purchase or rent from iTunes, and videos you've synced from your computer. You can also watch video you've downloaded from iTunes U here too, including video podcasts. The Videos app supports high-definition and standard-definition videos and movies, supports closed captioning, and can be viewed in wide-screen mode, among other things.

The YouTube app, also included, enables you to easily browse YouTube videos. If you have a YouTube account (it's free), you can sign in and access videos you've uploaded yourself; like, dislike, and comment on videos; view your subscriptions; and more. You can even email a link to a video to someone to share it. If you have video you'd like to upload to YouTube on your iPad, you can do that from the Photos app.

Of course, there are myriad third-party apps that are related to video; these are apps that you'll need to download and install yourself, because these apps aren't included by default on your iPad. One seriously worth considering is the Netflix app. This app (along with a monthly membership fee) enables you to watch movies and recorded TV shows right from your iPad, and there are literally thousands to choose from. If you want to avoid another monthly charge, though, try the ABC Player for the iPad. This free app enables you to watch recorded TV shows, such as *Lost* and *Grey's Anatomy* (for no cost). Of course, new apps appear every day, so you'll need to keep your eyes open for upcoming apps like those that are expected from Hulu, NBC, and various other TV-related entities, as you can be sure new apps will be arriving regularly!

Lastly, the iPad 2 comes with FaceTime, an app that enables you to hold video chats with others who have compatible hardware and software, specifically the iPad 2, iPhone 4, new iPod touch, or a Mac, when connected to a Wi-Fi network. With FaceTime, you use the iPad's video camera to send live video to others, and you, in return, can view their live video. The iPad 2 also supports video mirroring using the optional Digital AV Adapter, available from Apple, which enables you to display everything on your iPad screen on your TV (connected with an HDMI cable).

Explore the Videos App

When you're ready to sit down with your favorite movie, you'll sit down with the Videos app. You can watch almost any type of video, including those filmed in high definition (HD). You can watch complete movies, podcasts, music videos, and TV shows, as well as media you download from iTunes U. You can even watch videos you've recorded yourself, provided you've synced those videos using iTunes. Because there are no buttons or controls that remain on the screen all the time, you can watch media without visual interruptions, giving you a more "at-the-movies" feel. Figure 11-1 shows how the Videos app might look on your iPad. We've selected the iTunes U tab.

FIGURE 11-1   The Videos app offers tabs to hold various kinds of video. Tabs appear when you've acquired media that fits in the category.

Tip If you're really into movies on your iPad, consider buying a second-generation Apple TV. With it you can stream the movies you have stored on your iPad to a compatible TV using AirPlay. You'll need a widescreen TV, a home network with Wi-Fi, a computer that runs iTunes, and the appropriate cables. Of course, you'll need an iPad running iOS 4.2 or later. You'll also need AirPlay and a Wi-Fi network with both the Apple TV and the iPad connected. Once you've completed your setup, you'll see the AirPlay icon next to the Fast Forward button when a video is playing in the Video app. (Or you could just use the Digital AV Adapter and an HDMI cable to connect to any TV with an HDMI input jack! It won't be wireless, but it's a lot easier!)

Open and Navigate the Videos App

To open the Videos app, you simply tap it. Once the app is open, you will see tabs that apply to the type of video you've acquired. Here are some of the tabs you'll see.

Note that tabs will appear as media becomes available that belongs in these categories, and tabs disappear when that media is no longer available:

- **Movies** The Movies tab holds movies you've purchased or rented. Tap the Movies tab to see what's there. Other video may appear here too, including home videos you've synced using iTunes.

- **TV Shows** The TV Shows tab holds TV shows you've acquired. You won't see this tab if you don't have any TV shows.
- **Podcasts** The Podcasts tab holds video podcasts you've acquired. You won't see this tab if you haven't downloaded any video podcasts.
- **Music Videos** The Music Videos tab holds music videos you've purchased from iTunes. You won't see this tab if you don't have any music videos.
- **iTunes U** The iTunes U tab holds media obtained from iTunes U. You won't see this tab if you don't have any iTunes U media.
- **Shared** The Shared tab is only available if you've enabled sharing as detailed at the end of Chapter 8. That section is entitled "Stream Music over Your Home Wi-Fi Network." When you set up sharing and streaming, you can also opt to share and stream video.

Did You Know? Certain Videos Will Appear in the Photos App

If you record video with a stand-alone digital camera and upload that video to your iPad with the optional Camera Connection Kit or Media Card Reader, or if you take video with the Camera app using your iPad, those videos will appear in the Photos app, not the Videos app.

Get Movies or Videos on Your iPad

Computers have specific folders to hold videos. On a PC, that's the Videos or My Videos folder. If you know that you have videos and movies on your computer but you don't see any on your iPad, then you'll need to tell iTunes where to find those movies and videos so it can offer you the option to sync them.

To begin, point iTunes to the folder where you store the videos and movies on your PC. Here are the instructions for a Windows-based computer:

1. Connect your iPad to your PC.
2. In iTunes, under Library, click Movies.
3. Click File, and click Add Folder to Library.
4. Browse to the location on your computer where you save the videos you'd like to sync. This may be a Public Videos folder, or your personal Videos or My Videos folder. See Figure 11-2.
5. Click Select Folder, or something similar.
6. With your iPad connected, in iTunes, click your iPad in the navigation pane.
7. Under Movies, tick Sync Movies.
8. Configure syncing as desired. Figure 11-3 shows an example.
9. Click Apply.

If you don't have any videos or movies to put on your iPad, but you'd like to work through this chapter, you can get a free video podcast from iTunes:

1. Tap iTunes from the iPad's Home screen.
2. Tap the Podcasts tab.
3. Locate a free video podcast.
4. Tap it to view the Information page.
5. Tap Free, and then tap Get Episode.
6. When the download completes, open the Videos app and tap the Podcasts tab.

FIGURE 11-2   You can add folders for iTunes to sync to your iPad, if they aren't included in the sync process by default.

☑ **Sync Movies**   3 movi

☐ Automatically include [all   ◆] movies

Movies

☑ **Avatar (2009)**
🕐 161 minutes
2.35 GB
PG-13

☐ **Flying over the desert**
● 14 seconds
978 KB

☑ **Flying over the desert**
● 14 seconds
978 KB

☑ **Flying over the Hoover Dam**
● 45 seconds
3 MB

☐ **Flying over the Hoover Dam**
45 seconds
3 MB

☐ **Helicopter ride over Hoover Dam - Landing**
● 1 minute
4.3 MB

FIGURE 11-3 Select the movies to sync, or opt to sync all of them.

 Note If you haven't set up iTunes to automatically sync all podcasts, the podcasts you download directly will disappear when you sync your iPad to your computer.

Play a Video

Hopefully you now have some video, or at the very least, you have downloaded a free video podcast from iTunes. Now you're ready to find and play your video using the Videos app.

To find and play a video using the Videos app:

1. Tap the Videos app on the Home screen.
2. Tap the tab that contains the media to view.
3. Tap any video to see more information.
4. Turn the iPad so you're in Landscape view.
5. Tap the Play button, shown here.

Movies   Info   Chapters

Avatar (2009)
PG-13, 20th Century Fox, 2010   ▶

To use the video controls while watching a movie:

1. Tap the screen one time. The controls you'll see and experiment with here are shown in Figure 11-4.
2. Tap the Rewind button to start the video again or skip to the previous scene in a movie. Tap and hold the button to skim backward through the video.

FIGURE 11-4   Experiment with each control to see how it works when you tap it and when you tap and hold.

3. Tap the Fast Forward button to skip to the next video in the playlist (such as a multi-episode TV series) or skip scenes within a movie. Tap and hold the button to fast forward through the video.
4. Tap the Pause button to pause the video; tap it again to resume playing.
5. Use the slider to adjust the volume.
6. Tap the button in the top right of the page to switch to wide-screen view, and back. See Figure 11-5. You can also accomplish this by double-tapping anywhere on the screen. Note that this button won't be available if the video is a full-screen video, natively.
7. Drag across the Scrubber Bar at the top of the video to pinpoint a new location.

Watch Media You've Acquired from iTunes

In Chapter 9, you learned all about browsing the iTunes Store for movies, TV shows, music videos, and even college lectures. In that chapter you also learned how to rent and buy movies and TV shows, and how to browse the hottest movies of the day. If you made any purchases at the iTunes Store while reading that chapter that are video-related (movies, TV, and so on), you'll find that video in the Videos app. Just tap it once to play it.

If you have not yet purchased anything from iTunes, consider doing it, at least once, so that you can get the full iPad–iTunes experience. (If you're on the fence about a movie, you can preview it before buying, or rent it.) You can even purchase a single TV show if you like.

FIGURE 11-5   Note the Scrubber Bar and the option to change the view.

To watch media you've purchased from iTunes (note that you might have to tap the Video app's "back" button to return to the default screen with tabs):

1. Open the Videos app.
2. Tap the appropriate tab to locate the media in it.
3. Tap the thumbnail for the media, as shown in the following illustration.

4. Tap Play.

 If you buy a movie or TV show, it's yours (unlike renting). The next time you open the Videos app on your iPad, it'll still be there.

Show Closed Captioning

Closed captioning is the text version of the dialogue in a show or movie, and the text appears across the top or bottom of the movie while you watch it. Closed captions are embedded in a video or TV show and can be enabled when needed. Closed captioning was originally created for people who are hearing-impaired, but it can also be quite useful when you can't hear the movie dialogue because of a noisy environment or don't have headphones available. Along with the text, closed captions can also include descriptions of sounds played in the background, like a song playing, a person singing, or a door creaking.

 You have to be careful to purchase or download media that includes closed captions to have access to it.

You can enable closed captioning for the videos you watch on your iPad. Here's how:

1. On the Home screen, tap Settings.
2. Tap Video.

3. Move the slider for Closed Captioning from Off to On.
4. Make a note of the other settings here, including where to start playing the video by default. You can choose Where Left Off or From Beginning.
5. If closed captions are available for a movie, TV show, podcast, or the like, you'll see them when you play the video in the Videos app.

Work with Homemade Video

You can record live video with the iPad's camera and view it in the Photos app and/or upload it to YouTube. You can do the same with video you've uploaded using the Camera Connection Kit. You can also delete any video you've taken with the camera (or uploaded) if you no longer want it using the Photos app. You delete media you've obtained from iTunes using the Videos app or iTunes on your computer (provided you've synced it).

Take Video with the Camera and View It

You may already know how to record video; it's intuitive, especially if you have already used the camera to take digital pictures as outlined in Chapter 10. For the most part, you simply select the front- or rear-facing camera, make sure the slider is set to video mode, and tap the Record button that appears when the video camera is enabled. Tap the Record button again to stop recording. Figure 11-6 shows these controls.

As with taking digital pictures, a thumbnail appears after you've recorded some video. Tap it to view the recording (and share it) in the Photos app. Playing the video is as simple as tapping the Play button, tapping the screen, and tapping Done when finished.

Tap to see the last video taken.

Tap to record video and to stop recording.

Tap to choose a camera.

FIGURE 11-6   Recording is as simple as tapping the Record button.

You can also share the video via YouTube, by email, or even by copying the video, as shown here. Just tap the Share button.

Upload a Video to YouTube

You can take video with your iPad's video camera and upload it to YouTube, provided you have a YouTube account, and that the video is smaller than 2GB and is in an acceptable file format. You can also upload other video you have in the Photos app, perhaps video you obtained by uploading it using the optional Camera Connection Kit.

To upload video from your iPad to YouTube:

1. Tap the Photos app.
2. Locate the video and tap it.
3. Tap the Share button, and tap Send to YouTube. (Sign in if required.)

4. Type a title and description, choose a quality setting, include tags, choose a category, and choose who can view the video (Public or Unlisted).

5. Tap Publish.

6. When prompted, tap View on YouTube, Tell a Friend, or Close.

Delete a Video

You can delete videos from the iPad to save space. Videos can consume quite a bit of free space. When you delete a video on your iPad that you've synced from your computer, it is removed from your iPad, but it is not removed from your computer. To delete a video from your computer, delete it from the Movies or Videos folder manually, or delete it (or remove it) using iTunes.

To delete a video on your iPad:

1. From the Photos app:
   a. Locate the video to delete and tap it.
   b. Tap the Trash icon.
   c. Tap Delete Video.

2. From the Videos app:
   a. Tap and hold a video until an X appears on it.
   b. Tap the X to remove the video.
   c. Tap Delete to confirm.

 If you delete a rented movie from your iPad, it's deleted permanently.

Explore the YouTube App

YouTube is a video-sharing web site where users can upload and share videos they take or movies they create. Companies and artists also use YouTube to share clips of movies they produce, commercials they create for their products, TV show teasers, and music videos. Most of the video on YouTube is created and uploaded by individuals, though, and runs the gamut from funny to serious to downright filthy.

You can access YouTube videos from the YouTube app on your iPad. You'll need to be connected to the Internet, either using free Wi-Fi or a gracious 3G data plan. (If you have a limited data plan, make sure you're connected to a free network before continuing.) While you can browse all you want on YouTube without creating a user account, if you want to like or dislike videos, post comments, or perform similar tasks, you'll have to create one. (You'll also need a user account to upload videos from your iPad to YouTube.) For now, go ahead and browse without an account, and if you decide later that you need one, you can create one.

As with other apps, there are familiar buttons across the bottom:

- **Featured**   These are apps that are featured by YouTube because they're unique, meaningful, funny, or exhibit some other reason for featured status.
- **Top Rated**   When viewers view videos, they also often rate them. The videos in this category are the highest-rated videos of the day, the week, and all time.
- **Most Viewed**   YouTube keeps track of how often viewers watch a video, and the videos in this category have more views than the others.
- **Favorites**   The videos here are ones you bookmark as videos you like. (The bookmark icon is the same icon you have access to in Safari.) You can then access your favorite videos anytime you want to watch them again or show them to a friend. You will need to sign in with your YouTube account to access every feature here.
- **Subscriptions**   If you like a particular YouTube user, you can subscribe to him or her. You can then view all videos posted by that person easily, as well as any new videos he or she posts. This requires a YouTube account.
- **My Videos**   If you've uploaded any of your own video to YouTube, you'll have easy access to it here. You can also see how many people have viewed your videos, and read any comments that have been posted, as shown in the following illustration. Here you can see the video I uploaded in the previous section. This requires a YouTube account.

- **History**   The videos you've viewed on YouTube are listed here. This offers an easy way to access a video again, should you desire.

Create a YouTube Account

Here's how to create your own YouTube account:

1. Open Safari and navigate to www.youtube.com.
2. At the bottom of the page, tap Sign In.
3. If you have an account with Google, you can use it to sign in. Otherwise, tap Sign Up for YouTube!
4. Fill in the required information.

Play and Navigate a Video

Now that you're familiar with the YouTube interface, let's find a video and play it. The controls you'll use once a video is playing will look familiar, just like what you're used to in the Videos app.

To navigate to and play a video:

1. Open the YouTube app. Log in if you like. Note that you won't have access to all that YouTube has to offer unless you log in.
2. Click the Top Rated button at the bottom of the screen.
3. Tap any video to play it. The video should play in full-screen mode when the iPad is held in Landscape orientation. If a video is not playing in full-screen mode, pinch outward to have it fill the entire screen. Likewise, pinch inward to switch from full-screen mode to a smaller mode, shown in Figure 11-7.

FIGURE 11-7 You can view videos in two ways, full-screen mode or this smaller mode, where you can also view related videos and have the option to share, like or dislike, bookmark, or flag the video.

4. Turn the iPad to view the video in Portrait or Landscape mode.
5. Tap the video, then tap pause, and then Play.
6. Continue exploring as time allows.

To access the YouTube controls while watching any video or while the video is paused:

1. Tap while in full-screen mode to access the available controls. They include Bookmark, Repeat, Play/Pause, and Skip (to the next video), shown in Figure 11-8. You can also access the Scrubber Bar at the top of the page to quickly locate a specific part of a video.
2. Pinch inward to return to the smaller mode.
3. Tap while in the smaller mode to access the available controls. They include: + Add (to add a bookmark), Share, Like, Dislike, and Flag, and options to play or move through the video with the Scrubber bar provided. From this view you'll also see Related, More From, and Comments on the right side.

 If there's a specific event in a video you like, note how far into the video the event occurs. Then use the Scrubber Bar to quickly move there.

FIGURE 11-8   In full-screen mode, tap to view the controls.

Search for a Video

You've seen the Search window in the YouTube interface, and it works just like the Search window in any other iPad app. Just tap it to type in keywords for videos you'd like to see.

- Search for "Standing Cat – Mon chat" to see how to search for a specific video. Tap the video once to play it.
- Perform a broader search. In the Search box, type **news bloopers**. Note all of the results. Read the ratings to decide which ones you'd like to view.
- Finally, type a username. Try mine, **JoliBallew**, with no spaces. You can then browse the videos uploaded by that YouTube user. Note that usernames are unique, so if you want to see all of the videos a friend has posted, simply ask for his or her username.

Bookmark a Video

Every so often you'll run across a video you know you're going to want to watch again. When that happens, you'll want to bookmark that video so it'll be easily accessible. Once you have bookmarked the video, you can access it from the Favorites button at the bottom of the YouTube interface. So first, find a video you absolutely love, and then:

1. In full-screen mode, tap once to bring up the controls, and then, tap the Bookmark icon. It looks like an open book.
2. In the smaller screen mode, tap the video once to bring up the controls, and click + (Add). Tap Favorites.
3. Tap the Favorites button to view your bookmarks and access them.
4. While in the Favorites view, note the Edit button. Tap it to remove videos from your Favorites list.

Like and Comment on Videos

Once you have created your YouTube account and signed in, you're ready to like, dislike, and comment on videos. Both are really easy, and both can be done from the smaller mode, discussed throughout this chapter.

To rate and comment on YouTube videos:

1. Locate a video to comment on, like, or dislike.
2. Pinch inward to access the smaller mode, if applicable.
3. Tap the video screen while in the smaller mode, and tap Like or Dislike.
4. Tap Comments in the right pane to write your own comments. Press ENTER on the keyboard.
5. You can also flag a video if you find it offensive.

Share a Video

You can tap Share to email a link to a video to someone you think would enjoy it. Of course, you'll need to have Mail set up (see Chapter 4), and you'll need the email address of the person you'd like to send the link to, but you probably already have all of that.

Explore Third-Party Video-Related Apps

One of the greatest things about the iPhone and the iPod Touch, and ultimately the iPad, is and will continue to be third-party apps and the optional apps provided by Apple (like iWork). You can find apps in the App Store, as detailed in Chapter 7. While you may have previously focused on apps for social networking, increasing productivity, shopping, or finding your way around town, there are plenty of apps directed specifically at video and TV. There are two that are "must-have" apps for TV and movies that have already been released, and as time passes, you can be sure that more will be introduced.

Install the ABC Player for the iPad

The ABC Player for the iPad is a great third-party app available from ABC Television. You can use the app to watch TV shows that ABC makes available. Not all television shows are available, only some, but it's a great start for TV on the iPad. As time goes on, watch for other networks to release their own apps.

To install the ABC Player for the iPad:

1. Click the App Store icon on the Home screen.
2. Click the Search window.
3. Type **ABC Player**.
4. Tap Free, and tap Get App.

Watch a TV Show from ABC

With the ABC Player installed, you can now watch a TV show on your iPad. Just open the app and look for the available shows. You can browse shows by Featured, Schedule, All Shows, Me, or Info. Figure 11-9 shows the Featured option. When you tap a show, you can often pick which episode you'd like to see.

Tap the arrow to play any show. It'll take a minute or so to load, but once it begins you'll have access to familiar controls (once the initial commercials have finished playing), including Play/Pause, view in wide screen, and the Scrubber Bar for moving forward or backward in the show.

FIGURE 11-9 The ABC Player lets you watch television shows on your iPad.

Search for Additional Internet TV Programming

As noted, as time passes, new TV apps are sure to be released. You'll want to check occasionally to see if there are any that interest you. The best way to search for new apps from your iPad is to open the App Store, and search TV, TV programming, Watch TV, or Television. Look for apps that have been released by the actual networks, like NBC, FOX, CBS, TNT, and the like. Read the reviews before you download and install, to make sure they are worth the trouble, space, and so on.

Tip If you have Time Warner for your cable TV service at home, try the Time Warner Cable app. It's incredible and offers quite a bit of the programming offered by Time Warner, which you can access directly from your iPad.

Sign Up for Netflix

Netflix is a subscription service that, for under $10 a month, offers DVDs by mail that you can keep as long as you want, and a long list of movies and television shows you can watch instantly on your TV, computer, or iPad, if you have the right equipment and/or apps.

Netflix is something to seriously consider if you're in any of the following situations:

- You are planning to use Netflix when you're connected to a wireless network. If you're connected to 3G, you'll use up your data plan very quickly.
- You watch a lot of movies or television shows, and you want to watch those on your iPad.
- You want to watch network TV series you missed and series previously on premium channels like HBO and Showtime that you never had the opportunity to watch before.
- You don't want to purchase movies from iTunes, and you feel that the price for renting from iTunes is too expensive.
- You want to spend less than $10 a month to watch an unlimited number of movies and TV shows on your iPad (and you enjoy movies and television shows that have been out for a while).

You're not going to be able to watch just-released movies or TV shows on your iPad using the Netflix "Watch Instantly" options, so if that's what you're looking for, you'll probably want to stick with iTunes. Netflix offers brand-new movies on DVD only, and it takes some time to get the production company's permission to offer TV shows and movies over the Internet as well as a bit of time to make that transition. However, if you're OK with the classics like *Guess Who's Coming to Dinner*, *Planet of the Apes*, *Doctor Doolittle*, and *Cool Hand Luke*, and if you're okay with not being the first on your block to see the most recently released movies, you can get your fill here.

Tip   When browsing Netflix Watch Instantly options, check out New Arrivals. You'll find newly released movies, TV shows, and other media here.

Netflix fills a television void too. If you missed the first season of *Bones*, you can watch it on your iPad with Netflix. If you never got to watch Showtime's *Weeds* or *Dead Like Me*, you can watch it now. If you need to catch up on some of your favorite specials on The History Channel, there's an entire section dedicated to that. You can also watch made-for-TV movies, TV documentaries, miniseries, and even British TV. You can watch older episodes of *Mythbusters*, *King of the Hill*, *My Name Is Earl*, and a host of other shows. You'll certainly never run out of things to watch.

To watch media with the Netflix app, you'll need to sign up and sign in. This will require a credit card that can be billed each month. You can sign up from a computer or your iPad. To sign up for a free trial of Netflix to try out on your iPad:

1. Get the Netflix app from the App Store. It's free.
2. Tap the app to open it.
3. Sign in or create a new account.

Watch a Movie with Netflix

Watching a movie on Netflix is simple. From the Watch Instantly tab, locate the movie to watch, and tap Play:

1. Open the Netflix app.
2. Tap Home if applicable.
3. Browse until you've found a movie to watch.
4. Tap any movie to play it.

Watch TV Shows with Netflix

Watching a TV show with your Netflix app is similar to watching a movie, but this time, from Genres, tap Television. Once in the Television section, browse to find a show you'd like to watch. As with Movies, you can tap Play to play it immediately. Note that you can do much more with Netflix; this is only an introduction.

Explore FaceTime

FaceTime is an app that lets you hold video chats with others. People you want to video chat with must have an iPad 2, iPhone 4, new iPod touch, or a Mac over Wi-Fi. Because calls are placed by tapping a contact's email address, when you first tap FaceTime, you'll be prompted to input your own Apple ID and password, and then tell FaceTime what email address you want to use when people call you. When that's done, FaceTime will be ready to use.

To have a video chat using FaceTime:

1. Tap FaceTime on the Home screen.
2. If this is your first time to use FaceTime, input your Apple ID and password, tap Next, and verify the email address (or type a new one). Tap Done.
3. In the All Contacts list that appears, tap the contact to send a FaceTime invitation to. If the contact has a blue camera by their name, they're available for FaceTime (and have the required hardware).

4. Tap that email to initiate the call. A call in progress offers controls to switch from the front to the rear-facing camera, to mute the sound, and to end the conversation, shown in Figure 11-10.

 Tap Settings and FaceTime to change or add an email address, or turn on or off FaceTime.

FIGURE 11-10   FaceTime offers controls while in a call, including one to end it.

Use Video Mirroring Using the Digital AV Adapter

You can share what's on your iPad on a larger screen if you purchase the optional Digital AV Adapter from Apple. It's called *video mirroring*. You can share a presentation at work using a compatible projector, your favorite app on an HDTV, your personal photos on an external display, and more. One end of the AV adapter plugs into the 30-pin connector on the iPad, and the other end plugs into your HDMI cable. And the HDMI cable plugs into your HDTV, projector, or other HDMI-friendly monitors. There's also a second 30-pin connector to USB cable to charge your iPad, so you can leave your iPad plugged in while you screen your presentation or movie. There's no setup either; you just make the connection and you're ready to view!

PART V

Productivity

12

Manage Contacts

HOW TO...

- Sync Contacts
- Open and explore the Contacts app
- Add a contact manually
- Add a picture for a contact
- Change the order in which contacts are listed
- Scroll and search to locate a contact
- Get a map to a contact's address
- Email a contact
- Edit a contact
- Share contact information

If you've ever used an email program, cell phone, instant messaging program, or even an old-fashioned Rolodex, you're familiar with contacts. A contact is a person or company that you... well, contact, via email, phone, text message, instant message, letter, fax, or other medium.

Your iPad comes with a Contacts app that allows you to keep digital contacts. When you add a contact manually, you can input the usual information: email address, phone number, street address, zip code, and the like, but you can also add personal information such as birthdays, anniversaries, and even children's names. You can add a picture. Beyond adding the information, though, you can access contact information from various other apps, like Mail and Calendar. You can even have the Calendar app send you a reminder on a person's birthday or anniversary.

Add, Access, and Edit Contacts

The Contacts app is located on the Home screen of your iPad. You'll use this app to easily browse the contacts on your iPad. You may already have contacts if you've synced them from your computer, or if you've manually added them from Mail. You can also add contacts simply by touching the + sign and inputting information.

Sync Contacts

If you haven't synced contacts on your iPad, you can do so from iTunes on your computer. As with other syncing tasks, connect your iPad, select your iPad in the left pane, and configure your syncing preferences. iTunes enables you to sync contacts from various sources including:

- **On a Mac**   Sync contacts from Mac OS X Address Book, Yahoo! Address Book, and Google Contacts. You can sync with all of these at the same time if you like.
- **On a PC**   Sync with Microsoft Outlook 2003, 2007, 2010, Google Contacts, Windows Vista Contacts, Windows Address Book (Outlook Express), and Yahoo! Address Book. Unlike on a Mac where you can sync with multiple applications at the same time, on a PC, you can only sync with one of these at a time. You can merge the information, though; for instance, you can sync all of your Outlook Contacts, and then switch to Google and merge those contacts with the ones already on your iPad. You'll see the option to merge, shown in Figure 12-1, when you click Apply in iTunes.

If you haven't synced any contacts yet, first, on your computer, clean up your Contacts list. Make sure the people in the list are people you still communicate with, that there aren't any duplicates, and that the email addresses are valid. Then, configure the settings as desired, and click Sync. Figure 12-2 shows the options from the Info tab of iTunes on a PC.

Open and Explore the Contacts App

The Contacts app is one of the simpler apps to use. It looks like the physical address book you're probably already familiar with, and includes alphabetical tabs to let you access a page quickly. The + sign lets you add a contact manually, and you can tap

FIGURE 12-1   You can sync and merge contacts from various sources using iTunes.

MobileMe

Learn More   You can use MobileMe to sync your email, calendars, contacts, and bookmarks with your iPad.

☑ **Sync Contacts with** [Outlook   ⬍]

    ⦿ All contacts
    ◯ Selected groups

       ☐ Collected Contacts

☐ Add contacts created outside of groups on this iPad to : [⬍]

FIGURE 12-2   Connect your iPad, and in iTunes, click the Info tab to view syncing options for Contacts.

any existing contact and then Edit to add information if you wish. Figure 12-3 shows these two options, at the bottom of the Contacts interface.

To open and explore the Contacts app:

1. Touch the Contacts icon on the Home screen.
2. If you have contacts in your Contacts list, use your finger to scroll through them.
3. Touch any contact to view it. See Figure 12-4.
4. Rotate the iPad 90 degrees to explore Landscape view.
5. Note the + sign. This is where you'll add a new contact.

FIGURE 12-3   You'll find both the Add Contact option and the Edit option at the bottom of the Contacts interface on your iPad.

FIGURE 12-4 Contacts are listed alphabetically; you can set the sort and display order in the Settings app.

Add a Contact

As noted, to add a contact you simply click the + sign in the Contacts app. When you do, an empty Contact card will appear, where you can add information to your heart's content. Make sure to add an address if you have one; later you can touch the address to open the Maps app and get directions to the contact's location.

Did You Know?

You Can Use MobileMe or Microsoft Exchange

You can set up MobileMe on your iPad and enable Contacts. You can then sync contacts over the air with other MobileMe devices. You can also set up a Microsoft Exchange account, and obtain and sync contacts with your Exchange server at work.

To add basic contact information:

1. Open the Contacts app.
2. Click the + sign, located at the bottom of the page.
3. Fill in the basic information, including but not limited to:
   a. First and last name
   b. Phone number
   c. Email address
   d. Street address
   e. City, state, and zip

 As you begin typing in the phone, email, or URL fields, additional fields will appear. For instance, as you start to type a mobile phone number, a new field will appear under it, iPhone. If you start typing an iPhone number, a new field will appear under that, home.

 When entering information in the phone, email, and URL fields, tap the name of the field in the box on the left for more choices. For instance, next to the Email field, prior to typing any email, tap "home." You can then change the field to work, other, or even add a custom label.

4. To add additional information, scroll down to the bottom of the Contact card and click the green + sign next to Add Field. See Figure 12-5. Note all the fields you can add, shown in the illustration, including but not limited to
   a. Prefix
   b. Phonetic First Name
   c. Phonetic Last Name
   d. Nickname
   e. Job Title
   f. Birthday
5. Depending on the option you choose in Step 4, you'll have the option to input information regarding that field.
6. You can click Done now, or continue to the next set of steps to add a photo.

To add a picture for a contact:

1. If you closed the Contact card you were working on earlier, tap the contact in the left pane, and tap Edit in the right. With a Contact card open, tap Add Photo in the top-left corner.

add photo	Pico
	Ballew
	Company

To add a picture for a different contact, tap the contact name in the Contacts list and tap Edit.

FIGURE 12-5 The green + sign next to Add Field lets you add additional information.

2. You have two options, Tap Photo and Choose Photo. For now, tap Choose Photo.
3. Tap the folder that contains the picture to add.
4. Tap the picture to use.
5. If you like, drag to move and scale the picture. Note that you can also pinch to resize it.
6. Tap Use.
7. Tap Done.

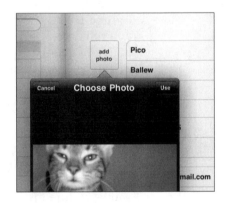

Brightness & Wallpaper	**Default Account** Joli_Ballew@tx.rr.com ❯
Picture Frame	Messages created outside of Mail will be sent from the default account.
General	Contacts
Mail, Contacts, Calendars	**Sort Order** First, Last ❯
Safari	**Display Order** First, Last ❯
	Calendars

FIGURE 12-6   You can change how contacts are sorted and displayed in Settings.

Change How Contacts Appear in the List

By default, the names in the Contacts list are listed alphabetically, sorted by a person's last name. But the names are displayed in the list with their first name listed first. To us, this is not the optimal setup. If you like, you can change the order in which the contacts are sorted and/or how they are displayed. You do that from Settings:

1. Tap Settings on the Home screen.
2. Tap Mail, Contacts, Calendars.
3. If desired, under Contacts, next to Sort Order, tap Last, First to change it to First, Last. See Figure 12-6.
4. If desired, under Contacts, next to Display Order, tap First, Last to change it to Last, First. See Figure 12-6.

Locate Contacts

You know you can scroll through your list of contacts to locate the one you want, but as your contact list grows, scrolling may not be the best way to locate the person you want. There are a few other ways to locate a contact. One is to tap the first letter of the contact's first or last name (depending on how you have your Contacts list configured) to skip to that part of the alphabet in your Contacts list. You can then locate the contact alphabetically, minus the scrolling. However, what may be the fastest way of all is searching for the contact.

To scroll or tap to find a contact:

1. In the All Contacts list, flick up or down to scroll the list.
2. Tap any letter on the left side to go to that section of the Contacts list.

Search to Locate a Contact

At the top of the Contacts list is a Search window. You can use this window to type in a part of your contact's name, and view the results in a list. If you have four contacts with a first name of Brittany, you can type **Brit**, and then select the desired contact from the list.

To search for a contact:

1. In the Contacts app, locate the Search window.
2. Touch inside the Search window to bring up the virtual keyboard.
3. Type the first few letters of the name of the contact you'd like to find, as shown in this illustration.

4. Touch the desired contact to view the Contact card.

Get a Map to a Contact's Address

You can get a map to any contact's home or place of business quickly, provided you've previously input that information in the Contact card. Just locate the contact in the Contacts app and touch the address. Here's the step-by-step example:

1. Open the Contacts app.
2. Use any method you like to locate the contact.
3. Touch the contact to open their Contact card.

4. Touch the address.
5. Maps will open and you'll have the directions you wanted.

 Note   For more information on using Maps, see Chapter 14.

Get in Touch with a Contact

The main reason you add contacts on your iPad is almost always to make it easier to email them. You may add yourself as a contact too, so that you can easily share your contact information with others, and you may add a contact just so you'll have easy access to a map to their home. However, for the most part, contacts you add are for emailing. In Mail, most of the time you only need to type a few letters of the contact's name and the information for that contact appears wherever it's needed (like the To line in an email).

Email a Contact

You have a couple of options for sending email to a contact. You can open the Contact card for a person you'd like to email in Contacts, and click their email address to open a new message in Mail, or you can open the Mail app and start a new email, and type part of the contact's name in the To line to add them.

To send an email to a contact from the Contacts app:

1. Open Contacts and locate the contact to email.
2. Tap their name to open their Contact card.
3. Tap their email address, as shown in the following illustration, to have Mail open automatically and insert the email address in the To line.

work   **Joli_Ballew@hotmail.com**

other   **joli_ballew@tx.rr.com**

home   **joli_ballew@hotmail.com**

Note   Feel free to email me at any of these addresses, at any time!

FIGURE 12-7 One way to select a contact from your Contacts list is to tap the + sign in an email and select the contact from a list.

To send an email from the Mail app:

1. Tap Mail to open it.
2. Tap the Compose button.
3. Tap the + sign to locate a contact to add, shown in Figure 12-7, or simply type the first letter of their first or last name to select them from another list that appears.

Note For more information on using email, see Chapter 4.

How to... Add a Contact from an Email

If you receive an email from someone you do not yet have in your contact list, tap the sender in the From line and tap Create New Contact. Alternatively, you can tap Add to Existing Contact.

Manage Contacts

You really don't have to do much to manage your contacts except update contact information when it changes, delete contacts you no longer need, and sync contacts to your computer. You can share a contact if you like, to send the information to someone else, but for the most part, your job is to keep the contact information up to date. Your iPad does the rest. It keeps your contacts alphabetized, enables you to easily access contacts from various apps, and makes syncing contacts with a computer (with iTunes) a breeze.

When contact information changes, you should edit the contact accordingly and in a timely manner. You never know when you may need to contact a person! To edit a contact:

1. Open the Contacts app.
2. Locate the contact to edit.
3. Tap Edit.
4. Replace the desired information.
5. Tap Done.

To delete a contact:

1. Open the Contacts app.
2. Locate the contact to delete.
3. Tap Edit.
4. Scroll down to the bottom of the page and tap Delete Contact, as shown here.

To share a contact via email:

1. Open the Contacts app.
2. Locate the contact to share.

3. Tap Share Contact.

4. Mail opens to a new mail message. Complete the message and tap Send.

Although you can initiate a FaceTime call in the Contacts app, you can also make the contact a favorite in the FaceTime app. Once marked a Favorite, it's easy to initiate a call there. To make the contact appear as a Favorite in FaceTime:

1. Open the Contacts app.
2. Locate the contact to denote as a favorite.
3. Tap Add to Favorites.

13

Manage Your Schedule

HOW TO...

- Open Calendar and explore views
- Create a Calendar event
- Add an alert for an event or set it to repeat
- Tap an event to edit it
- Navigate the Calendar
- Search the Calendar
- Add new calendars
- View a single calendar and show multiple calendars at once
- Subscribe to someone else's calendar
- Sync to verify that all calendars are updated

Perhaps (like us), you've given digital calendars a try, only to be turned off by how difficult it is to add and edit events, sync with your computer, or maintain the calendar in the long term. It's a big step—depending on a device to remember important dates like birthdays, anniversaries, interviews, and the like can be unnerving. It's difficult to completely let go of your written calendar. Those days just might be over, though. You know you can depend on your iPad; it has a long battery life, it doesn't crash or freeze up, and it's easy to sync with your computer. Starting today, you can make the transition. You can trust the Calendar app to maintain your schedule with minimal effort from you.

 Your iPad isn't going to send out an alarm or otherwise notify you of an event if you don't turn it on and use it. Once you move the slider to unlock the iPad, then you can see event notifications.

Explore the Calendar and Set Events

The Calendar app is available from the Home screen; tap it once to open it. If you haven't already synced calendar events through iTunes, an empty calendar awaits. Once in the Calendar app, you can explore different views, tap to see different calendars and calendar layouts, and add events.

To open the Calendar and explore the interface:

1. Tap the Calendar app on the Home screen.
2. At the top of the Calendar app, click Day, Week, Month, or List, as shown in the following illustration. If you've synced Calendar data with your computer, you may see existing entries, as shown here.
3. Turn the iPad 90 degrees to rotate from Landscape view to Portrait and back again.

If you keep a calendar on your computer, and if you've already synced that calendar data, you'll see entries on your calendar. If you're a PC user, you may have already synced some data from your Microsoft Outlook Calendar. If you use a Mac, you may have synced data from iCal or Microsoft Entourage. If you have a Microsoft Exchange account, you can incorporate that and receive and respond to meeting invitations too, and you can enable calendar syncing if you use MobileMe. (In fact, you may even see an Invitations button next to the Calendars button, depending on how and what you sync, although this is rare.)

You Can Incorporate Other Calendar Data

It's important to note that while the Calendar app and iTunes support only a handful of calendar applications via iTunes, you can incorporate other calendars. For instance, if you have a Gmail account and keep a calendar at Google, you can incorporate your Google Calendar with Outlook on your computer, and any events you create on your Google Calendar will be synced with Outlook, which will ultimately be synced with your iPad.

Create an Event

If you're ready to immerse yourself in the Calendar, you'll start by inputting data. Think about all of the things you could input, and make a list of dates you'd like to keep track of:

- **Birthdays and anniversaries**   Create birthdays and anniversaries as once-a-year events, and set reminders for a couple of days before the date. Then you'll have plenty of time to buy a present or card. Because you create a yearly event, you won't have to input it again.
- **Doctor and dental visits**   We all go to the doctor and dentist once or twice a year for a checkup (or we should). Create an event for this so you won't forget to make that appointment when the time is near.
- **Goals**   Create an event that is really a goal, such as what you'd like to weigh at the start of next month, the month after that, and the month after that. Your goals may include how much you'll walk, run, or bike. Of course, goals can be many other things, and only you know what you input here. Whatever you add, it'll be easier to stay on top of the things you want to achieve.
- **Deadlines**   Create events that are common deadlines, such as when quarterly taxes are due. Create events for deadlines for work projects, home projects, or the like too.
- **Travel plans**   Create events for travel dates and include flight information, rental car information, and gate information. With the information in your calendar, you can easily access it no matter where you are.
- **Yearly events**   Create events for yearly events like Election Day, National Night Out, Tax Day, golf tournaments, marathons, and even the date your cell phone subscription renews.
- **Weekly events**   Create recurring events for things that happen each week, like going to an aerobics class every Tuesday night or meeting with your parents or kids every Thursday. If you try to plan additional events, you can easily see that you already have plans. You may even want to input information about your favorite TV shows, so you can try to watch them if you're out of town.
- **Children's events**   Input your kids' soccer and baseball games, rehearsals, and recitals, and for best results, create a separate calendar for their events. You can always overlap your calendar with theirs, if you need to compare the two.
- **"Me" Time**   While you're scheduling, pencil in some "me" time. Mark off a little time each week just for yourself.

Tip Before you create an event, consider whether or not you need to create multiple calendars to organize your events. You can create a calendar for your own schedule, a separate schedule for your kids, and a third just for work. You can merge the calendars when necessary too, so you can see all of your obligations. If you think you'd benefit from multiple calendars, read the section "Work with Multiple Calendars" later in the chapter first, and then return here.

Now, create entries for every event you can. Set reminders too, and open the Calendar each day to view those entries. Before you know it, you'll be totally organized! To add an event to the calendar and add alerts and reminders:

1. Open the Calendar app.
2. Locate the + sign at the bottom of the page on the right.
3. Type the desired information:

Note If you saw an Invitations button next to the Calendar button when you opened the Calendar app, you'll likely also see an Invitees option in the Add Event window that's shown here.

   a. **Title** Tap to add a descriptive title for the event. If you're adding a birthday, for instance, type something like *Andrew's Birthday*.

   b. **Location** Tap to add a location, if applicable.

   c. **Start and End Times (or All Day Event)** Tap to configure the start and end times, or to create an all day event. Click Done after entering the desired information.

d. **Repeat**   Tap to set the event to repeat. Choose from None, Every Day, Every Week, Every 2 Weeks, Every Month, or Every Year. Click Done when finished. Use the End Repeat setting to determine when an event no longer needs to repeat.

e. **Alert**   Tap Alert to set an alert. Choose from None, 5 Minutes Before, 15 Minutes Before, 30 Minutes Before, 1 Hour Before, 2 Hours Before, 1 Day Before, 2 Days Before, or On Date of Event. Tap Done when finished.

f. **Calendar**   Tap Calendar to choose a calendar. What you see here will differ based on the calendars you have access to. You'll notice colors associated with each calendar option if you have more than one calendar. When you add an event to a specific calendar, it will appear on the calendar in that color. Click Done when finished. (If you only have one calendar, you will not see this option.)

g. **Notes**   Tap to type notes regarding the event.

4. After all the information is added, tap Done.

5. Notice the new event on the calendar, as shown in the following illustration. Tap Edit to edit the event, if desired.

Browse Events and Dates

Now that you've input some data, you can browse the calendar and your upcoming events. You can also browse the calendar for free time. There are several ways to browse the calendar and access events. You can

- Tap any event that you've already input to view the complete event. You can do this in any calendar, in Day, Week, Month, or List mode.
- In Month view, double-tap any date to view that date in the calendar in an expanded two-page Day view.

- In Day view, use your finger to scroll through events.
- Use your finger to scroll through dates using the bar that runs across the bottom of the Calendar app, or simply tap a date to jump to a specific day.
- In any view, tap an event to edit it. Note that you can delete an event in the Edit window.
- In any view, tap the Today button (bottom left) to return to the page for the current day.

Search a Calendar

When you have a lot of information in the Calendar app on your iPad, you may find that you need to search for something on it (versus scanning and scrolling). Like other apps on your iPad, Calendar has a Search window. Just type what you're looking for, and when it appears in the list, tap it to go to that event, as shown in the following illustration.

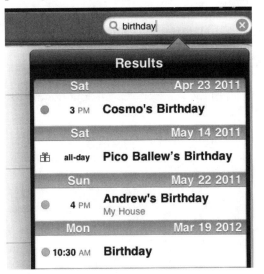

Work with Multiple Calendars

You may wear multiple hats. You could be a full-time employee, a mom or dad, a coach, a hobbyist, an athlete, and/or a caregiver. When you have multiple types of responsibilities and interests, you also have multiple schedules. That's where multiple calendars come in. To help you keep your priorities in order, you can create a calendar just for work, one just for your kid's games and your own athletic endeavors, one for the hours when you're responsible for taking care of an aging parent, and another for "me" time.

If you'd rather put all of your personal responsibilities on one calendar, though, you can. There's still a reason for keeping two or more calendars, though. You can create another calendar for your children or a spouse. You can add their events to a separate calendar, and view that calendar when you need to know where they are and what they are doing. Of course, with this plan you have to actively involve them, and make sure they input what they have planned, but they can do that on a computer that can then be synced to your iPad daily. You may even create a separate calendar for your boss.

Each calendar you create stands alone. Each calendar has events listed in its own color, and each calendar can be viewed with any other calendar when needed. With multiple calendars on a single device, you can keep track of everything.

Create Additional Calendars for Your iPad

Creating a second or third calendar isn't something you do on your iPad. You create additional calendars in the calendar application you use on your computer. For instance, in Microsoft Outlook

1. Open Calendar view in Outlook.
2. Right-click in the Calendar area in the left pane, and click New Calendar, as shown here.

3. Type the name of the new calendar, and select the appropriate Calendar folder to place it in. Click OK.

Now you can sync that calendar to your iPad, using iTunes:

1. Connect your iPad to your computer.
2. In iTunes, click the Info tab.
3. Locate Sync Calendars, and, in this example, select Outlook.
4. Click Selected Calendars.
5. Click the calendars to sync.
6. Click Apply.

To view a single calendar and show multiple calendars at once on your iPad after syncing:

1. In the Calendar app, tap Calendars.
2. Tap any calendar to show or hide it. If it has a check by it, the calendar will show; if not, it will be hidden.

Subscribe to Someone Else's Calendar

You can subscribe to compatible calendars on the Internet and have those calendar events included with the calendar you keep on your iPad. You'll find calendars everywhere and for almost anything, including calendars for your favorite sports teams, calendars for your kid's lunch program at school, calendars that detail work-related holidays, and more. Apple provides a number of free calendars if you'd like to try them out, including calendars for national holidays and sports events.

To subscribe to a calendar available from Apple:

1. Open Safari and navigate to icalshare.com.
2. Note the Calendar categories, shown in Figure 13-1.
3. Locate a calendar you'd like to include, and tap it. We'll choose US Holidays.

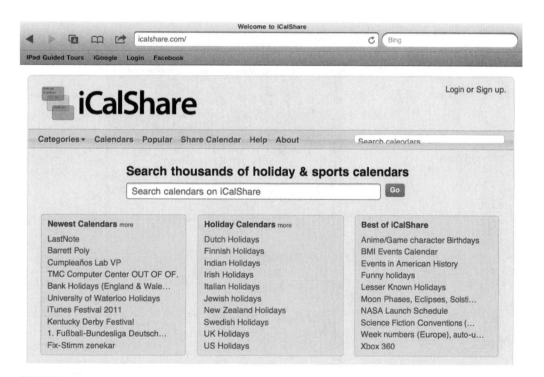

FIGURE 13-1   You can subscribe to all kinds of calendars from the iCalShare web site.

4. Tap Subscribe to Calendar.

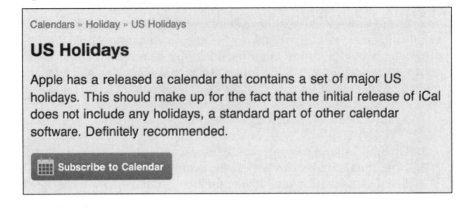

Calendars » Holiday » US Holidays

US Holidays

Apple has a released a calendar that contains a set of major US holidays. This should make up for the fact that the initial release of iCal does not include any holidays, a standard part of other calendar software. Definitely recommended.

🔳 **Subscribe to Calendar**

5. Tap Subscribe.
6. Tap View Events to see the new entries in Calendar.
7. If prompted, tap View Events again.
8. Verify that the new calendar will appear by tapping Calendar and noting that US Holidays is checked.
9. Tap outside the list to view the entries.

Set Up and Verify Syncing

In order to truly trust your calendar, you need to verify that syncing works between your iPad and your computer. This involves creating events on your iPad, connecting your iPad to your computer, and verifying that events are copied back to the calendar program on your computer. You should also find out just where those events are stored on your computer, and then configure an appointment there and verify that it is transferred to your iPad when you sync. You should be able to create events at either place and sync them automatically each time you connect your iPad to your computer.

To verify that the events you create on your iPad are copied to your computer, and to locate them:

1. Connect your iPad to your computer.
2. Click your iPad in the source pane of iTunes.
3. Click the Info tab.
4. Verify that syncing is enabled for the application you use on your computer.
5. Click Sync.
6. Open the Calendar app on your computer.
7. Locate the calendars you've created on your iPad and verify that they are enabled in your Calendar app.

14

Use Maps

HOW TO...

- Open Maps and explore the interface
- Find your present location
- Explore all views—satellite, topography, street, and terrain
- Pinch and scroll to change views
- Find a location and drive there
- Explore Street View
- Find a nearby restaurant and walk to it
- Find a route using public transportation
- Share a location
- Find a business and get information about that business
- Mark a location
- Add a bookmark

The Maps app is one of the most awesome apps on the iPad, at least in our opinion, and (unlike the iPhone), the iPad has a large enough screen that you can actually use the app effectively. You can incorporate Maps with Google's Street View when available to view a picture of your destination, and access driving routes, walking routes, and public transportation routes easily. You can search for points of interest, landmarks, businesses, restaurants, or even a specific intersection. You can easily find your present location, and if a location isn't marked on a map, such as a friend's house or park, you can mark it yourself, and save it as a bookmark. You can even share destinations and locations with others via email.

You can use Maps with either version of the iPad. The Wi-Fi model finds your location using known Wi-Fi hotspots. This means that when you want to know where you are, your iPad will gauge this based on how close or far you are from any stable known Wi-Fi hotspots. The Wi-Fi + 3G models use Wi-Fi hotspots too, but they also use GPS (Global Positioning System) and cellular towers to provide location information. Although it can all be rather complicated to explain, suffice it to say that you can use Maps no matter which iPad you own.

Explore the Maps App

You open the Maps app the same way you open any app, by tapping it once. There are several interface features to explore, and they are arranged familiarly with buttons and tabs. These include

- **Search** Tap Search when you want to view something on the map, including your present location. In contrast, tap Directions to get directions from one place to another.
- **Directions** Tap Directions to access two windows you can fill in to get directions from one place to another. You can get directions from your present location to a new location, or using any two addresses. (You don't have to input an address, though; you can input a restaurant name, street name, and more.) In between the two windows is an icon that enables you to reverse the route, if desired.

- **Location icon** Tap the Location icon (it looks like an arrow) to the left of the Bookmark icon to show your present location on a map. A blue dot appears to denote where you are.
- **Bookmarks** Tap to see bookmarks you've saved and to access them. Bookmarks are like your Favorites list in Internet Explorer, or, well, Bookmarks in Safari. There are three tabs available in the Bookmarks window:
  - **Bookmarks** A list of Bookmarks you've saved in Maps.
  - **Recents** A list of places you've recently looked up with Maps.
  - **Contacts** A list of the contacts you have in the Contacts app. You can tap any contact that has an address associated with it to access a map of the contact's location or to get directions to it.
- **The Search window(s)** When Search is selected, you'll see one Search window; when Directions is selected, two. Type the name of a location, business, or geographical feature here to perform a search for it. You can type exact street names and addresses or generic ones. See Figure 14-1.
- **Page turner/Dog ear** Tap or pull back the bottom-right corner of the Maps interface so that you can see "underneath" the Maps interface, shown in Figure 14-2. Here, you'll find options to change the view and additional options:
  - **Classic** To view a graphical representation of the map with street names, parks, and water included. See Figure 14-1.
  - **Satellite** To view the location as it appears from the sky. You can pinch and double-tap to zoom in or out, as you can with other views.

FIGURE 14-1   The Search window offers a place to type the name of a location, business, or geographical feature and find it on the map. This map is in Classic view.

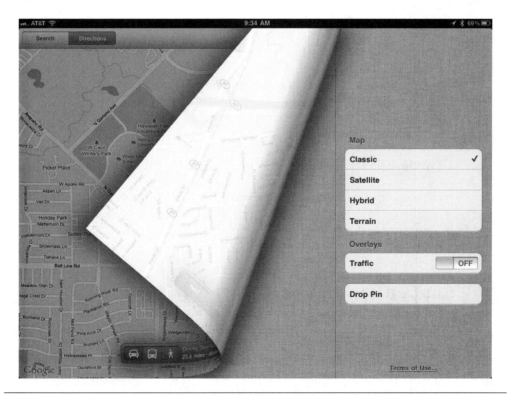

FIGURE 14-2   Additional options are offered "below" the current map.

- **Hybrid** To view a map in Classic and Satellite view, together.
- **Terrain** To view the map in another graphical representation that includes terrain features, such as elevation. In this view you'll also see street names as well.
- **Traffic** To show traffic conditions, if available, for the current map. Colors that denote traffic are red, yellow, and green.
- **Drop Pin** To drop a pin anywhere on a map, tap this and then tap and hold where you'd like the pin to appear. You can then tap the pin and the associated "i" to add it to your Contacts, Share the location, and more.

The best way to explore the Maps app is to first find your current location, and then, tap the various options for views to see how they look. Because you're probably familiar with your surroundings, you can easily recognize what's around you. Once the iPad knows your current location, you can easily browse nearby streets, businesses, and even the current traffic, if available.

To find your present location:

1. Open Maps.
2. Tap the Location icon, shown here.
3. Tap the blue letter "i" to learn more about your location, including the address and the option to share your location with others, create a bookmark, and even view a picture, if available.

With a map on the page, you're ready to explore views. To switch views:

1. Touch the bottom-right corner of the map to turn the page and see what's underneath.
2. Touch any view option to see that view on the map.
3. Repeat to explore all views.
4. In any view, use your finger to scroll through the map. You'll learn more navigational techniques next.

While in any map and in any view, try out these navigational techniques:

- Pinch your fingers toward each other to zoom out on a map.
- Pull your fingers outward to zoom in on an area on a map.
- Tap twice to zoom in. (Pinch to zoom back out.)

Did You Know?

You Can Tap the Blue Location Icon to Reorient the Map

When the location icon is gray, tapping it drops a pin on the map at your current location and the Location icon turns blue. Tap the blue Location icon and the map will be reoriented with the direction you are facing. Tapping the Location icon once again returns the map to its "standard" orientation.

- Reposition the iPad from Landscape to Portrait view and back by turning the iPad 90 degrees left or right.
- Tap and drag across the screen to see more of the map.

Go Places and Do Things

So you know where you are and how to navigate the map by pinching or scrolling, and by tapping to zoom in. Now it's time to actually use Maps to perform tasks. In this section you'll learn several things including how to get driving directions to a specific address, how to locate a business and restaurant on a map and view pictures of them, how to locate a nearby restaurant and get walking directions or directions using available public transportation, and how to locate a business, among other things. Once you've found a location, you can tap to see the Information screen, where you can get directions, a phone number, and other information regarding it. Finally, you'll learn how to mark a site on a map that isn't currently marked as a business, park, restaurant, landmark, or the like. You can mark your own house, where you work, a friend's house, a park, or anything else you like so that you can more easily share it or access it. By marking and then bookmarking your favorite locations, you'll have easy access to them later.

Find a Location and Drive There

You can replace all of your physical maps and map books with your iPad, provided you are certain that you will be able to access satellite information and the Internet from wherever you are (an iPad 3G model is ideal for this). You can type in any address to obtain driving directions to the address from your present location, and scroll through maps digitally to view the terrain or route. If you need directions from one place to another, but one of those places is not available in Contacts or any recent lists, you can also type in two addresses. This enables you to obtain directions from a starting point to an end point; from anywhere to anywhere.

Caution If you are going to be travelling in remote areas where you may not have Internet access, you may want to bring along those physical maps, just in case you need them.

To find an address and get directions to that address:

1. In Maps, tap Directions.
2. By default, the starting point is your current location. For best results, tap the Location icon to make sure Maps knows where you are before going any further. If you want to start from a different address, tap in that window and type a new address.
3. Tap in the second window to type the ending address. Note that you can type something other than an address, though. As you can see in Figure 14-3, I've searched for Chase Place, a local bar and grill.

FIGURE 14-3 It's easy to get directions using Maps, especially if you start from your current location.

4. At the bottom of the page, tap the driving icon. It looks like a car.
5. Click Start, and then advance through the directions using the arrow buttons.

 You can open the Contacts app and touch a contact's address to get a map of that location.

You Can Use a Digital Compass to Find Which Way Is North

Tap the Location icon two times. This enables the digital compass. The map is "freed" to orient itself to your position when the compass is called on. You'll see a small compass icon in the top right of the screen when the compass is enabled. To test it out, turn in a circle while holding the iPad. You'll see the map orient itself to your relative position.

If you get a message about recalibrating the compass or that the compass can't be enabled because of interference, hold the iPad firmly with two hands and move it in a figure-eight motion. This recalibrates the compass and may resolve any problems you have with it.

Explore Street View

Street View is a view available via Google Maps that allows you to view pictures of a location or your destination. This feature provides 360-degree views of many locations across the world. You can access these images from the information window that appears in the pin associated with a location. (You have to tap the small "i" that appears when you tap the pin to get to this window.) When Street View is available, you'll see a thumbnail in the information window, as shown here.

If you tap the thumbnail, you'll enter full-screen mode. While in full-screen mode, you can drag your finger across the screen to see what's to the left and right of the location, or even what's across the street. When you're finished exploring, tap the small icon in the bottom-right corner to return to Maps, as shown here.

 Tip   To hide an information window, tap outside of it. To show it again, tap the pin on the map.

Find a Nearby Restaurant and Walk to It

Another way you can use Maps is to locate your current position in a city, tap the Search button in the top-left corner, and then search for nearby restaurants. To search, simply tap inside the Search window and type **Restaurants**. Touch any pin on a restaurant result, and tap the "i" to view the phone number and address, and if available, the restaurant's web site. Once you find a restaurant you like, you can get directions to it easily. As with other Maps results, you can get driving directions, but you can also get walking directions or directions using public transportation.

To search for and find a nearby restaurant:

1. In Maps, click the Location icon to pinpoint your present location.
2. Tap Search.
3. Touch inside the Search window to bring up the keyboard.
4. Type **Restaurants**. Tap Search on the keyboard.
5. Tap any pin on the map to see the restaurant name, address, and to get directions.

To get walking directions to the restaurant:

1. In any restaurant's information page (which you access by tapping the pin for it), tap Directions To Here.
2. On the map, tap the icon to get walking directions. The icon looks like a man walking, as shown in this illustration.

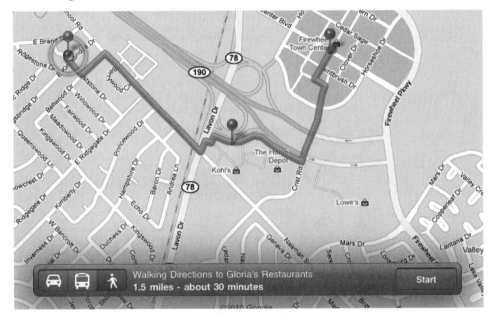

Find a Route Using Public Transportation

You can also get directions using a route that incorporates public transportation. If you're in a city, and on foot, but the restaurant or business you need to get to is too far to walk, this is a good alternative. You find a public transportation route using the same method you use to find a walking route, except you tap the icon that looks like a bus instead of tapping the icon that looks like a man walking.

FIGURE 14-4   Look for the bus icon to get information about the route you need to take.

Once the route is on the screen, look for icons that detail how to get there. You'll see icons that show you where you must walk, and icons that tell you where you can ride. Tap the icon to see more information. Figure 14-4 shows an example. Although it's hard to see, we've tapped a very small blue icon of a bus. Then, we tapped the "i" that was associated with it. Finally, we see that we need to get on the DART bus, #513.

Share a Location via Email

If you'd like to invite others to meet you at a location, you can click Share Location from the information page. You'll see the option Share Location on every information page, as shown in this illustration. Tap it and a new email will open, where you can complete the invitation.

Locate a Business

Chances are when you need the phone number or address of a business, you head to your computer or cell phone and not the stack of phone books piled up in your laundry room. Phone books are cumbersome (and often unavailable), and after you find the address and phone number you still have to drag out a map, call the business, or head back to your computer to get directions to it. That's all changed with Google Maps, always-on Internet, and computer technology. Now when you want to contact a business, you simply search for it online.

You can use Maps and your iPad to locate a business, obtain the phone number and address, and get directions, all with only a few taps of your finger.

To find a business and get a phone number, address, and directions:

1. Open Maps.
2. Tap the Search window.
3. Type the name of the business.
4. Locate the business on the map. Tap the small letter "i" to access the business's information page.
5. Call the number, get directions, add to bookmarks, or share the location, as desired.

Mark a Location of Your Own

You know now that when you search for a restaurant or business, Maps sets down a pin in its location. You touch the pin to get more information about it, including directions. You probably also know that not all locations have pins. A brand new restaurant won't, for instance, since the information about it has not had time to get to the Internet servers responsible for providing the information to Google Services. There may not be a pin for the establishment where you work, and maybe not even for your home. You can add your own pins, though, simply by tapping and holding an area of the screen.

To mark a location (and save it as a bookmark):

1. Locate the location on a map.
2. Tap and hold to drop a pin.
3. Click the letter "i" to open the information page.

4. To name the location and save it, tap Add to Bookmarks, and name the bookmark as desired.
5. Tap Save.

Find a Landmark

You can locate (and often view) landmarks, points of interest, and even museums and art galleries, by searching for them in Maps. For instance, you can search Maps for University of Texas, Austin, and view the campus in Maps using Street View. You can have Maps locate your current location and type **Museum of Art** to locate the nearest art museum. You can even search for the White House or the Statue of Liberty, although we can't guarantee there's a picture of that available.

To find a landmark and attempt to view it in Street View:

1. In Maps, type the name of the landmark you'd like to view.
2. Tap the letter "i" to bring up the information page.
3. If a picture is available, click it. If a picture is not available but a web site is, click that.

Bookmark a Location

It takes a little bit of effort to locate a place on a map. Generally you have to search for it, and on occasion you type in an address. It's not a big deal, but if it's a location you think you'll need to look up again, you may as well make a note of it. So, once you've located a site you want to revisit, you should bookmark it. A bookmark enables you to easily access the location again without having to search for it. Bookmarks act like Favorites for web sites. You click the bookmark and you're offered the location you marked. This makes it very easy to share a location later, or revisit it should you need to.

To add a bookmark for a location:

1. Locate any place in Maps you'd like to bookmark via search or dropping a pin.
2. Tap to open the information page.
3. Tap Add to Bookmarks.
4. Accept the name of the bookmark or type your own.

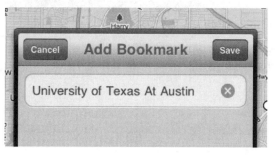

5. Tap Save.
6. Tap outside the Information window to close it.

How to... ## Access a Bookmark

After you've saved bookmarks, you have easy access to them:

1. Tap the Bookmarks icon in Maps.
2. Note the three tabs at the bottom of the Bookmarks window. Tap Bookmarks. See Figure 14-5.
3. Tap the bookmark to visit.

FIGURE 14-5 The Bookmarks window offers a place to access saved bookmarks as well as recent places and contacts.

15

Use Notes

HOW TO...

- Open Notes and explore views
- Create a note
- Fix spelling errors
- Use accelerated typing tools
- Paste text copied from Contacts and Maps
- Delete a note
- Review notes
- Edit a note
- Sync notes
- Email a note

The Notes app is like having a legal pad with you all the time. It looks like the familiar legal pad you're used to, and once you write down a note, it stays there, just as a note on a legal pad would (meaning that you don't have to click Save and name the note). You can review notes you've written, and even if you stop taking notes to listen to music or check your email, when you come back to the Notes app, the note you were working on is there, ready to complete or edit, just where you left off. You can easily delete a note, just as you can with a legal pad, and you can carry notes on your iPad with you anywhere you go, even to the grocery store.

Unlike a legal pad, though, the Notes app will let you know when you misspell something and may add punctuation while you type. It'll even offer advice when replacing misspelled words. And, unlike with a legal pad, you can email notes to others or to yourself, and you can sync notes to your computer using iTunes.

Creating a note is easy; you simply tap anywhere in a note and use the keyboard to write what needs to be written. The beauty of Notes is just that—the simplicity of it.

Create Notes

Think of all the things you write down in a day. You probably jot down phone numbers, grocery lists, to-do lists, and all kinds of reminders that need to be dealt with immediately, or at least within a couple of days. You may write down a recipe, a gift idea, or an ongoing list of items you need at the home improvement store. If you keep these notes on bits of paper, you will likely misplace them often. At the very least, your notes are mismanaged and in various places around your home, office, car, or purse, making them difficult to use efficiently.

You can use your iPad and the Notes app to get organized and to stay organized. You can type your most recent notes while working through this chapter, and make it a point to keep new notes on your iPad from here forward. When you choose to do this, you simplify your life by having everything in one place; everything is neat and orderly, and easily accessible. You'll never lose a note again.

First, open Notes and explore the available views:

1. Tap Notes on the Home screen.
2. View the Notes app in Portrait view. Note that there's a + sign for creating a new note, and icons at the bottom of the page. Now, turn the iPad sideways to view it in Landscape mode. You can see a list of any existing notes in this view.

To create a note:

1. If you've never created a note, simply tap inside the blank note already on the screen. If there's a note there already, tap the + sign to create a new note.
2. Use the keyboard to type. You do not have to save the note; it will remain in your Notes list until you delete it.
3. The title of your note (in the list in the left pane in Landscape mode) is whatever you typed into the first line of the note, so you should make it descriptive so it's easy to find the note you need later.

Correct Errors in Notes

Although the Notes you keep in the Notes app are often personal notes to yourself such as grocery lists and to-do lists, Notes will still track spelling and suggest punctuation for you as you type. This only works if you have Auto-Correction enabled in Settings, under General, and Keyboard. When Notes finds spelling errors, it will underline them using a red dotted line, giving you the option to fix them.

To see how spelling correction works in Notes:

1. Open Notes and start a new note. (Click the + sign to create a new note.)
2. Use the keyboard to type the note, creating misspelled words while typing. Type **Pick up mcbrini** (which is our really misspelled version of "macaroni") and press the Space bar to let your iPad know you think *mcbrini* is a word. You should now see the red, dotted line.
3. If you see a red dotted line underneath a word, tap it to view the suggested correction (that is, if it isn't corrected for you).
4. Tap the correction to apply it. The red dotted line will disappear when you do. Figure 15-1 shows another example.

FIGURE 15-1 When you misspell a word and then tap it, you'll see suggestions for replacing the word.

Use Advanced Notes Tools

The Notes app includes a few tools to help you type faster and incorporate data from other applications. The accelerated typing tools track what you write and suggest words, among other things. You can also use your finger to place the cursor anywhere in a note to edit it. You can also copy text from other apps, including Mail, Safari, Calendar, Contacts, and Maps to paste that text into a Note.

You'll learn about the available accelerated typing tools as you type. For instance, if, while typing, you misspell a word that the iPad's dictionary knows, it will either fix the spelling error automatically or offer a suggestion. Press the Space bar to accept the suggestion. If Notes makes a suggestion that isn't right, tap the X next to the suggested word (shown in the following illustration) to "teach" your iPad that this is not what you want, or just keep typing. Most of the time, you'll find that the iPad has guessed the word correctly, as shown here.

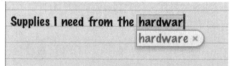

As with other apps, you can tap and hold to see options to select text. Once selected, you can tap Cut, Copy, or Paste. If you've selected a single word, you may also see Replace, if the dictionary has any suggestions for the word. (Note that you won't see the Replace option if you have Auto-Correction and Check Spelling turned off in Settings.) And tapping and holding produces the magnifying glass, which you can use to navigate to a specific word in the note by dragging it to the appropriate area of the note. There's more on this later, but here's a teaser.

Note There are typing tips scattered throughout this book, and you can incorporate many of them here.

Incorporate Text from Contacts and Maps

You know how to copy text and how to paste it. This topic has been covered throughout the book, and had its own section in Chapter 4. You may not know that you can copy text from other apps and paste it into Notes, though. You can't paste pictures into a note, but you can paste text.

To copy an address from Maps and paste it in Notes:

1. Tap Maps and locate an address. For more information on Maps, refer to Chapter 14.
2. Tap the address from the Information window, and tap Copy, as shown here. Copying data from a Contact card looks very similar to this.

phone	**+1 (214) 571-1000**
home page	http: Copy sitdallas.com/
address	**325 North. St. Paul Street Dallas TX United States**

3. Tap the Home button and open Notes.
4. Tap inside an existing note or create a new note (and then tap inside it).
5. Tap Paste.
6. The text will be pasted, using the default font selected in Settings, under Notes.

> Today
>
> 325 North. St. Paul Street
> Dallas TX
> United States

To copy an email address in Contacts and paste it in Notes:

1. Open Contacts and locate the contact to copy.
2. Tap and hold on the email address for the contact.
3. Tap Copy.
4. Close Contacts and open Notes.
5. Tap inside an existing note or create a new note (and then tap inside it).
6. Tap Paste.

Did You Know? Your iPad Can "MultiTask"

You can double-tap the Home button to leave one app open while accessing another, provided that the app has already been opened and is capable of "multitasking."

Manage Notes

If you think about the Notes app as a glorified legal pad, it'll be easy to visualize deleting a note, locating existing notes, and editing notes. The Notes app offers a Trash Can icon on every note you create to make it easy to get rid of notes you no longer need. The source pane (available in Landscape view) makes it just as easy to locate notes you've previously written, and by flicking upward you can scroll notes that extend more than one page. Finally, editing a note is as simple as touching the note and typing, or touching and holding to access cut, copy, paste, replace, and additional items.

Shortcut   If you prefer Portrait view for your notes, use the left and right arrow keys at the bottom of the page to see other notes you've written (also available in Landscape view).

To access previous notes and delete a note:

1. Locate the note to delete:
   a. In Portrait view, use the left and right arrow keys to find the note.
   b. In Landscape view, tap the note in the source pane.
2. Once you've found the note to delete, click the Trash Can icon, as shown here.

To edit a note:

1. Locate the note to edit.
2. To add something to a note:
   a. Tap inside the note where you'd like to start typing.
   b. Type the additional information.
3. To erase something that's on a note:
   a. Tap any note and hold briefly.
   b. Tap Select or Select All.
   c. Tap Cut to delete the selected text, noting that you can use the blue grab points to select more or less text.

325 North. St. Paul Street
Dallas TX   Cut   Copy   Paste   Replace...
United States-
=====9999999999999999999999999999999999999999
9999999999999999999999999999999999999999puoiu09
90880hg

4. To correct a single letter in a note or to add text in the middle of a note or sentence:
   a. Tap and hold until the magnifying glass appears.

   b. Drag the magnifying glass to the location to perform the edits. Lift up your finger.

   c. Use the Back button on the keyboard to erase letters one at a time, and use the keyboard to type.

5. To replace a word in a note with another word:

   a. Tap the word to replace.

   b. Tap Select.

   c. Tap Replace. (You won't always see this option.)

   d. Choose a word from the list or tap outside the options to make the suggestions go away.

6. To cut or copy text:

   a. Tap any word that's included in what you'd like to cut or copy.

   b. Tap Select to select a single word or Select All to select everything.

   c. Use the blue circles at the beginning and end of the selected text to choose more or less text.

   d. Tap Cut or Copy.

Share Notes

There are several ways to share notes, and one of them is to sync them with your computer (in essence, sharing them with yourself). You sync notes the same way you sync music, contacts, and pictures; you connect your iPad to your computer, tell iTunes you want to sync notes, and let iTunes manage the rest. You can then access the notes on your computer, and even change data on them. The next time you sync, the changes will be synced to the notes on your iPad.

There are other ways to share notes. Although you'll probably mostly create notes for your own personal use, you may occasionally want to share a note with others. Perhaps you've found the perfect banana cream pie recipe, have a phone number to share, or want to delegate a to-do list to your spouse. You can share these notes via email.

Finally, you can email yourself a note. That email can arrive just about anywhere you need it, including on your home computer, your email-enabled cell phone (such as a BlackBerry or iPhone), or even a handheld PDA you use for work. This is a great option when you need to get a note to another device quickly, and beats any other option that includes syncing the note to your phone and somehow transferring it using another method.

Sync Notes

If you use a compatible program on your computer (like Microsoft Outlook, for instance) that allows you to create and view notes, you can sync the notes you create on your iPad to your computer. Any changes you make to any notes, whether they are on your computer or your iPad, will be synced when you connect the two next time. You have to set up iTunes to sync Notes, as you do with other data.

To set up iTunes to sync Notes data and to sync existing notes:

1. Create a few notes on your iPad.
2. Connect your iPad to your computer.
3. When iTunes opens, click the iPad in the source pane.
4. From the Info tab, set Notes to sync automatically.
5. Select a source to sync notes with, if you have more than one option. See Figure 15-2.
6. Click Sync.

FIGURE 15-2 You have to tell iTunes you want to sync notes.

To verify that syncing is working properly:

1. Disconnect your iPad from your computer.
2. Locate a note on your computer, open it, and make changes to it.
3. Save the changes.
4. Connect your iPad to the computer, and sync again.
5. On your iPad, open Notes to verify that changes to the note were applied and synced.

 Tip If you have trouble syncing, you may have to wait for an update. There seem to be some problems with syncing, especially with 64-bit machines running Microsoft Outlook 2010.

Email a Note

You may need to email a note to someone, or you may want to email a note to yourself to get it on another device (like a BlackBerry) quickly. Emailing a note is as simple as tapping the Mail icon in any note and filling out the new email that appears.

To send a note via email:

1. Make sure your iPad is connected to the Internet.
2. In Notes, open the note to email.
3. Click the Mail button.
4. Complete the email and tap Send.

PART VI

Accessibility and Security

16

Accessibility

HOW TO...

- Enable and explore VoiceOver
- Disable VoiceOver
- Enable and use Zoom
- Use Large Text
- Enable and use White-on-Black display
- Enable and use Mono Audio
- Explore additional accessibility options
- Enable and use closed captioning
- Explore hardware options

If you have any kind of disability, be it vision, hearing, or mobility, you can rest easy knowing that the iPad offers at least a few accessibility options. And, if you've purchased accessibility apps for an existing iPhone, those apps should work on the iPad too. There are several accessibility options that come with your iPad: VoiceOver, Zoom, Large Text, White on Black, Mono Audio, Speak Auto-Text, and Triple-Click Home. Of course, the iPad's size is a boon too; because the device is larger than many other mobile devices, it's easier for those with vision, hearing, and mobility disabilities to use. And there are a few things that you can configure to help you use your iPad that aren't technically accessibility options, such as setting a minimum font size for emails or zooming in on faces during a Picture Frame slideshow.

There are also hardware options to explore. If you have trouble typing on the iPad's virtual keyboard, you can purchase an optional wireless keyboard. If you have a vision problem, the feel of the tactile keyboard may be just what you need to type effectively. Beyond keyboards, the iPad supports more than 30 Bluetooth wireless Braille displays right out of the box. For more information, visit http://www.apple.com/accessibility/iphone/braille-display.html. And, although the iPad's speaker is pretty loud, there is still an option to connect external speakers. This means you can connect headphones too. If you have a hearing disability, one of these options may work for you.

The iPad Can Be Part of a Therapy Program or Perfect for the Elderly

The iPad is not a complex device. For those with cognitive disabilities, this is a plus. You tap to open an app, and you tap to make that app do something. This makes the iPad the perfect device for those with a brain injury, intellectual disability, or neurological impairments. This also makes it a great device for older individuals who are overwhelmed by the idea of using a computer. The iPad is not intimidating, and you never hear of one "crashing" or ceasing to work because you've pressed the wrong buttons or key combinations. iPads shouldn't get viruses either, and they don't need a lot of attention when it comes to updates and staying secure. It's just what the doctor ordered!

Enable and Use VoiceOver

Your iPad includes VoiceOver, a feature that will read what's on the screen if you're blind or visually impaired (or learning a new language). Once VoiceOver is activated, to use it, you simply tap the screen. When you tap, you'll hear a description of the item under your finger and a black rectangle will appear (called the VoiceOver cursor). You can then drag, double-tap, or flick to control the iPad. VoiceOver speaks 21 languages, so you can have it speak to you in your native tongue, and it works with all of the applications built into iPad.

Note VoiceOver only works with the built-in iPad apps and third-party apps that specifically support it.

VoiceOver offers a lot of features, too many to detail here. But it's all spelled out in the *iPad User Guide*, which is bookmarked in Safari. However, to help you get started, here are a few introductory steps you can take:

1. To enable VoiceOver, tap Settings, General, and then Accessibility.
2. Tap VoiceOver; it's off by default. See Figure 16-1.
3. Move the slider from Off to On.
4. Note the practice tips underneath the slider. Tap any item to have the item read out loud (for instance, tap *To select an item*).
5. Note the other settings. You can change the speaking rate, use phonetics, and even change what happens when you type.

Tip To access the options for Typing Feedback, tap it once to select it, and then double-tap quickly to access the page that offers the options. To return to the VoiceOver options, tap once to select the VoiceOver button, then quickly twice to move back to it.

6. Press the iPad's Home button to exit Settings.

Settings	General	Accessibility	
Notifications	On		
Location Services	On	VoiceOver	Off >
Cellular Data		Zoom	Off >
Brightness & Wallpaper		Large Text	Off >
Picture Frame		White on Black	OFF
General			
Mail, Contacts, Calendars		Mono Audio	OFF
Safari		Speak Auto-text	OFF
iPod		Automatically speak auto-corrections and auto-capitalizations.	
Video		Triple-click Home	Off >

FIGURE 16-1   There are several Accessibility options in Settings, General.

Note   We're not going to address all of the Accessibility features available on your iPad, especially all of the things available in the VoiceOver section. We just wanted you to know that they're available should you be interested. Apple has devoted several web pages to this, though, and we encourage you to visit www.apple.com/accessibility/iPad to learn more.

Here are a few things to experiment with while VoiceOver is enabled:

- Use a three-finger swiping motion to move to another screen on the iPad.
- Tap once to select Safari; tap two times to open it. Tap any words on the page to have them read to you.
- Double-tap anywhere on the screen to activate a selected app once it's selected, even on another app's icon.
- Tap the Home button to return to the Home screen.
- Tap Settings. Tap Settings twice more, quickly, to enter Settings.
- Tap Include in Rotor. Double-tap to enable this feature.
- With the Rotor enabled, you can rotate two fingers on the screen to make a gesture, as if you were turning a dial. These options can be used to change how VoiceOver moves through a document. As an example, a flick up or down might move the cursor through the text one word at a time. But when the Character setting is selected, the same gesture will move the cursor through the text character by character instead. You can also use the rotor to navigate web pages. When you're on a web page, the rotor will show the names of elements like headers, links, form boxes, images, and more. You select a setting, then flick up and down to move to the previous or next occurrence of that item on the page. This lets you skip the items in between.

To disable VoiceOver, you'll have to use specific gestures to get back to the Settings options and the VoiceOver On/Off slider:

1. If you aren't on the Home screen that offers access to Settings, use three fingers to flick to that page, or simply double-tap the iPad's Home button.
2. Tap Settings one time.
3. Double-tap to open Settings.
4. Turn the iPad to Portrait view to have access to the Accessibility settings.
5. Tap the Accessibility button once to select it, and twice to open it.
6. Tap the VoiceOver option once to select it, and then double-tap to access the slider.
7. Tap the slider once to select it. Double-tap to turn VoiceOver off.

How to... **Enable VoiceOver in iTunes**

To enable VoiceOver in iTunes, connect your iPad, and under the Summary tab, click Configure Universal Access. Click VoiceOver, as shown here.

Version

Check for Update

Restore

Options

Manually manage music and videos

Encrypt iPad backup | Change Password...

Configure Universal Access...

Universal Access

Seeing: ● VoiceOver
○ Zoom
○ Neither

☐ Use white-on-black display
☐ Speak Auto-text

Hearing: ☐ Use mono audio
☐ Show closed captions when available

OK | Cancel

Did You Know?

The iPad Has Built-in Braille Displays

Your iPad includes built-in support for Braille displays that use Bluetooth wireless technology. Braille displays with input keys and other controls can be used to control the iPad when VoiceOver is turned on.

Enable and Use Zoom

Another option if you are visually impaired is Zoom. Zoom lets you magnify the iPad's entire screen up to five times its original size, and it works with any application. Once you've zoomed in, you can move the screen in any direction to view what's on it. Zoom works with every app and in every screen, including the Unlock and Spotlight screens.

To enable and use Zoom:

1. Tap Settings, General, and then Accessibility.
2. Tap the Zoom option.
3. Move the slider from Off to On.

Accessibility	Zoom	
Zoom		OFF

Zoom magnifies the entire screen.

To zoom
Double-tap with three fingers.

To move around the screen
Drag three fingers while zoomed.

To change zoom
With three fingers, double-tap and drag up or down.

4. Note the gestures to move around the screen:
   a. Double-tap with three fingers to zoom in one time.
   b. Drag three fingers to move around the screen.
   c. Double-tap with three fingers, and on the last tap, drag up or down to increase or decrease the zoom level.
5. To disable Zoom, move the slider from On to Off in Settings | General | Accessibility, and Zoom.

FIGURE 16-2 Select one of the Large Text options to make viewing Contacts, Mail, and Notes easier.

Use Large Text

You can make text larger in Contacts, Mail, and Notes. In Settings, tap General, tap Accessibility, and then tap Large Text, and tap one of the options shown in Figure 16-2. Here you can see how much larger the information is in Notes.

Enable and Use White-on-Black Display

White-on-Black display is a high-contrast display for the visually impaired. The name tells the story; when this feature is enabled, you'll see white letters on a black background. If colors and fonts make it difficult for you to read what's on the screen, try this option.

To enable and use White-on-Black display:

1. Tap Settings, General, and Accessibility.
2. Tap the slider for White on Black.
3. Tap again to disable it.

Enable and Use Mono Audio

If you have a hearing disability that affects only one ear, you can enable Mono Audio. When you enable Mono Audio, you tell the iPad to combine the left and right channels of stereo audio so that the sound is identical for each ear. When you wear headphones, you can be sure that all parts of a recording are being broadcast identically to both ears.

To enable and use Mono Audio, tap Settings, tap General, tap Accessibility, and tap the slider for Mono Audio to enable it. See Figure 16-3.

Explore Additional Accessibility Features

There are a handful of additional Accessibility features available from Accessibility, including Speak Auto-Text and Triple-Click Home. There are a few more scattered about the iPad, including changing the minimum font size for email messages, changing the font and font size in iBooks, and if you want to stretch it a little, zooming in on faces when showing pictures with Picture Frame. You can also set a maximum volume limit for your iPad (should your hearing aids distort or buzz if you play music too loudly), or change how quickly slides change in a slideshow so you'll have time to view the picture and make it out.

 If you want to protect your children's hearing, enable a volume limit.

Mono Audio	OFF
Speak Auto-text	OFF
Automatically speak auto-corrections and auto-capitalizations.	

FIGURE 16-3   Enable Mono Audio to combine audio channels.

Speak Auto-Text

When you enable Speak Auto-Text, your iPad will automatically speak auto-corrections and auto-capitalizations when they are made. This gives you an opportunity to accept or reject those changes, and to note what changes have been made for you. You access this feature from Settings | General | Accessibility.

Triple-Click Home

You can enable Triple-Click Home to have an easier way to turn some Accessibility features on or off by pressing the Home button three times. When you turn on this feature, you can configure it so that a triple-click toggles VoiceOver, White on Black, or Zoom, or you can set it to ask what you want to do. You access this feature from Settings | General | Accessibility.

Accessibility	Home	
Triple-click the Home Button:		
Off		✓
Toggle VoiceOver		
Toggle White on Black		
Toggle Zoom		
Ask		

Minimum Font Size for Email

From Settings, and then Mail, Contacts, Calendars, under Mail, set a minimum font size for email messages. Options include Small, Medium, Large, Extra Large, and Giant. Giant isn't as large as you might expect it to be, but at least it's quite a bit bigger, than say, Medium.

Change Font Size and Type in iBooks

When reading a book in iBooks, tap the Font button and tap Fonts to have access to the options. Tap the larger A to make the text larger, and if desired, select a new font.

Show Faces in Picture Frame

In the Picture Frame settings, you have the option to zoom in on faces during the Picture Frame show. During a Picture Frame show, faces will be easier to see if they are zoomed in on. The iPad can't discern all faces and won't zoom in on every one, but it will be able to zoom in on some of them.

You can only access this setting if the Transition is set to Dissolve, and it is not available if the Transition is set to Origami. To configure this, from Settings in Picture Frame, set the Transition to Dissolve, and then move the slider for Zoom In On Faces from Off to On.

 If the pictures in a slideshow move too quickly and you can't make out what's on each slide, change the slideshow duration to its maximum, 20 seconds.

Maximum Volume Limit in iPod

From Settings, in iPod, tap Off next to Volume Limit to set a volume limit with a slider and to lock it. If you opt to lock the volume limit, you'll need to input a code before you can change it.

Enable and Use Closed Captioning

We talked a little about closed captioning in Chapter 11. This chapter wouldn't be complete without addressing closed captioning again, though. Closed captioning displays subtitles on movies and videos that explain what's going on (if music is playing or there are creaking sounds on the stairwell), and also provides the dialogue for the movie or video in text provided at the top or bottom of the screen. If you are deaf or hard of hearing, this allows you to watch a movie without missing any of the dialogue or background noises.

Closed captions are built into media, so you have to make sure you're obtaining media with closed captions included in them to use this feature. Movies and podcasts with closed captioning are available at the iTunes Store. You won't yet find closed captions at places like Netflix, though. This is because Netflix would have to (basically) duplicate each movie, and insert closed captions in the copy. This is prohibitive in terms of time, cost, and technology.

To enable and use closed captioning:

1. Tap Settings, and tap Video.
2. Move the slider for Closed Captioning from Off to On.

Explore Hardware Options

As noted in the introduction, there are several hardware options you can employ to assist you in accessing your iPad. There are keyboards for typing, and you can attach speakers and headphones. If you're having trouble using your iPad or hearing what you play on it, consider these optional items. Watch for additional hardware devices in the future, including those that will allow users with more severe disabilities to access the iPad using third-party devices.

Explore Apple's iPad 2 Dock, the Smart Cover, and Wireless Keyboards

Apple's iPad 2 Dock is useful if you have trouble physically holding the iPad. The Dock offers easy access to charging, and an audio out port for connecting speakers. You can attach the Camera Connection Kit and the Digital AV Adapter to the Dock, which is a plus as well. There are a few problems with the Dock, though, so before you run out and buy one, consider this; it can only hold the iPad in Portrait mode, so it's not great for watching movies, and the viewing angle isn't adjustable. If you want a stand that can hold the iPad in Landscape mode, consider the Smart Cover. It protects the screen, can automatically wake/sleep the iPad when you open/close the cover, and it folds into a triangular shape (held securely with magnets) that can support the iPad in Landscape mode.

In addition to purchasing something that can hold the iPad for you, you might also want to consider a wireless keyboard. Wireless keyboards, should you opt for one, often offer buttons to change the volume, skip to the next song or a previous one, enable Caps Lock, and more. There are lots of keyboards to choose from too, and some (from Zagg for instance) also come with a stand to hold the iPad and house the keyboard.

Explore Speakers and Headphones

If you visit the Apple Store online to shop specifically for iPad accessories, and perform a search for "iPad speakers," you'll find several listed. The same is true if you shop for headphones. You don't have to buy these products from the Apple store, though. This is because just about any speakers and headphones will work with the iPad, and you likely already have something you can use. If you want to buy either from the Apple Store, though, simply search the store for what you want.

A search for speakers provides all kinds of options including:

- Rechargeable mini-speakers perfect for traveling
- Speaker systems perfect for viewing movies at home
- Wireless speakers to be used with AirPlay
- Docking stations that have built-in speakers

Tip Before purchasing Bluetooth devices or docks, verify that they are compatible with the iPad.

A search for headphones provides plenty of options too, including:

- Small, in-ear ear buds
- Travel headphones
- Over-ear or on-ear headphones
- Behind-the-head headphones

And speaking of headphones, as you know, you can use stereo Bluetooth headphones with the iPad, but there are also headphones made specifically for the iPad, iPhone, and iPod, which include remote controls and a microphone built onto the cable. Apple's latest In-Ear headphones, for instance, include an iPad-compatible remote built into the cable that controls volume, play, pause, and track skip, and also includes a microphone. This remote functionality might be just what you need.

17

Security

HOW TO...

- Protect your iPad with a passcode
- Enable restrictions
- Configure parental controls
- Sign out of iTunes, the App Store, and web sites
- Secure Safari
- Avoid phishing scams
- View usage data settings
- Set up Find My iPad

There are a few features available on your iPad to help you secure it, like the ability to create a passcode that must be entered to unlock your iPad and the option to disable apps, including Safari, YouTube, iTunes, and others. You can also set parental controls to disallow movies, music, and other media that have a specific rating you select.

You can do things to keep you and your iPad safe too, including signing out of iTunes and the App Store when you aren't using them (as well as other web sites), and disabling Safari's AutoFill option, which automatically inputs personal data like your name and address. You can explore Safari's security settings and leave them enabled to protect you from fraud. You can also sign up for and enable Find My iPad, which enables you to send a message to your iPad if you lose it (and hope the finder will return it), have it play an alarm so you can find it (if you've left it in your car or under a couch), and even wipe all the data off your iPad remotely, should it ever be lost or stolen. Find My iPad is free, but requires that you manually set it up.

By far, though, the best thing you can do is to keep track of and protect your iPad. If you have to leave it in a car, at least put it in the trunk. Turn it completely off if you think it's going to be hot in there. And if you have to leave it in a hotel room, consider putting it in the hotel room's safe. Even when your iPad is in your home, you should keep it hidden from people you don't know, like handymen and the like. You know people are going to want your iPad; who wouldn't?

Use a Passcode

You can set a passcode for your iPad. A *passcode* is a four-digit number that must be input to unlock your iPad once it's locked due to inactivity or after you press the Sleep/Wake button to manually lock it. When a passcode is applied, you must know the passcode to get to the data on the iPad, and to use it. We can't encourage you strongly enough to do this.

To enable Passcode Lock and create your own passcode:

1. Tap Settings.
2. Tap General.
3. Tap Passcode Lock.
4. Tap Turn Passcode On.
5. Type a four-digit passcode, and type it again to verify.

FIGURE 17-1   Once a passcode is created, you'll have options to configure including how long to wait until the passcode is required.

6. Once the Passcode is enabled, you can configure additional options, shown in Figure 17-1.
   - **Change Passcode**   Tap to change your passcode. You must know your old passcode to change it to a new one.
   - **Require Passcode**   Tap to choose Immediately, After 1 Minute, After 5 Minutes, After 15 Minutes, After 1 Hour, or After 4 Hours of Inactivity.

Did You Know?

Apple's Smart Cover Is Indeed, Pretty Smart!

If you purchased Apple's Smart Cover, you can use it to put the iPad to sleep and wake it up by opening and closing the cover. This also locks and unlocks the iPad. What this means is that you get to forgo using the slider on the Lock screen to access the iPad, when the feature is enabled. If you have a passcode lock configured, you'll still have to type it, though, provided the time limit set for the lock has been reached. You can change this behavior in Settings | General.

- **Simple Passcode** Tap to change what kind of passcode you use. By default, it's a four-digit number. If you turn Simple Passcode from On to Off, you can input any password you like, including one that contains letters and numbers.
- **Picture Frame** To require a passcode (or not) when showing pictures with Picture Frame.
- **Erase Data** To opt to erase all data on the iPad after ten failed passcode attempts.

Enable Restrictions

When you enable restrictions, you have the option to allow or disallow access to specific apps and content. When you disallow specific apps, those apps disappear from the Home screen. For instance, if you disallow Safari, only Mail, Photos, and iPod will appear across the bottom of the Home screen, as shown here—Safari will be unavailable and Safari won't appear in the Settings app.

You can allow or disallow the following features:

- **Safari** When this option is disabled, the user cannot access Safari to surf the Internet.
- **YouTube** When this option is disabled, the user cannot access the YouTube icon to watch YouTube videos. (However, if Safari is left available, the user can still go to www.youtube.com in Safari to view YouTube videos.)
- **Camera** When this option is disabled, the user cannot access the camera (or use it).
- **FaceTime** When this option is disabled, the user cannot hold FaceTime conversations or open the FaceTime app. Figure 17-2 shows this restriction and others.
- **iTunes** When this option is disabled, the user cannot open the iTunes app, and thus, can't make any iTunes Store purchases.
- **Ping** When this option is disabled, the user cannot access Ping or perform any "Ping" activities.
- **Installing Apps** When this option is disabled, the user cannot install any apps from the App Store.
- **Deleting Apps** When this option is enabled, the user cannot delete apps from the iPad.
- **Location** When this option is disabled, the user cannot use Maps or another location-based app to pinpoint or broadcast his or her location. Location data is not provided. These options are shown in Figure 17-3.
- **Accounts** When this option is enabled, the user can't make changes to the accounts configured on the iPad.

Wi-Fi	3802
Notifications	On
Location Services	On
Cellular Data	
Brightness & Wallpaper	
Picture Frame	
General	
Mail, Contacts, Calendars	
Safari	
iPod	
Video	
Photos	
FaceTime	
Notes	

Disable Restrictions

Allow:

Safari	ON
YouTube	ON
Camera	ON
FaceTime	ON
iTunes	ON
Ping	ON
Installing Apps	ON
Deleting Apps	ON

Allow Changes:

Location	>
Accounts	>

FIGURE 17-2   To enable or disable a restriction, simply tap the On/Off button.

Allow Changes ✓

Don't Allow Changes

Disallowing changes locks the settings shown below and prevents new apps from using location services.

Location Services ON

Allow the apps below to determine your approximate location.

Bing for iPad	ON
Camera	ON
LIFETIME	ON
Maps	✈ ON
Twitter	ON

An app that has requested your location within the last 24 hours will show the location services icon next to its name.

FIGURE 17-3   You can decide if you want apps to learn your location.

You can also enable and disable specific content:

- **In-App Purchases** Some apps offer an option to make additional purchases to add features or to upgrade the app. When you disable this feature, you disable the option to purchase upgrades, features, and additional apps.
- **Ratings For** Choose the country you want to draw ratings from. If you're in the United States, make sure United States is selected. Tap it to select something else.
- **Music and Podcasts** In the United States, music and podcasts can be rated Explicit. Tap this setting to access a switch that toggles Explicit content playback on or off.
- **Movies** Tap Movies to set the type of movies you'll allow to be played. As shown here, you can allow or disallow all types.

Allow Movies Rated	
Don't Allow Movies	
G	✓
PG	✓
PG-13	✓
R	✓
NC-17	✓
Allow All Movies	✓

- **TV Shows** Tap TV Shows to choose what kinds of TV shows to allow. You may want to disallow TV – MA, for instance. (MA stands for Mature Audiences.)
- **Apps** Tap Apps to enable and disable apps based on their age-appropriateness.
- **Multiplayer Games** Tap to enable or disable the ability to play multiplayer games in the Game Center.
- **Adding Friends** Tap to enable or disable the ability to add friends in the Game Center.

To enable restrictions and configure allowed and disallowed content (and you can perform similar steps to disable restrictions once enabled):

1. Tap Settings, and tap General.
2. Tap Restrictions.
3. Tap Enable Restrictions.
4. Input a passcode and input it again to verify it.

Did You Know?

iBooks and the iBookstore Are Unrestricted

There are no restrictions on the iPad for books from the iBookstore. That's because there is no ratings system for books. If you're letting children use your iPad to read and obtain books, keep a watchful eye on them.

5. Move the slider for any app to allow or disallow.
6. Tap any option under allowed content to change what's allowed and what isn't. Tap the Restrictions button to return to the Restrictions page.
7. When finished, press the iPad's Home button.

Sign Out of Stores and Web Sites

If you've created a web clip for an email provider (such as one from Yahoo!), and you've told that provider to keep you logged in for two weeks, then anyone with access to your iPad also has access to your email. All they have to do is tap the web clip on your Home screen. The same is true of sites like Facebook. If someone gets access to your iPad and taps your Facebook web clip, they can change your status or send messages to their heart's content. If you want to be really secure but don't want to apply a passcode, you'll want to sign out of these types of sites when you're finished using them. Figure 17-4 shows the option to log out of Facebook on the Account drop-down menu.

FIGURE 17-4   To be safe, log out of web sites when you're finished using them.

Additionally, you can easily log out of the App Store and iTunes by tapping your account at the bottom of just about any page, as shown here. You can then tap Sign Out.

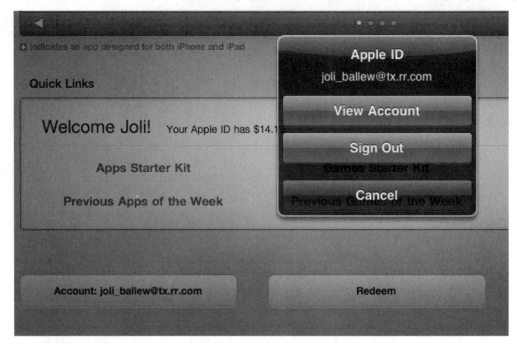

Be Careful on the Internet

As you learned in Chapter 3, Safari is what you use to surf the Internet on your iPad. Safari has a Fraud Warning option that is enabled by default. Additionally, there's a pop-up blocker that's also enabled. You can still take a look at these to be sure, though, and we'll show you how in a minute.

There are steps you can take too; you can preview a web link before you click it, to make sure that you're actually going to the site you want to, and not a fraudulent site set up to look like a real one. You can monitor your data usage so you can see how much data you're using, and keep track of how much more data you can use if you're on a limited plan. And you can clear your History, if you've visited sites you probably shouldn't have, or if you've been searching for the perfect birthday gift for your spouse, who also uses the iPad.

Secure Safari

By default, Safari is set to show features of the web, such as some movies, animation, and web applications. You may wish to change the security settings to help protect your iPad from possible security risks on the Internet. You configure security settings under Settings, Safari. Options include;

Note These are the security features of Safari, and do not include options like changing the Search Engine or showing the Bookmark Bar.

- **AutoFill** Leave this option disabled to keep Safari from automatically inputting contact info, and usernames and passwords. See Figure 17-5.
- **Fraud Warning** Leave this option enabled to have Safari warn you when visiting web sites reported as fraudulent.
- **JavaScript** Disable this option to disable JavaScript on web pages, which lets web programmers add sophisticated elements to a page, but can also be potentially exploited by hackers and computer viruses. We leave JavaScript enabled, though, so that we can enjoy all the web has to offer. JavaScript, in this setting, should not harm your iPad.

General

| Search Engine | Bing > |

| AutoFill | Off > |

| Always Show Bookmarks Bar | ON |

Security

| Fraud Warning | ON |

Warn when visiting fraudulent websites.

| JavaScript | ON |

| Block Pop-ups | ON |

| Accept Cookies | From visited > |

Clear History

Clear Cookies

Clear Cache

FIGURE 17-5 It's best to leave AutoFill Off, especially if you don't protect your iPad with a passcode.

- **Block Pop-ups**   Enable this option to block pop-ups that could possibly appear when you close or open a web page.
- **Accept Cookies**   Disable or change this option to keep Safari from accepting cookies from web sites. Cookies tell web sites your preferences when you visit, such as your name, what you like to purchase or look for while on the site, and similar, generally harmless, information. The web site puts a cookie on your iPad so the web site can remember you the next time you visit. This allows web pages to be customized for you. Note that some web pages won't work correctly if you completely disable cookies.
- **Clear History**   Tap to clear the history of web pages you've visited.
- **Clear Cookies**   Tap to clear all cookies from Safari.
- **Clear Cache**   Tap to clear the browser cache. The browser cache stores things like pictures, so the pages will open faster the next time you visit them. If a page doesn't show new content, it's offering the page cache. Clear the cache to pull new data from the page.

Avoid Phishing

Phishing is a term used when an unscrupulous person tries to get you to input personal information by tricking you into thinking the web site or web form you're using is official, when in reality, it isn't. You may be familiar with phishing emails. The email says that your bank account, PayPal account, instant messaging account, or something similar has been compromised, and you need to visit the company's web site to fix the problem. If you go to that site, you may be asked for information including name and address, social security number, birth date, and even bank account numbers, usernames, and passwords. The bad guys then use that information to purchase things using your account or to steal your identity.

There are also phishing web sites. These are links to other web pages that appear on a web page that imply they'll take you to an official web site, but once you're there, you become suspicious because the page seems a little off or the web address doesn't match the address you expect.

Before you visit any web site from an email or another web page, if you feel suspicious of the page, you can preview the web address before going there. Here's an example. This email looks as if it's from Amazon.com, a valid online company, but how can you be sure that the link in the email will take you to www.amazon.com, and not some phishing web site like www .westealyouridentity.com? Easy, just tap and hold to view the web address of the link. In this illustration, notice that the web link starts with http://www.amazon.com, which indeed is a valid web page for Amazon. (If it didn't start with amazon.com, you'd have to be suspicious.)

You can perform the same test on any web page in Safari. Simply tap and hold to see where the link will really take you.

Monitor Data Usage

If you have an iPad Wi-Fi + 3G model and a limited-use cellular data plan, you can check your data usage from Settings:

1. Tap Settings.
2. Tap General.
3. Tap Usage.
4. You can easily see your Sent and Received Cellular Network Data usage, and reset the statistics.

You can also tap Settings, tap Cellular Data, and tap View Account to get much more detailed information. You'll have to log in, and then you can see information including how many days you have left until your monthly data plan renews.

Set Up Find My iPad

You can protect your iPad with a feature called Find My iPad. You set it up through the Settings app, under Mail, Contacts, Calendars. Find My iPad offers the following features:

- It helps you locate your iPad if you lose or misplace it. Once Find My iPad has been set up and enabled, should your iPad ever be misplaced, you can visit www.me.com to get its approximate location, provided the iPad is powered on.
- You can display a message on your iPad to help someone return it to you if it's lost.
- The Remote Passcode Lock feature lets you remotely lock your iPad. If your iPad is stolen while it is unlocked, you can easily lock it.
- The Remote Wipe feature lets you erase all content and settings on your iPad if it's stolen. This resets all settings to their original value and erases all your information, data, and media.

To set up Find My iPad:

1. Tap Settings.
2. Tap Mail, Contacts, Calendars.
3. Tap Add Account.
4. Tap MobileMe.
5. Sign in with your existing Apple ID and password.
6. Tap Next.
7. Tap OK to allow MobileMe to incorporate Location Services so that your iPad can be located if lost.

8. Tap Save.
9. If your MobileMe account says "Not Verified," check your email Inbox for an email from Apple.
10. Click Verify Now when the email arrives.
11. Return to the Settings app, in Mail, Contacts, Calendars, and switch the Find My iPad from Off to On.

To try out Find My iPad:

1. Place your iPad in another room in your home or office.
2. From any computer, visit www.me.com.
3. Type your Apple ID and password.

MobileMe	Done
MobileMe	
Account	joli_ballew@tx.rr.com >
Find My iPad	ON
Allow this iPad to be shown on a map or remotely wiped.	

4. Click Sign In.

mobile me

Sign in with your Apple ID

| joli_ballew@tx.rr.com | •••••••• | Sign In |

5. Click the arrow beside your iPad.

6. Click Display Message or Play Sound. Note the other options, though, including Lock and Wipe.
7. Type a message if desired, then tap Send.
8. Locate your iPad, read the message (if applicable), and click OK.
9. In a few minutes, check your email Inbox. You'll get a message about your iPad telling you that it was located.

PART VII

Appendixes

A

Settings

The Settings icon enables you to customize your iPad's apps and set preferences. This is where you'll go to change your Wallpaper, configure settings for Safari, and configure preferences for Picture Frame, among other things. There's a wide range of settings to choose from and lots of preferences you can set. You can configure preferences and settings in the following categories: Airplane Mode, Wi-Fi, Notifications, Location Services, Cellular Data (iPad 3G only), Brightness and Wallpaper, Picture Frame, General, Mail, Contacts, Calendars, Safari, iPod, Video, Photos, FaceTime, Notes, and Store. Each time you change a setting here, it is applied immediately.

Although we've introduced some of these settings in this book, this chapter outlines what you can do within each category of settings. The chapter is organized by *what you can do*; it is not simply a list of settings and how to enable or disable them (which was covered throughout this book).

Airplane Mode

When you are on an airplane, you'll often be advised when you can use "approved devices." The iPad is one of those approved devices, provided you disable the wireless features of the device. You may also want to enable Airplane Mode to increase battery life when you know you won't be connecting to any networks. Airplane Mode turns off wireless features, Bluetooth, and GPS reception.

Airplane options include the ability to:

- **Turn Airplane Mode on or off**   Here you can easily turn Airplane Mode on or off.

Wi-Fi

You configure Wi-Fi settings to state how the iPad should use local Wi-Fi networks to connect to the Internet. You'll want to leave Wi-Fi enabled when you know you'll be accessing the Internet from your home network or a wireless hotspot. If no Wi-Fi networks are available, or you turn Wi-Fi off, the iPad will connect to the Internet over your cellular data network (on iPad Wi-Fi + 3G only), if it's available and if you subscribe to a cellular data service. When Wi-Fi is off, you'll see "Off" at the end of the Wi-Fi line in the left pane of Settings. When Wi-Fi is on, you'll see the name of the network you're connected to.

Wi-Fi options include the ability to:

- **Turn Wi-Fi on or off**   To turn Wi-Fi on or off.
- **Join a Wi-Fi network**   To join a Wi-Fi network in range. You first select a network from the list, and then you may be required to enter a password.
- **Set the iPad to ask if you want to join a new network**   To be notified when networks are available (or not).

- **Forget a network, so iPad doesn't join it automatically**   You want to "forget" networks you know you'll never use because your iPad works through all of the networks when looking for one. This uses battery power and takes time. It's best to keep the list short, and only filled with networks you recognize. To do this, tap next to a network you've joined before, then tap Forget This Network.

- **Join a closed Wi-Fi network**   To join a Wi-Fi network that isn't shown in the list of networks. To enter a network manually, tap Other, and then enter the network name and other required information, such as a password.

- **Adjust settings to connect to a Wi-Fi network**   To change settings for your current Wi-Fi network.

Notifications

When you configure the Game Center or install certain third-party apps, you'll be asked to allow the app to send notifications to your iPad automatically. These notifications can include badges, alerts, and sounds. When notifications are enabled, apps can alert you about new information, even when the application isn't running. Most notifications play a sound, offer text, or place a number on the app's icon on the Home screen. To maximize battery life, you can turn these notifications off.

 To save on data usage, disable unnecessary alerts.

Notifications options include the ability to:

- **Turn all notifications on or off**   To turn off all notifications (or turn them all on).
- **Turn sounds, alerts, or badges on or off for an application**   To turn off notifications for a specific app. (Note that "badges" are the notifications that appear on an icon, such as the number of new Facebook status updates.)

Configure Location Services

Location Services is what enables an app, say Maps, the Camera, and others (including third-party apps), to determine your approximate location. You may want to disable this to maintain your privacy. However, most apps that want information regarding your location want it to make your experience with the app more valuable. For instance, when Location Services for Maps is enabled, you can tap the Location icon to let Maps figure out where you are, perhaps to use as a starting point for directions you'd like to acquire. Third-party apps, such as Bing for iPad, shown here, use your location to offer information about the weather and local businesses, among other things.

Location Services options include the ability to:

- **Turn Location Services on or off**   To enable or disable Location Services for all apps (or turn them all on).
- **Turn off or on Location Services for specific apps**   To turn on or off Location Services for only the apps you want.

Cellular Data

Cellular Data settings are available only on the iPad Wi-Fi + 3G model, and enable you to change settings related to your current cellular data network, and turn cellular data and/or roaming on or off.

 To avoid unwanted charges, turn off data roaming.

Cellular Data options include the ability to:

- **Turn the cellular data network connection on or off**   To turn on or off access to the cellular network. You may want to turn off cellular network access when you've reached your monthly quota of bandwidth, and turn it back on at the beginning of your next payment cycle.
- **Turn data roaming on or off**   To turn data roaming on or off. Data roaming may cost extra if you're out of the country. It's best to leave this off until you fully understand your plan.
- **View your account information**   To see or change your account information.
- **Add a SIM PIN**   To add a PIN to lock your micro-SIM card. If your iPad is stolen, a thief could possibly pull the SIM card and obtain data from it.

Brightness & Wallpaper

Use Brightness settings to adjust the screen brightness and Wallpaper settings to personalize your iPad's Home screen wallpaper and the picture you see when you unlock your iPad.

Tip   Reduce brightness to increase battery life.

Brightness and Wallpaper options include the ability to:

- **Adjust the screen brightness**   To change the screen's brightness using a slider.
- **Set whether iPad adjusts screen brightness automatically**   To enable or disable Auto-Brightness. When Auto-Brightness is enabled, your iPad will adjust the brightness automatically using the built-in ambient light sensor.

- **Set wallpaper**   To select a wallpaper for the Lock screen, Home screen, or both. In addition to the wallpapers provided by Apple, you can choose any of the pictures in your Photos as wallpaper.

Picture Frame

You can use your iPad as a digital picture frame. You can enhance this by also incorporating the optional dock to hold the frame in place on a mantle or table. Picture Frame mode lets you also apply transitions in between photos, and choose what photos to display. You can even zoom in on faces and shuffle photos when playing them.

Picture Frame options include the ability to:

- **Select a transition**   To choose the type of transition to use between photos.
- **Show a picture for a specific time**   Set the amount of time that a picture should remain on the screen until it moves to the next one.
- **Zoom in on faces during a Picture Frame show**   To zoom in on faces during a show using Picture Frame. You must choose Dissolve under Transition for this option to be available.
- **Shuffle**   Turn shuffle on or off. Randomizes the order photos are displayed.
- **Choose what pictures to show**   To select a folder or all photos to use when Picture Frame is playing.

General

General settings include those related to the date and time, security, network, and other things that affect every part of your iPad. This is also where you can find information about your iPad, or reset your iPad to its original state. The General settings offer subcategories, that, when selected, offer even more options. Listed next are the subcategories and what they include.

General	
About	>
Usage	>
Sounds	>
Network	>
Bluetooth	Off >
Spotlight Search	>
Auto-Lock	5 Minutes >
Passcode Lock	On >
Restrictions	Off >
Use Side Switch to:	
Lock Rotation	
Mute	✓

 To enhance battery life, turn off Bluetooth when you aren't using it.

About

Click About to get information about your iPad including but not limited to total storage capacity; space available; number of songs, videos, and photos; serial number; and software version.

General	About	
Joli's iPad		
Network		AT&T
Songs		162
Videos		4
Photos		655
Applications		16
Capacity		14.0 GB
Available		8.7 GB
Version		4.3.1 (8G4)
Carrier		AT&T 10.0
Model		MC982LL

Usage

This setting is available on the iPad 3G model only. Click the Usage category to obtain information about your battery and the amount of cellular data you've sent and received.
   Usage options include the ability to:

- **Show battery percentage**   To display the percentage of battery charge next to the battery icon on the Home screen. On iPad Wi-Fi models, this setting is available on the General settings menu, above the Reset option.
- **See cellular network data**   To view the amount of data sent and received over the cellular data network (on iPad Wi-Fi + 3G only) since the last time you reset your usage statistics.
- **Reset your usage statistics**   To clear accumulated data and statistics.

Sounds

Click Sounds to make changes to settings related to sounds.

Sounds options include the ability to:

- **Adjust the ringer and alerts volume** To change the volume of the ringer and alert sounds.
- **Adjust the volume bar with the Volume buttons on the outside of the iPad** When this option is enabled, you can change the volume under Ringer and Alerts using the buttons on the outside of the iPad. If this option is disabled, you can't.
- **Set alert and effects sounds** To turn specific sounds on or off. You can enable or disable sounds when you do the following:
  - Set a ringtone for alarms
  - Get an email message
  - Send an email message
  - Have an event that you've set to alert you
  - Lock the iPad
  - Type using the keyboard

Network

Network settings enable you to access and change settings related to the various networks you use, including Wi-Fi and VPNs. A VPN is a Virtual Private Network. VPNs offer secure connections to networks using the Internet.

Network options include the ability to:

- **Add a new VPN configuration** To add a new VPN configuration. (You'll have to drill down into VPN settings to access this command.)
- **Change a VPN configuration** To change a VPN's configuration settings.
- **Turn VPN on or off** To turn VPN on or off.
- **Delete a VPN configuration** To delete a VPN.
- **Access Wi-Fi Settings** To access Wi-Fi settings, as detailed earlier.

Bluetooth

Your iPad can connect to Bluetooth devices such as headphones and keyboards. Bluetooth devices allow you to listen or type without wires. There are three options for Bluetooth:

- **Turn Bluetooth on or off** To turn on and off Bluetooth capabilities.
- **Search for Bluetooth devices** To watch while your iPad searches for Bluetooth devices, once Bluetooth is enabled.
- **Connect to a Bluetooth device** To pair your iPad with a Bluetooth device in range. You first select a device from the list, and then you may be required to enter a password.

Spotlight Search

When you search with Spotlight, the iPad searches through the data on it to find what you need. You can state which data the Spotlight Search should consider. You can choose to enable or disable Contacts, Applications, Music, Podcasts, Videos, Audiobooks, Notes, Mail, and Events. You can also drag any item to the top of the list or the bottom, to have it searched first or last, or in any order you like.

- **Tell Spotlight Search what data to look through**   To enable and disable what types of data Spotlight Search looks through when searching the iPad for criteria you type.

Auto-Lock

Locking the iPad turns the display off. There's a button on the outside of your iPad for locking it. You can turn the display off to maximize battery life, but it will lock itself after a few minutes of idle time anyway. Locking the iPad also keeps it safe from unintended operation, by preventing taps on the screen from activating an app. You can also require a passcode when you're ready to unlock your iPad. Passcode features are not enabled by default. By setting a passcode, you can prevent your iPad from being accessed without your permission, detailed in the next section.

Auto-Lock options include the ability to:

- **Set the amount of time before the iPad locks**   To change how long the iPad is idle before it is locked automatically. You also have the option of disabling Auto-Lock.

 Set a short idle time and configure a Passcode Lock (detailed next) to activate the lock quickly and prevent unauthorized access to your iPad.

Passcode Lock

You can secure your iPad by requiring a Passcode Lock. When this feature is enabled, each time you unlock your iPad, you have to input this code. This keeps it safe from unauthorized users.

Passcode Lock options include the ability to:

- **Set a passcode**   To enter a four-digit passcode.
- **Turn passcode lock off**   To turn the Passcode Lock off and on again.
- **Require more than a "simple" passcode**   When Simple Passcode is disabled, you can create a passcode that requires more than four numbers to unlock the iPad.
- **Change the passcode**   To change the passcode.
- **Set how long before your passcode is required**   To set how long the iPad should be idle before you need to enter a passcode to unlock it. Choosing Immediately is the only way to really secure your iPad.

- **Picture Frame** To require a passcode (or not) when showing pictures with Picture Frame.
- **Erase data after ten failed passcode attempts** To turn on this feature (or to turn it off later). If you turn on this feature, after ten failed Passcode attempts, the iPad will erase all your information and media.
- **Automatically lock and unlock your iPad when you close and open the iPad Smart Cover** Turn this feature on to automatically lock and unlock your iPad when using the iPad Smart Cover. When this feature is enabled, you don't have to move the slider to unlock the iPad when you open the cover. You'll still have to type your passcode to unlock it if you've set one, though. Turning it off and opening and closing the Smart Cover doesn't wake or sleep the iPad.

Restrictions

Restrictions on the iPad are kind of like parental controls on other devices. You can set restrictions for iPod content on the iPad, as well as a few other applications like YouTube or iTunes.

Restriction options include the ability to:

- **Enable restrictions** To enable restrictions. You'll have to create and enter a four-digit Passcode.
- **Turn off restrictions** To disable restrictions.
- **Set application restrictions** To set restrictions for Safari, YouTube, Camera, FaceTime, iTunes, Ping, Installing Apps, and Deleting Apps. You can also allow changes to Location and Accounts, or not.
- **Set allowed content** To set restrictions on the type of content that can be played with regard to ratings. These include In-App purchases, ratings for a specific country, music and podcasts, movies, TV shows, apps, and Game Center's multiplayer games. The ability to add friends can also be set here.

Side Switch

Here you configure what you want the side switch to do. It can be a rotation lock or it can mute the iPad.
Side Switch includes the ability to:

- **Set the side switch controls**   To configure the side switch to lock the iPad's ability to rotate when you move it, or mute the device.

Date and Time

There are settings available to personalize the date and time information on your iPad. Date and Time options include the ability to:

- **Set whether the iPad shows 24-hour time or 12-hour time**   To turn 24-Hour Time on or off.
- **Set Automatically**   To have the iPad set the time automatically, if this option is available. If this option is turned off or unavailable:
  - **Set the time zone**   To set a time zone
  - **Set the date and time**   To set the date and time

Keyboard

You can change various settings for the keyboard and set preferences for how you type. For instance, you can turn on or off the Auto-Capitalization feature if you'd rather not have the iPad automatically capitalize the beginning of sentences.

Keyboard options include the ability to:

- **Turn Auto-Correction on or off**   To turn Auto-Correction on or off.
- **Turn Auto-Capitalization on or off**   To turn Auto-Capitalization on or off.
- **Check Spelling**   To turn on or off spell check.
- **Set whether the Caps Lock feature is enabled**   Enabling this setting lets you double-tap the Shift key to engage Caps Lock mode.
- **Turn the "." shortcut on or off**   To turn the "." shortcut on or off. (The "." shortcut lets you double-tap the Space bar to enter a period followed by a space when you're typing.)
- **Set up international keyboards**   To add and configure keyboards for multiple languages.

International

Your iPad comes with various international settings. With these, you can set the language for the iPad, turn keyboards for different languages on or off, and configure similar preferences for your preferred language.

International options include the ability to:

- **Set the language for the iPad**   To choose the language you want to use.
- **Set up international keyboards**   Access to the same international keyboard settings that were described in the preceding section. To add and configure keyboards for multiple languages.
- **Set region formats**   To choose your region and set regional defaults for date, time, and other data.
- **Set calendar**   To set your calendar. You can currently choose from Gregorian, Japanese, and Buddhist.

Accessibility

Accessibility options make it easier for a person with visual, mobility, or hearing issues to use the iPad.

Accessibility options include the ability to:

- **Have what's on your iPad's screen read to you**   Enable VoiceOver.
- **Zoom in on your iPad's screen**   Enable Zoom.
- **Use Large text**   To make text larger in Contacts, Mail, and Notes.
- **Use a high-contrast screen**   To use the White on Black screen mode.
- **Use Mono Audio**   To combine stereo audio channels so that identical sound is heard in both channels.
- **Speak Auto-text**   To have the iPad speak auto-corrections and auto-capitalizations to you.

- **Triple-click Home** To enable a feature that allows you to triple-click the Home button to toggle some Accessibility features.

General	Accessibility	
VoiceOver		Off >
Zoom		Off >
Large Text		Off >
White on Black		OFF
Mono Audio		OFF
Speak Auto-text		OFF
Automatically speak auto-corrections and auto-capitalizations.		
Triple-click Home		Off >

Resetting the iPad

You will change the default values for various settings on your iPad as you use it. You'll likely reorder the Home screen, add words to the Dictionary while typing, or change Network settings. You can reset these items if desired. You can also reset your iPad, and delete everything on it, restoring it to factory settings.

Resetting iPad options include the ability to:

- **Reset all settings** To reset all settings. This only applies to settings on the iPad, not your data (like contacts, calendars, and media).
- **Erase all content and settings** To completely reset your iPad and delete all of the data on it.

Tip Before you sell, trade, give, or donate your iPad, erase all content and settings.

- **Reset network settings** To reset only the network settings.
- **Reset the keyboard dictionary** To reset the Keyboard Dictionary.
- **Reset the Home screen layout** To reset the Home screen layout.
- **Reset the location warnings** To reset Location Warnings.

Mail, Contacts, Calendars

You'll use the Mail, Contacts, Calendars settings to set up email accounts and MobileMe, and to set up Find My iPad. You can also customize preferences for these accounts and related features, including Contacts and Calendars.

Mail, Contacts, Calendars	
Accounts	
MobileMe Find My iPad	>
Joli_Ballew@tx.rr.com Mail	>
joli@joliballew.com Mail	>
joliballew@gmail.com Mail, Notes	>
Subscribed Calendars UK Holidays	>
Add Account...	>
Fetch New Data	Push >
Mail	
Show	25 Recent Messages >
Preview	2 Lines >

Accounts

This is where you configure the email accounts and calendar subscriptions on your iPad. You can change your account settings, stop using an account, or even delete an account.

Account options include the ability to:

- **Change an account's settings** To choose an existing account and make changes to it.
- **Stop using an account** To disable an account.
- **Adjust advanced settings** For email accounts, configure options such as mailbox behaviors and settings for incoming messages.
- **Delete an account from the iPad** To delete an account completely. If you want to use the account again, you'll have to re-enter it.

Fetch New Data

Fetch and Push are two ways to obtain your email. Push is a technology that allows Internet servers to send information to your iPad as soon as the message is received by your email provider on their email servers. Some email servers will push email to you, while others won't. Be aware that using Push will use battery power to obtain the updates and, because of the data it transfers, can minimize battery life. Transfers while connected via 3G are counted towards your monthly data usage as well. This isn't a problem if you have a generous data plan access, but it can be if you have a limited plan.

Other email accounts such as POP, IMAP, AOL, and Gmail accounts aren't Push-compatible on the iPad. This means that no email will arrive at your Inbox in Mail until you open Mail and access the Inbox. At that time, Mail will check for email and obtain mail from your email servers. If this is inconvenient and you'd rather have Mail check for email automatically, even when you aren't using it, you can configure your iPad to fetch your email on a schedule, such as every 15, 30, or 60 minutes. You can also set Fetch settings to Manually so that no fetch occurs by default. Like Push, Fetch will drain your battery more quickly on than off. To maximize battery life, fetch less often or fetch manually. Fetch also kicks in for Push email accounts if Push is turned off, so if you're watching your data usage, you may need to turn off Push and set Fetch to Manually.

Fetch options include the ability to:

- **Turn Push on**   To turn on Push.
- **Set the interval to fetch data**   To set how often you want to fetch data.

Mail

You can configure lots of Mail settings. You can add a signature to all outgoing emails, set the minimum font size for email messages, set a default email account, and more.

 To change the sounds associated with Mail, in Settings, go to the General options, under Sounds.

Mail options include the ability to:

- **Set the number of messages shown on the iPad**   You can opt to see the most recent 25, 50, 75, 100, or 200 messages.
- **Set how many lines of each message are previewed in the message list**
  To change email preview options, specifically, how many lines of text you'd like to preview (up to five lines).
- **Set a minimum font size for messages**   To set a font size, choosing from Small, Medium, Large, Extra Large, or Giant.
- **Set whether the iPad shows To and Cc labels in message lists**   To show or hide the To/Cc Labels.

- **Set whether the iPad confirms that you want to delete a message**   To confirm that you want to delete a message (or not).
- **Set whether the iPad automatically loads remote images**   To load remote images (which will cause the email to take longer to load) or to turn off this feature. (You can manually load the images while reading the email if you want to see them.)
- **Organize by thread**   To have the iPad organize your emails by thread (conversation). A thread is created when you send emails back and forth to a person and the subject line remains the same.

Brightness & Wallpaper	Preview — 2 Lines >
Picture Frame	Minimum Font Size — Medium >
General	Show To/Cc Label — OFF
Mail, Contacts, Calendars	Ask Before Deleting — OFF
Safari	Load Remote Images — ON
iPod	Organize By Thread — ON
Video	Always Bcc Myself — OFF
Photos	Signature — Sent from my iPad >
FaceTime	Default Account — Joli_Ballew@tx.rr.com >
Notes	Messages created outside of Mail will be sent from the default account.

- **Set whether the iPad sends you a copy of every message you send**   To always send a blind carbon copy (Bcc) to yourself each time you send an email.
- **Add a signature to your messages**   To add, change, or delete the automatic signature for outgoing messages. By default, the signature is "Sent from my iPad."
- **Set the default email account**   To set your default email account. The default account is the one that will be used automatically each time you compose an email.

Contacts

You can change how your contacts are sorted.
Contacts options include the ability to:

- **Set how contacts are sorted**   To change the sorting option for contacts. You can sort contacts by first name or last name.
- **Set how contacts are displayed**   To change the display order for contacts. You can display contacts by first name or last name.

Calendar

The Calendar helps you keep track of appointments and important dates. You can change how the Calendar sends you alerts, among other options.

Calendar options include the ability to:

- **Set alerts to sound when you receive meeting invitations** You can turn this on or off. You may need to be alerted for each meeting invitation, or you may not.
- **Set how far back in the past to show your calendar events on the iPad** To select a period of time for how far back to show events on your calendar.
- **Turn on Calendar time zone support** To enable Time Zone Support. When Time Zone Support is enabled, the Calendar always displays your event dates and times using a specific time zone. When Time Zone Support is turned off, event dates and times are determined by the time zone of your current location.
- **Choose a default calendar** If you have more than one calendar configured on your iPad, you can set which of them is the default here.

Safari

There are a few things you can configure regarding Safari. You can choose a specific Search engine, enable AutoFill, always show the Bookmarks Bar, and change Security settings. There are also "Developer" settings, which you can likely ignore.

Safari	
General	
Search Engine	Google >
AutoFill	Off >
Always Show Bookmarks Bar	ON
Security	
Fraud Warning	ON
Warn when visiting fraudulent websites.	

General

General options include the ability to:

- **Select a search engine** To select the search engine you want to use. Options include Google, Bing, and Yahoo!.
- **Enable AutoFill** To set Safari to automatically fill out web forms. Safari remembers data you've previously entered into web pages.
- **Show the Bookmarks Bar** To permanently show a bar with bookmarks on it in Safari. When the Bookmarks Bar is left off, you can still reveal it by clicking Safari's address bar or search box.

Security

Security options include the ability to:

- **Change security settings** To turn Fraud Warning on or off; to enable or disable JavaScript; to block or allow pop-ups; to set whether Safari accepts cookies; to clear the history of web pages you've visited; to clear all cookies from Safari; or to clear Safari's cache.

Developer

If you want to know when a web page has errors, and if you're interested in resolving those errors because you develop apps or web sites for the iPad, the Debug Console can help.

Developer options include the ability to:

- **Turn the Debug Console on or off** Get help regarding web page errors using the Debug Console.

iPod

The iPod app is the app you use to play music. You can configure various settings for the iPod, including playing all songs at the same sound level and setting a volume limit, among other things. Some of these options must be set at your computer.

iPod	
Sound Check	OFF
EQ	Off >
Volume Limit	Off >
Lyrics & Podcast Info	ON
Home Sharing	
Apple ID	joli_ballew@tx.rr.com
Password	••••••••
An Apple ID is required to use Home Sharing.	

iPod options include the ability to:

- **Set iPod to play songs at the same sound level** Enable Sound Check.
- **Use EQ to customize the sound** To select an equalizer from a list of predefined settings.
- **Set a volume limit** To set the maximum volume for the iPod and to lock it, if desired.
- **Display song lyrics and information about podcasts** To display lyrics and information when applicable.
- **Home Sharing** To set up home sharing using your Apple ID and password. You'll need to enable Home Sharing in the same manner on your other iOS devices, and you can include up to five devices in any Home Sharing situation. Sharing will occur over your home Wi-Fi network, and you can then share media easily.

Video

Video settings offer options that apply to all video content, including rented movies. Some of the things you can configure include enabling closed captioning and widescreen.

Video	
Start Playing	Where Left Off >
Closed Captioning	OFF
TV Out	
Widescreen	OFF
TV Signal	NTSC >

Video options include:

- **Set where to resume playing** To set where videos that you previously started watching begin. You can resume playing from the beginning or where you left off.
- **Turn closed captioning on or off** To turn Closed Captioning on or off.
- **Turn widescreen on or off** To turn Widescreen on or off when using video output accessories. Turn this on to preserve the widescreen aspect ratio when watching a video made specifically for the wide screen.
- **Set the TV output signal to NTSC or PAL** If you're using the iPad with a video output accessory, use this setting to determine what video format you'll output. If you're in the United States, NTSC is the correct choice. Elsewhere, try PAL.

Photos

The settings in Photos are those related only to slideshows.

Photos	
Slideshow	
Play Each Slide For	3 Seconds ›
Repeat	OFF
Shuffle	OFF

Photos options include:

- **Set the length of time each slide is shown**   To specify the length of time each photo in a slideshow should appear before the next photo appears.
- **Set whether to repeat slideshows**   To repeat slideshows once they are completed. Turn repeat on to repeat, or off to end.
- **Set photos to appear randomly or in order**   To randomly shuffle photos in a slideshow.

Set FaceTime Defaults

You'll use the FaceTime options to enable or disable FaceTime and to configure the account to use and the email associated with your account. You can also add another email if you wish.

FaceTime	
FaceTime	ON
Account joli_ballew@tx.rr.com	
You can be reached for video calls at:	
Email joli_ballew@tx.rr.com	›
Add Another Email...	

FaceTime options include:

- **Enable or disable FaceTime**   To enable or disable the FaceTime app.
- **Change account information**   To change information associated with your FaceTime account, including your email and password.

Set Notes Defaults

Tap any font name to change the default font used for Notes. There are three: Noteworthy, Helvetica, and Marker Felt. To create a note, tap Notes on the Home screen and tap to begin typing. Notes will be saved automatically, and will appear in the left pane in Landscape view. Controls appear at the bottom of the screen.

Notes	
Font	
Noteworthy	✓
Helvetica	
Marker Felt	

Store

The Store settings offer a place to change or create an iTunes Store account.

Apple ID: joli_ballew@tx.rr.com

Store options include:

- **Sign in to or out of an account**   To enter your user name and password, and to sign out if desired. While signed out, users have the option to create a new iTunes account.
- **View your iTunes Store account information**   To view information regarding your account, including your Apple ID, payment information, billing address, country or region, and more.

Manage Apps

Apps you've acquired that offer settings options appear under the Apps section. What you see here will be specific to your iPad. Tap any app in the list to view the settings available. The following illustration shows the settings for iBooks.

 You may have more categories listed. For instance, if you've downloaded iBooks, it'll be listed, as will various other apps you acquire. Not all apps place a listing here, though.

iBooks	
iBooks 1.2.1 (335)	
Full Justification	ON
Auto-hyphenation	ON
Auto-hyphenation requires iOS 4.2	
Tap Left Margin	Previous Page ›
Sync Bookmarks	ON
Sync Collections	ON
Copyright © 2011 Apple Inc. All rights reserved.	

B

Troubleshooting

You may not know that you can call Apple at 1-800-My-Apple and get help for free during the first 90 days you have your iPad. You can call for help about setting up email, using Safari, or downloading an app. We've called a couple of times and it's a short wait on hold, the people who answer the phone are easy to understand and are extremely helpful, and they'll even call you back if they need more time to resolve your problem or if you're disconnected. So, if you'd rather simply call someone than look through this Appendix, and you're still in the 90-day support window, help is just a phone call away.

You can also get help on the Internet. Visit www.apple.com/support/ipad/ if you'd rather look there. The Support pages can help you set up and use all of the apps available on the iPad, including Wi-Fi, Mail, and more. You can also access links to "carrier support" from AT&T and Verizon. There's no way we can include here everything that can go wrong and what to do about it, so that may be a good place to look if you don't see what you're looking for. At Apple's Support site you can access troubleshooting guides, discuss your problem with other iPad users, and troubleshoot problems that are less common than the ones here.

To use this Appendix, locate the heading that relates most closely to your problem, and read the information in that section to resolve it. The sections include

- I am having a problem related to email
- I can't get connected to the Internet
- I have a hardware problem
- I have a backup, sync, update, or restore question
- I have a problem not listed here

I Am Having a Problem Related to Email

There are two separate issues with regard to email:

- You have previously set up email and sent and received email successfully, but are now having a problem.

  or

- You have just set up an email account and are receiving errors and/or cannot send or receive email.

I Used to Be Able to Get My Email, But Now I Can't

There could be a few things going on here: First, you must be connected to the Internet to get your mail. This may mean that Wi-Fi or cellular data needs to be enabled, and that you need to be within range of a free Wi-Fi network or within your provider's data coverage area. So first, open Safari and see if you're connected to the Internet. If you aren't, take steps to resolve that problem first.

If you're connected to the Internet, consider or try the following:

- Verify that you have enough battery power. If your battery is low, plug it in to charge it, and after 10 or 20 minutes, try again.
- If you get email on your iPad and on another device like an iPhone, BlackBerry, or computer, you may experience difficulty downloading your mail at the exact same time as another device. That's because the mail server could be busy sending your mail to one of your other devices and can't accommodate your request right now. Wait. Your mail may come in shortly.
- Open Settings, and then Mail, Contacts, Calendars, and verify that you haven't accidentally deleted or disabled your email account(s). While there, consider letting Mail show more or fewer recent messages.
- If your iPad uses a cellular data network (iPad Wi-Fi + 3G only), turn off Wi-Fi. This will force the iPad to connect to the Internet through the cellular data network. This will resolve the problem if it's caused by the local Wi-Fi network connection (being too weak to get your email, for instance) or its settings. Note that if you're in a pinch and you use a web-based email account such as Gmail, Yahoo mail, or Hotmail, you can check your email using Safari.

I've Set Up a New Email Account, But I'm Not Getting Any Mail (or I Get Errors)

Setting up a new Mail account, especially if it's not one of the supported email accounts like Google or Yahoo!, can be trying. It's easy to make a mistake when you input the required data, like POP mail server names. Even with an account that's supported, you can easily misspell your password or email address. If there are any errors in your email setup, you won't be able to send or receive email. If you've set up a new email account and can't send and/or receive email:

- Work through the troubleshooting tips outlined in detail in the previous section. Make sure your battery has enough power to get your email; if you get email on another device such as an iPhone, other smartphone, or computer, wait a few minutes to see if both are trying to access the mail servers at the same time. If Mail is frozen, close and reopen the app. If you use a cellular data plan, disable Wi-Fi for a moment to rule out a problem with the wireless network. Finally, reboot your iPad, just in case. Sometimes this resolves problems immediately. (One way to reboot is to hold down the On/Off button and the Home button for 10 seconds and use the slider when it appears to power the device off. After the iPad turns off, tap the On/Off button to turn it back on.)
- If you can't find the problem using the tips in the previous bullet, and if your email works on the computer you sync your iPad with, consider syncing your Mail settings. You'll still have to input your password, but this may fix the problem. For more information refer to Chapter 4.
- If none of those actions resolves the issue or is appropriate, you'll need to verify your settings for your Mail accounts:
  - Click Settings, and click Mail, Contacts, Calendars.
  - Tap the problematic account.
  - Review the information for the POP servers, username, password, and so on. If necessary, call your provider to verify you have the correct settings.
- If you still can't get your email to work, contact your service provider and ask them to walk you through it. If they tell you they don't support the iPad, ask them for the following information and write it down very carefully:
  - Incoming mail server host name
  - Outgoing mail server host name
  - Your account type, such as IMAP or POP
  - Any special requirements such as whether you need to enable secure logon or type a special port number
- If you have a cellular data plan, and you can receive email but not send it, in your email account's SMTP settings, turn on one of the additional email servers. Try these servers both with and without SSL. Alternatively, you can add a new server to the problematic account's Other SMTP Servers list, such as the one you use for Hotmail, Gmail, or another web-based email.
- Finally, search for people on the Internet who have had similar problems. Not all accounts are supported yet, but with the right amount of finagling, you can likely get it to work.

I Can't Open an Email Attachment

Your iPad can only be used to open certain types of attachments. The iPad can display picture attachments in many commonly used formats (JPEG, GIF, and TIFF) inline with the text in email messages. The iPad can play many audio attachments (such as MP3, AAC, WAV, and AIFF). You can download and view files (such as PDF, web page, text, Pages, Keynote, Numbers, and Microsoft Word, Excel, and PowerPoint documents) attached to messages you receive, as well. If you're having trouble opening an attachment, it's likely because it's not compatible.

I Can't Get Connected to the Internet

If you can't connect to the Internet on a Wi-Fi only iPad, it's one of two things. Either you don't have Wi-Fi enabled or you aren't within range of and connected to a Wi-Fi network. To resolve this problem, enable Wi-Fi in Settings, under Wi-Fi. There you'll see if networks are available, and you can attempt to connect to them. If you're not within range or if the signal is weak, move closer to the Wi-Fi "access point." Sometimes, even if you're connected to a Wi-Fi network, email can't be downloaded because the signal is simply too weak.

If you can't connect to the Internet on a Wi-Fi + 3G iPad, it's one of a few things. You may not have Wi-Fi enabled, or you may not be within range of and connected to a Wi-Fi network, as detailed earlier. Try to connect using the methods outlined there.

If you are unsuccessful connecting to a Wi-Fi network, you can try using your cellular data connection. For this to work:

- You must have signed up with AT&T or Verizon for cellular data service and have minutes remaining on your data plan.
- You must have Cellular Data enabled in Settings.
- You must be inside your provider's coverage area.

I Have a Hardware Problem

If you're having a problem with your hardware, first, make sure everything is connected properly and fully charged. Most of the time if a cable is involved, the problem is that it's not firmly connected. As an example, often the 30-pin connector that you use to connect the iPad to the computer via USB looks and feels connected even though it is not. You should remove the connection and start again, to be sure. If the problem persists, turn on and off the device.

As with all troubleshooting steps, make sure you have enough battery power, and that you have the proper features enabled on your iPad. If you're having trouble connecting a Bluetooth device, for instance, make sure that Bluetooth is enabled in Settings, General, and that the device to connect is turned on and ready. (If the device needs to be charged, such as is the case with an external keyboard, charge it.) If you're trying to pull pictures from a digital camera using the Camera Connection Kit, make sure the camera is turned on and set to the proper position (often Play). Often hardware problems can be resolved by putting in fresh batteries too, as is often the case with keyboards.

My iPad Doesn't Respond and Is "Frozen"

If your iPad isn't responding and seems to be "frozen," there are several things you can try:

- If your screen won't rotate, verify the Screen Rotation Lock is not enabled. Likewise, if there's no sound, make sure the Mute switch isn't enabled.
- If an app seems "buggy," and causes the iPad to freeze up, delete it.
- If the battery is low on power, charge the iPad by connecting it to a wall outlet using the power adapter. You can use the iPad while it's charging, although this will increase the time required to charge it.
- If the previous options don't work or are not the issue, you'll need to turn off the iPad and turn it back on. Press and hold the Sleep/Wake button, and when the red slider appears, drag the slider to turn off the iPad. Then press and hold the Sleep/ Wake button to turn the iPad back on.
- As a last resort, reset the iPad. Resetting won't cause data loss if you choose the right option; it's like rebooting a computer. Press and hold the Sleep/Wake button and the Home button simultaneously for 10 seconds. When the Apple logo appears, let go. The iPad will restart.

I'm Trying to Install Some Hardware, But a Message Says the Accessory Is "Not Supported by iPad"

The iPad only works with specific supported devices. Each device you purchase should say "compatible with the iPad 2" or something similar. If it does not, it may not work with your iPad. However, if you're sure the device is supposed to be compatible, or if it has previously worked with your iPad, check the cables and connections to verify that it is connected properly. If a setting needs to be enabled, like Bluetooth, enable it, and if possible, try to connect the device to another iPad 2 to verify that the device itself is not defective. If possible, try a different compatible cable. (Finally, if you receive an error that the device won't work, dismiss the error message and see if the device will work anyway.)

I Have a Problem with My Battery or the Battery Icon

If you see any error messages related to the battery or if your iPad won't charge, consider the following problems and solutions:

- If the battery is completely drained or is extremely low on power, it probably won't boot up, even if it's plugged into a wall outlet. Let the iPad charge (preferably connected to a wall outlet, not a computer) for 10 or 20 minutes and see if this resolves the issue.

- If the iPad is plugged in to a wall outlet but won't charge, try the following:
  - Test the outlet with another device to make sure the outlet is working properly.
  - Verify that all connections to the outlet and the iPad are secure.
  - Make sure you're using an Apple power adapter. Third-party adapters can cause problems.
- If the iPad won't charge while plugged in to a USB port on a computer:
  - Test the USB port with another device to make sure it's working properly.
  - Try a different USB port. The USB port you use must be a USB 2.0 type in order to charge the iPad. Older USB ports (1.0) will work for syncing data, but they don't provide enough power to charge the iPad.
  - Don't use a USB hub. Plug the iPad directly into a USB port.
- If the iPad still won't charge, turn it off and plug it in to a working wall outlet using the included power adapter. Wait an hour or so and try to turn it on again.

I Have a Backup, Sync, Update, or Restore Question

Backing up, syncing, updating, and restoring are all very important tasks with regard to your iPad. You should back up your iPad regularly, sync data between your computer and iPad often, and occasionally, check for updates. There are many reasons to do this, but one is to have a backup in case your iPad is lost, stolen, or broken. You can use your latest backup to restore your iPad, if you replace it with a new one.

I Want to Back Up My iPad in Case Something Happens to It

You use iTunes and your computer to create backups for your iPad, which includes your iPad's operating system, your apps, the settings you've configured, application data, and various other data that is directly related to the iPad. The backup doesn't include items you sync that are stored on your computer and that you've transferred to your iPad, though, such as songs, pictures, and videos, or songs, pictures, and videos you've pulled from the Internet and synced to your computer. This data is backed up via syncing through iTunes. So there are two tasks to backing up your data:

- Connect your iPad to your computer to back it up.
- Connect your iPad to your computer to sync it.

You can do both at the same time by simply connecting your iPad to your computer. If, after connecting your iPad to your computer, iTunes does not show that it (1) backs up your iPad and (2) syncs it, then in iTunes, click the iPad in the source pane of iTunes, and click each tab to verify that the items you want to be synced are selected. Then, click Sync or Apply.

To manually create a backup:

1. Connect your iPad to your computer.
2. Make sure your computer is connected to the Internet.
3. Right-click your iPad in the source pane of iTunes.
4. Click Back Up.

For extra security, you can set iTunes to encrypt your backups. When you encrypt your backups, you assign a password. You'll have to input the password to restore the data later. If you use a password, make sure you write it down and keep it in a safe place. Here's how to encrypt your backup:

1. Connect your iPad to your computer.
2. In iTunes, select iPad in the source pane.
3. In the Summary pane, tick Encrypt iPad Backup.
4. Select a password, then click Set Password.

I Created a Backup and Now I Want to Use That Backup to Restore My iPad

If you've created a backup using iTunes, you have a copy of your settings, application data, your iPad's operating system, and various other pertinent data that make your iPad run, and run the way you want. And if you've synced your iPad with your computer, you have a backup of all of your media too. You can restore from these two backups should you ever need to. You can restore the data to your existing iPad, or, if the iPad was lost, stolen, or damaged, you can restore to a new iPad.

To restore iPad from a backup:

1. At the computer where you manage your iPad, connect to the Internet.
2. Connect your iPad to the computer.
3. In iTunes, right-click on a PC or CTRL-CLICK on a Mac on the iPad in the source pane, then choose Restore from Backup from the menu that appears.
4. Choose the backup that you want to restore from the pop-up menu, then click Restore. If the backup is encrypted, you'll need to enter your password.
5. When the restore is complete, sync your iPad.

I Want to Sell My iPad or Give It to Someone Else, and Need to Delete All My Data and Personal Information

This is easy to do. First, call AT&T or Verizon, if you have an account with them for 3G data, and cancel the plan. Now, connect your iPad to your computer, and from the Summary tab in iTunes, click Restore. This will restore your iPad to factory settings. Once the restore is complete, do not sync your iPad. You can also do this directly on the iPad under Settings, General | Reset | Erase All Content and Settings.

I Want to Make Sure My iPad's Operating System Is Up to Date

Once in a while, Apple makes an update available for your iPad. You can easily check for updates by connecting your iPad to your computer, and in iTunes, from the Summary tab, clicking Check for Update. However, you should get a pop-up when a new update is available, making manually checking for updates unnecessary.

I Have a Problem Not Listed Here

There are a few problems that stand alone; perhaps you can't get your iPad to sync, or an application appears too small on the screen. Although we can't list everything here that you could encounter, here are a few common problems and their solutions.

I Can't Sync My iPad

If you can't sync your iPad, try the following, in this order:

- Restart your computer, with the iPad disconnected from it. When the boot process completes, connect the iPad. If that doesn't work, continue troubleshooting as follows:
- Completely disconnect and reconnect the iPad to the computer at both cable ends.
- Charge the iPad's battery from a wall outlet for about 20 minutes.
- Reboot your iPad.
- If you have another cable to connect your iPad to your computer, try it. If the cable has been damaged, syncing can't occur.
- Check iTunes for an update.
- Make sure you're syncing to the same computer you typically use to sync your iPad.

An Application Appears too Small

This often happens because you've acquired an app created for an iPhone or iPod Touch and it hasn't been updated for use with the iPad's larger screen. You can try tapping the "2x" button in the bottom-right corner of the screen to zoom in or look for an updated version at the App Store.

I've Authorized Five Computers and Need to Authorize Another One

If you've authorized five computers in iTunes and you need to authorize another, open iTunes, click iTunes Store in the left pane, and sign in to your account. Click your account name, enter your password, and click Deauthorize All. Now, reauthorize only the computers you still use (from the Store tab in iTunes on each computer you want to authorize). Deauthorize All won't appear if you have fewer than five authorized computers. You can do this once a year.

I Deleted an App, Movie, Book, or Other Data from My iPad and Now I Want It Back

Connect your iPad to your computer. Click your iPad in the source pane of iTunes. Click the appropriate tab, Apps, Movies, Books, or the like. Tick the option to sync these items, and in the list beneath, tick the apps to put back on your iPad. Click Sync. Alternatively, you can download the app again for free from the App Store from your iPad.

I Can't See the Virtual Keyboard

This happens when the iPad is paired with a Bluetooth keyboard, or if it's connected to the iPad Keyboard Dock. To show the virtual keyboard, press the Keyboard key on the Keyboard Dock, or press the Eject key on a Bluetooth keyboard.

Remember, I have a Facebook group entitled How to Do Everything: iPad. *If you'd like to post your problem there, I'll do my best to help you resolve it!*

Index

Numbers

30-pin dock connector, 13

3.5 mm stereo headphone mini jack, 13

3G services. *See also* Wi-Fi + 3G
    choosing data plan for Wi-Fi + 3G model, 22
    status icon for, 25

A

AAC (Advanced Audio Coding)
    audio formats supported, 145
    troubleshooting email attachment
      issues, 336

ABC Player app
    overview of, 210
    watching TV show from ABC network, 180,
      225–226

About category, General settings, 317

accelerometer sensor, built-in to iPad, 24

accessibility
    Apple resources for, 283
    Braille support, 285
    closed captioning, 289–290
    font settings, 288–289
    hardware options, 290–291
    Large Text option, 286
    Mono Audio for hearing disabled, 287
    overview of, 281
    settings, 322–323
    Speak Auto-Text feature, 288
    Triple-Click Home feature, 288
    VoiceOver, 282–284
    volume limits, 289
    White-on-Black display for
      visually impaired, 287

    Zoom feature for visually impaired, 285–286
    zooming in on faces in Picture
      Frame show, 289

accessories
    exploring and purchasing, 19–20
    shopping for speakers and headphones,
      290–291
    troubleshooting unsupported, 337

accounts
    email. *See* email accounts
    PayPal, 4
    restrictions on, 296
    YouTube, 222

accounts, iTunes Store
    exploring App store, 122
    setting up, 5, 7

accounts, Microsoft Exchange, 67, 236

activity status icon, 25

Address window, Safari, 48–49

addresses
    copying from maps and pasting into
      Notes app, 273
    finding addresses and getting directions,
      261–262

Administrator rights, required for installing
    iTunes, 4

Advanced Audio Coding. *See* AAC (Advanced
    Audio Coding)

AIFF (Audio Interchange File Format)
    audio formats supported, 145
    troubleshooting email attachment issues, 336

AIM (AOL Instant Messaging), 117

Airplane Mode
    preventing Wi-Fi connections, 12
    settings, 309
    status icon for, 25